Gypsy Scholar

Migrant Teacher

Global Academic

Adjunct Labour in Higher

 leeds metropolitan university

the last date

Gypsy Scholars,
Migrant Teachers and the
Global Academic Proletariat
Adjunct Labour in Higher Education

Edited by

Rudolphus Teeuwen
and
Steffen Hantke

Amsterdam - New York, NY 2007

The paper on which this book is printed meets the requirements of "ISO
9706:1994, Information and documentation - Paper for documents -
Requirements for permanence".

ISBN: 978-90-420-2309-3
©Editions Rodopi B.V., Amsterdam - New York, NY 2007
Printed in the Netherlands

Contents

Preface

Wanderers see more than settlers, but run greater risks of stumbling. In the academic year of 2000-2001 the two editors of this volume stumbled upon each other in the different courses of their academic migrations. They found themselves both in the Foreign Language and Literature Department of Sun Yat-sen University in Kaohsiung, Taiwan. Rudy Teeuwen had already been there for five years (he is still there and has lost his credentials as a wanderer although intellectual restlessness lingers); Steffen Hantke would leave again after that year, first to serve as a one-year visiting professor in the US, and then to sign on with Sogang University in Seoul, Korea where even he, in a manner of speaking, now is in danger of settling.

During this one academic year of shared affiliation, as we became friends, we talked much about our stumbling, about how our academic careers had seemed for the longest time to refuse to take flight. Of course we didn't start out talking about this. At first we talked "shop" and tried to impress each other with our intelligence, with what we knew and who we knew: we were academics, after all. We kept this up - and still do to some extent, through email and in a decidedly laid-back manner but at some point the question presented itself: if we're really so hip, why is it that nobody but ourselves seems to have taken notice of this?

The answer to this question, we felt, was blowin' in the wind. All over the world, the university had been changing and humanities departments had been bearing the brunt: "Done because we are too menny." As we expounded these institutional shifts to each other and grew angry, we also described our academic death and near-death experiences, told each other of our lives, and became friends. This is how it seems to go: stumbling yokes systemic analysis to personal story. One wonders: does settling join systemic compliance to personal excuse?

This, we assume, must take place in institutions of higher education all over the world: colleagues strike up friendships, and their conversations stray into more familiar, personal terrain. Because the demands of professional and collegial etiquette constrain us, the real lay of the land can sometimes only begin to emerge when we leap the bounds of such etiquette.

Hence, in 2003, we had the idea to collect more stories and critical analyses from academics such as we are, or were. Having listened to the personal conversations taking place alongside the professional ones, we wanted to bring the experience, expertise, and sentiments of the former back into the latter. A quick Call for Papers in *PMLA* and on various websites and a long search for a publisher - and now, in this volume, many more of the "too menny" present their analyses of the changes in the university systems and departments that they have known first hand. They tell of their brushes with academic death, rescues, and the impact this has had on their lives.

In this book we hear of gypsy scholars and adjunct teachers in various academic contexts the world over. Quite a few initial respondents, however, decided, after some deliberation, not to give us their stories for publication. Some did not want to be seen by their institutions as telling stories out of school. Some must have declined out of loyalty to their institutions and in their hope still to be embraced one day by the academy that spurns them now. Some, no doubt, did not feel up to the task of taking stock of their academic lives. If misery loves company, then there's some company for them in the pages of this book. And if universities are places that welcome courageous criticism and analysis (the "if" gets bigger here), then many of those who managed to settle in them will also appreciate these contributions of their "lesser colleagues."

RT
SH

Introduction:
Disappointed Hope - Adjunct Teachers
in the Two-Tier Academic Labour Market

Rudolphus Teeuwen

We have no hope and yet we live in longing
Dante, Inferno

There is a lot to be said for defining an academic discipline by its problems. This is not an unduly gloomy way of looking at academic activity because identifying, formulating, understanding, and pondering problems are at the heart of an academic's joy. There are usually, at a specific time and place, specific problems that seem crucial to the discipline, or to a strand within it, and specific approaches of dealing with them. Blessed mavericks aside, a discipline's most ambitious practitioners zero in on such problems or bring them up in the first place and then exhaust their own and others' ingenuity, interest, and patience on these problems. Sometimes, in some disciplines, they solve them. The discipline then moves on by moving away from those problems and approaches to other, often newly conceived, ones.

This view of a discipline as a collection of problems obtains not only for what occurs when people practice their discipline but also for the way a discipline organizes itself as a profession. How does it select and reward its professors and police the way they move through the ranks? How does it attract students, funds, and the respect of other disciplines, of governments, and of society at large? How does it determine excellence, or mere worthiness, in its professors and students?

We in the humanities justifiably think of our disciplines as especially prone to professional problems in a world that already questions our relevance as a practice. But perhaps we sometimes go too far in this conviction of singular woe, or fail to see ourselves in larger contexts. For example, there are surprisingly severe existential problems in the sciences as well. Chemistry and physics in the UK, for instance, have problems with attracting students in sufficient numbers and with the financial loss per student that responsibly teaching them entails. Chemistry departments get £5,923 per student whereas students of medicine and dentistry come to their departments with a government allotment of £13,963.[1] Chemistry departments can economize on their teaching costs by replacing live laboratory experiments by computer simulations, but that diminishes exactly what makes chemistry a "spectacular, dynamic and sensual subject."[2] "Since 1996," according to the Royal Society of Chemistry, "28 universities have stopped offering chemistry degrees."[3] These closures are partly the consequence of the RAE system, the Research Assessment Exercise that measures the quality of all academic departments throughout the UK, and awards departments a grade. A department that doesn't attain the highest grades of 5 or 5* will receive less government funding and less interest from potential students. Attempting to improve one's RAE rating may, ironically, hamper good, exciting chemistry teaching because RAE assessment criteria force the hands of imaginative and innovative teachers. "A tightly defined national curriculum with a lot of time spent on assessment has cut down the time available for imaginative experiments and pushed schools into using safe, formulaic practices that get the marks [in the RAE]."[4] UK chemistry departments are trying to deal with these problems of student numbers, teaching methods, and evaluative structures that deaden as they give life in various ways. One of them is to take the excitement of experiments, explosions, and bad smells to high schools, trying to hook 11-13 year-olds on a discipline that has been forced into tameness at the universities.[5]

-2-

There is no shortage of problems in departments of languages and literature throughout the world. The problems aren't exactly the same everywhere, and attempts at solutions sometimes take the perverse shape of importing another system's problems. It is in the nature of the power and prestige that US higher education now enjoys in much of the world that the importation of foreign problems as solutions to domestic ones is mostly a trade in US notions and practices. Adjunct labour is clearly such a case. European and Asian universities often adopt and adapt US hiring and labour practices or even actual US labour.

The crises that US humanities departments experience are so intractable in part because they are all facets of a wider problem. They do therefore not respond well to the piecemeal engineering that is often the most sensible manner (Karl Popper usefully pointed out) and also usually the only acceptable way of addressing problems in a system in which one has to function during repairs. That wider problem is that the humanities and sciences just cannot thrive in a university that models its virtues on the managerial rationality of commercial corporations. Individuals and committees within our profession have identified this as the main problem regularly and eloquently, before giving their recommendations for piecemeal reform. Cheryl Glenn, a member of the MLA Committee on Professional Employment, is quoted in that committee's final report as saying, "although efficiency and accountability are crucial to any educational system, institutions of higher education cannot make economic, capitalist, and corporate considerations their primary concerns [...]."[6] Exactly! But rather than ourselves, we need to remind university administrators and governments that society needs non-profit organizations as well in order to accommodate citizens' rightful aspirations and unfold the full scope of human capacities, and that universities should be such organizations. This task of reminding the managers that the free market needs tempering falls to the managed: it is part of being a humanities or science professor. And this task of reminding is best done as a concerted, cooperative effort across ranks and disciplines. That there is a faintly utopian aura to this task is less an indication of farfetchedness than of how far we have let things come already.

The mother of all our crises in higher education is the job crisis. This has been with us for at least thirty years now which makes the very word "crisis," with its promise of temporality and cure, a misnomer.[7] If our profession could offer new PhDs a fighting chance of a professorial career, we could stop our anxious fretting about whom to exempt from the consequences of our failure and whom to burden with them. One way of protecting the future of a discipline that overproduces PhDs is to limit student intake in graduate programmes artificially. This is a method widely used by governments in Europe and Asia, where universities are in overwhelming majority funded and overseen by national governments. In the US such central control would obviously be harder to realize. Besides, the practice violates an aspect of academic freedom - the freedom to choose what one wants to study - that is worth preserving, and societies often prove too dynamic to make limitations on student intake a very effective means of fitting current supply to future demand. The practice could also very well hasten our demise: the dynamics of our particular discipline and profession has been one of steady decline over the last few decades, and overproduction of PhDs might ironically be the surest way to guarantee our survival. A problematic presence is preferable to the assisted fade-out that could well be the result of a market economy reinforced (rather than tempered) by central planning. Meanwhile, in the US our profession only moves farther and farther away from being in the sort of shape to guarantee all comers full employment, or even a fair shot at it, as academic pursuits, in all their branches, are expected to bend more and more to the demands of the free market. Statistics indicate that less than 50 percent of new PhDs in languages and literature do find full-time tenure-track positions upon graduation; those who persist in seeking a job for five years after graduation have odds of two out of three of making it to such a position.[8] No one knows anything new to say about the job crisis anymore so that professional discussion is moving on to newer problems.

One such a newer one is the problem of early professionalization of PhD candidates. Patricia Meyer Spacks, when MLA president in 1994, drew our attention to how PhD candidates, in part in reaction to the job crisis, concentrate on turning out publishable papers instead of using their student years to deepen and broaden their knowledge. This crisis has also been going on without much direction for a decade now, although there have been interesting proposals to lessen the pressure on graduate students to be both students and professionals. Robert Scholes recently proposed that good graduates be offered three-year terminal positions. The first two years will consist of full-time teaching of basic courses at two-thirds pay, and in the third year the pay continues but the new PhDs can devote their time to research, scholarship, and writing. After these extra three apprentice years, a new PhD enters the job market with a broad and deep education, teaching experience, and work on a scholarly project underway (Scholes 122).[9]

The crisis in publishing and tenure is the one that currently generates the most vivid debate, especially in the US. The problem, in a nutshell, is one of circularity: if you need a book (or even two, and laudatory reviews as well) in order to get tenure, you'll need an academic publisher and laudatory reviewers. *Getting* good press should be the true difficulty in a healthy academic system but it isn't; *finding* a press is. Academic publishers, forced by administrators at their affiliated universities, need to turn themselves into profit-making ventures. All those tenure books with their pitiful numbers of buyers and readers are such a drain on the budgets of university presses that finding a publisher has become very hard indeed for all but the best-known scholars. Some look to new technologies such as electronic publishing and on-demand printing for solutions to this crisis,[10] but this would only prop up a system that needs serious questioning. Shouldn't we rather publish fewer books, but ones that have matured longer? Shouldn't we rethink criteria for tenure and promotion?[11]

By means of contrast (not an entirely bracing one) to current US academic practice, let us point out how differently most European universities deal with publications and promotions. The free market principle hasn't made such deep inroads there yet, although it is on its way because European universities look to it for solving budgetary problems of their own. The American system, after all, looks like the epitome of fairness: measurable achievement leads to corresponding incremental advancement in a scholarly career. Compared to this transparency and fairness, European universities offer a deeply flawed arbitrariness.

The faculty formation of individual departments at European universities is usually determined by a country's Ministry of Education, and not easily changed. The English department of a specific university might, for instance, be allowed one full professor, some more associate professors, and still some more assistant professors. The allowance of slots for the various professorial ranks might be different at the English department of another university elsewhere in the country, but it still would be just as fixed. Add to this that fresh PhDs might right away be appointed associate or, although unusual, even full professors, and that they might be appointed at the institution that granted them that degree, and you have a recipe for logjam. Anyone who isn't full professor and would like to become one (and mutatis mutandis for the lower ranks) is very much in the position of curates and clergymen in the eighteenth- and nineteenth-century Church of England, waiting for preferment once a living falls free. They are quite possibly at least as capable as current occupants of a living are, but there is just no help for it: if slots are filled, the pre-determined formation doesn't allow for a promotion. Publications are important in European universities, but the link between publications and preferment is less direct than in the US. True scholars in such a system, in whatever rank, do their work anyway. But if you find yourself in a low rank and think of the university as a career (and what's wrong with that?), then chances are that you'll be beset by dispiritedness over the absence of clear rules, equal chances, and just rewards. Think of it as just a job and you can coast as long as you creditably teach your courses and produce the occasional publication. The relatively weak correlation between ability or production and professorial position makes for a less cutthroat atmosphere in European humanities departments: everyone knows how much chance is part of the system. European academics do extraordinary things such as developing hobbies, taking early retirement, and going on vacation to places where there isn't a conference going on. But then again this academic system also favours the development of those same vices in European academics that were prevalent among their clergymen forebears: malicious gossiping, fawning, and nepotism.

To return to the US: the crisis in publishing and tenure there, unlike the crises of early professionalization and of adjunct labour, hits the profession's upper echelon of the tenured or tenure-track. That the rot has already risen so high might prove a blessing in disguise for those languishing at the profession's low end. The idea that our various crises are really mostly manifestations of the single phenomenon of misplaced free market ideals in the minds of university administrators becomes considerable even to those who until recently could afford to disregard it. In optimistic moods, solidarity of some depth across the ranks feels possible now, and initiatives to resist the absolute reign of managerial rationality have a much better chance of success if those who still have the ear of administrators join adjunct teachers and graduate students in complaint and protest.

It remains ironic, though, especially with respect to those who rose in the profession by their espousal and forceful expression of radical ideas of social equality, that manifestations of solidarity with adjunct teachers amount to so little in practical terms. In a review of books in the field of composition studies, James D. Williams notices how, in that field too, theoretical radicalism comes to stand in for radical action rather than that it leads to it. Williams asks of scholars committed to "resistance pedagogy": "If these scholars truly are committed to change and resistance, shouldn't we expect to see at least a few refuse to publish, refuse tenure, request to be relocated into graduate student offices, or insist that a significant portion of their salaries as full professors be donated to improve the pay of adjuncts?"[12] Indeed, you would expect "at least a few" academic radicals to apply their ideas of societal reform to their own place in society. Doesn't the university's two-tier labour market of designated insiders (the tenured and tenure-track) and designated outsiders (adjuncts) cry out for radical reform, even if, unreconstructed, the academy were indeed already so fruitful a launch pad of radical ideas? If academics were radicals without a blind spot for their own position, the two-tier academic labour market would long since have been in shatters. But because in the humanities, for better and for worse, every academic is a mandarin at heart, no academic insider would destroy the place that allows him to grow his fingernails.[13] So it is faux-naïve in Williams and me to taunt radical colleagues for not practicing what they preach, and to pretend to be taken aback by this. Radicalism always begins as a quality of ideas, and those ideas then have to contest the might of conformity and conservatism in societies and individuals, radical thinkers themselves included. In his diary entry for Saturday, 31 May 1824, Eugène Delacroix mentions meeting an old gentleman who had still personally known Voltaire, Diderot, and Rousseau. This man had once walked with Rousseau in the Tuileries where they saw some children play ball. "'There,' said Rousseau, 'that is how I should like Emile to take exercise,' and other similar remarks. But a ball belonging to one of the children happening to strike the philosopher on the leg, he flew into a violent passion and, abruptly leaving his friends, ran after the child with his cane."[14] (44).

In a manifestation of the "false consciousness" of which Steffen Hantke speaks in his contribution to this volume, being outsiders hardly removes adjuncts' own blind spot to the university's unfair two-tier system of employment. The method at once most realizable and most radical of removing the unfair differentiation between insiders and outsiders would be to give up the guild-like tenure system altogether and to apply the newer flexibility of contingent labour across the board. But many adjuncts too are mandarins at heart and what they want most of all is a fair shot at actually becoming mandarins themselves. It is this chance of moving up to the tenure track that becomes more and more illusory to adjuncts the world over as possible career paths progressively separate and lead toward mutually exclusive species of academic employment. We are now at the point at which the realization of this divide is beginning to sink in, but most adjuncts still find out the futility of their desire only after years of struggle and self-delusion, guided as their imaginations are by the examples of previous generations. In German universities (and in many other European ones modelled after them), for instance, there used to exist from at least the mid-eighteenth century until the middle of the twentieth the rank of *Privatdozent*. For much of this time this term applied to academics that held doctoral degrees, had written their *Habilitation* thesis, and were qualified and considered worthy to hold a professorial rank. Men of acknowledged brilliance - Immanuel Kant, for instance - as well as much lesser minds could find themselves in this position. In the absence of available professorial slots, however, many *Privatdozenten* couldn't become professors. [15] But, with their *Habilitation* came their official permission to teach ("*venia legendi*"), so teach they did even though they didn't earn a salary with it beyond, perhaps, a lecture fee (originally directly paid by such a teacher's students). Those who needed an income would, for instance, work as private tutors or high school teachers while hanging on to their university posts and the contacts and exposure that would come with it. And something would sometimes come of this exposure, often only long after *Privatdozenten* had passed the age of 40, with the seats of their pants long since having gone shiny and elbow patches having appeared on their jacket sleeves. A journal like *Germanisch-Romanische Monatschrift* (*GRM* for short) contained in its old series a section called "Hochshul- und Personalnachrichten" ("Academic and Personnel Announcements"). Quite regularly, it would carry the triumph of some *Privatdozent* in crisp and clipped prose proving that, for all its drawbacks, the system, on principle, respected the equal merits of those qualified academics it could not accommodate, and had not hardened into an unyielding two-tier one in which the eligibility of many academics is quietly dropped after a few short years. In *GRM* of 1909, the journal's first volume, for instance, we read on page 776: "Ernannt zum ao. Prof. a.d. Universität Berlin: Dr. R. Meister, bisher Privatdozent für klass. Philologie und indogerm. Sprachwissenschaft in Leipzig."[16]

But still, even though the two-tier employment system is in so little danger from within, it is worthwhile to consider how much useful havoc to the system tenured professors of literature could wreak by a concerted effort. They could force a concept of professorial excellence that would go beyond quantified scholarly production. They could assert adjunct teachers' membership of their scholarly community, and thus make them share in that community's rewards. By way of modest proposal tenured professors could, for instance, refuse to publish any scholarly work at all for agreed-upon black-out periods, staggered ones perhaps, of say seven years every fifteen or twenty years. Details would have to be worked out, but the benefits are clear. Departments would have to learn to judge their professors in new ways that are not borrowed from accountancy. The overproduction of scholarly books and articles would be dammed in: professors would continue to write, of course, to get ready for the end of the black-out period. But they would likely start to write differently, using the pressure-free fallow periods for the development of longer views. They would think, read, and study more before they published, and be less afraid of thinner CVs. Publication would no longer mainly serve the aim of professional advancement, but would participate in a truly disciplinary discussion in which other scholars' views, even disagreeing ones, are considered and responded to. Professors might well publish less, but in a profession that does not reward quantity per se this would cease to feel like a drawback. Some tenured professors might decide to teach more, simply because they have always liked that better but were afraid to admit to it. Or some might write for magazines and newspapers and revive that much-mourned figure of the public intellectual. The new ways in which departments will have to learn to judge their professors might well include an appreciation for these activities as well. To accommodate truly compulsive publicists a system might be devised analogous to tradable carbon dioxide emission allowances as this is in place under the Kyoto Protocol (academics from the US, Canada, and Australia would have to sign up too, though!). The untenured, meanwhile, would supply the pages of hungry periodicals with copy and develop a research profile that could get them noticed. The humanities would cease to be those dismal traps of disappointed hope, humiliation, and sour grapes for most of its practitioners.

Alternatively, much in the situation of adjunct teachers could already be gained if they organized themselves into bargaining positions with the administration of their universities. The contributions to this book by Carla Love and Janet Heller point in that hopeful direction, contributions in the spirit of (but written before the appearance of) Joe Berry's *Reclaiming the Ivory Tower*. This book is both a history of and handbook for contingent faculty organizing. It quotes from the author's interviews with many activists reflecting on their experiences in organizing and unionizing adjunct teachers and taking on university administrations (with most activists given made-up names to protect their identities!). It offers sensible advice ("We lose, ultimately, if we quit fighting. Remember that the administration never quits"). It isn't in thrall to the pinched gentility that still surrounds the teaching of history or literature but treats university teaching almost shockingly as just another job (thus seeing teachers very much as administrators do, and as teachers do not generally see themselves). It also holds out an adjunct's ultimate hope: union organizer "Tim Cook" mentions the fight "to make the distinction between contingent faculty and regular faculty 'look silly.'"[17] He says, among other things (and speaking, I think, of a dispute playing out in 1995), "I am very impressed by the former Columbia [College, Chicago] president's comment that if all part-timers were paid $3000 per course the board of trustees might have another look at the issue of use of part-time faculty...."[18]

It would be wonderful if unionization could make contingent faculty simply too expensive to make budgetary sense, thus effectively cancelling the category. But isn't it at least as likely that such a form of organizing would entrench and justify the academy's two-tier employment market and lock contingent faculty permanently in the position of professionally inferior colleagues even though, it is true, it would improve on current pay and working conditions? True, adjunct staff would no longer hang around the corner of the university's gated community, waiting for a day's work, but for them that gate still would read "Abandon all hope, ye who enter here," with no escape to higher ranks and academic recognition for even the most talented or ambitious among us. Adjunct experience as we know it now very clearly points out that any abilities we may have beyond teaching introductory courses, coming to classes on time, being polite, and keeping ourselves reasonably clean simply go unrecognized. Much easier to recognize us as lower division teachers with a contract to teach lower division courses only. We then become the pygmies or *nani* of which Homer speaks, kept in cages that not only stunt our growth but also sap our strength.[19] University administrations might come to like such a situation better than the upgraded adjuncts of this imagined future themselves would: adjuncts would be off their backs, or rather, off their chests as the shameful scarlet letter that we could readily become. Part of our power, such as it is, is the power of embarrassment: students, their parents, many in the general public have ideas of universities that are waiting to clash, once knowledge of it gets out, with what actually goes on there. Those ideas may be high ideals in the tradition of Cardinal Newman's turning students into gentlemen or Humboldt's building of the nation-state; they may be expectations of value for money; or they may be something vaguer in between those extremes. Universities encourage such ideas by publicly embracing forms of the educational sublime that they think will appeal to their target audience. In any event, the use of adjuncts on the scale now current scandalizes pretty much any idea of universities held dear by anyone inside or outside of them. Adjuncts find it hard to project their power of embarrassment because we ourselves are embarrassed by our own distance to ideals we too embrace, a distance of which we are forced to be an embodiment.

Much of the impetus for the US debate on the crisis in publishing and tenure comes from Lindsay Waters, executive editor for the Humanities at Harvard University Press. In a pamphlet that borrows Cyril Connolly's great title, *Enemies of Promise*, Waters argues that humanities scholars have turned into their own worst enemies by letting the demands of administrators for standards and yardsticks dictate their conception of scholarship. "Modern, highly sophisticated accounting methods have been brought to bear on the work of the scholarly community and are having the unintended consequence of hollowing out the work of the academy."[20] Waters' criticism is reminiscent of that of UK chemistry professors with respect to the RAE system that is killing their departments. Scholarship has become a "quest for credentials" rather than a form of learning,[21] and books have become things to be counted rather than read. Humanities professors have become "grasping, short-sighted, and intensely competitive,"[22] "crafty and slippery characters,"[23] disguising their timidity as boldness and innovation. One form this timidity takes is the unwillingness to read and judge the work of colleagues coming up for tenure. This task of judging is "outsourced" to the university presses and their review processes. The judging is over once the book is published, and so is the need to read and ponder the book. Books stop being transmitters of revolutionary ideas and therefore do not really have to contain any in the first place. Waters ends his polemic by calling on departments "to tell the administrators in some nice, but forceful way, 'no.'"[24]

-3-

The technique of outsourcing as well as the need of a nice but forceful "no" to administrators is eminently relevant with respect to adjunct labour as well. Adjuncts are "attached to a faculty or staff in a temporary or auxiliary capacity," the *American Heritage Dictionary* helpfully explains. *Webster's New World Dictionary* defines adjunct (*adj.*) as "connected or attached in a secondary or subordinate way, or in a temporary or part-time position." These definitions imply that, if you are looking for a career, being an adjunct professor is not a state to strive for. Still, it is mostly in the humanities that being an adjunct is so heavily laden with perceptions and actualities of misery, worthlessness, abjection, and failure. The list of consultants and contributors to the *Merck Manual of Medical Information*, for instance, contains the names of many medical men and women who, in their self-descriptions, list their specializations and affiliations with hospitals, medical schools, and a particular pharmaceutical company. There are professors, associate professors and emeritus professors among them, but also quite a handful of adjunct professors. Ercem S. Attillasoy, specialist in Noncancerous Skin Growths, Andrew J. Fletcher, specialist in Genetics, Mitchell H. Friedlaender, who covers Eyelid and Tear Glands Disorders and Mark Monane (Drugs and Aging) are professionals in their fields, medical researchers or directors at pharmaceutical companies who take pride, it seems, in their adjunct affiliation with medical schools throughout the USA. In the humanities, you wouldn't see adjuncts anywhere near an authoritative guide to anything we do (Norton Anthologies, Cambridge Guides) - except perhaps when they carry such a guide under their arm as they walk to their seventh class of the day.

As professional pursuits, the humanities differ, of course, from Oncology or Obstetrics (and most other fields) in that the latter are disciplines with a wide range of employment possibilities away from colleges and universities. Being in English or History, and staying in it, mostly means teaching it. To Ercem Attillasoy and Andrew Fletcher, an affiliation with the dermatology department of Thomas Jefferson University or the Temple University School of Pharmacy is a form of professional acknowledgment and success, and a way to stay close to medical research and research facilities wonderfully auxiliary to their own further development. More power to them: they'll likely be better doctors, directors, or researchers for it, and the system of adjunct teaching seems a perfect vehicle to satisfy both personal and societal demands. The very fact that it isn't likely that the university will ever become auxiliary to teachers of literature, language, and history should require the university to have some special care for those it educates as its future core of educators.

In *Profession 2001*, the MLA's David Laurence reports the results of a survey, done in the fall of 1999, of staffing in English and foreign language departments. The survey was designed as a "census of all modern language departments in the United States and Canada," and all known two- and four-year institutions were contacted (with a 42% response rate).[25] "Across responding departments, tenured and tenure-track faculty members made up only 35 % of the total number of instructors teaching undergraduate courses in fall 1999 and less than half the faculty (i.e., after graduate TAs were excluded). Faculty members holding part-time appointments accounted for 32% of all instructors in the English departments and 29% in the foreign language departments."[26] In doctorate-granting departments, part-time or full-time non-tenure-track teachers make up smaller percentages, but that is because in those departments graduate student TAs make up the majority of teachers of undergraduate courses. "[I]f graduate student TAs are combined with part-time faculty members as an overall category of part-time instructors, this category in doctorate-granting departments (61% in English and 60% in foreign language) resembles the part-time instructor head count percentage for two-year colleges."[27] The survey is full of other salient statistics. Two-thirds of the courses taught by part-time faculty members are first-year writing or first year language; 70% of English departments do not offer their part-time non-tenure-track faculty members health, retirement, or life insurance benefits (but at least 75% do to full-time non-tenure-track faculty members). One piece of information that the survey does not offer is what percentage of part-time or full-time faculty members holds a PhD.

These figures are dispiriting to anyone trying to imagine them as actual lives led by adjunct teachers in the US. In fact, the first part of this collection of essays testifies to what such figures mean for the lives of a large number of well-educated Americans, mute inglorious Miltonists buried in their campus churchyards, and never an elegy written for them.

These figures also bring up various questions, some not to be taken up here (such as: "Should an English Department in an English-speaking country really offer all those years of composition?" In other parts of the world native language departments leave students largely to their own devices in figuring out how to move beyond their high school prose. Results are just as spotty there).[28] Another question, more germane here, is: "If lower-level courses are so essential to a humanities department, why outsource them?" And if the answer to this question is so clear ("because it's cheaper"; "because tenured faculty members are better qualified for the higher-level courses"), the question then becomes a matter of conscience: shouldn't such useful worker bees be decently treated? This doesn't seem too hard a case to make to administrators, and can be brought up together with plans for a review of tenure criteria and a floating of Robert Scholes' idea to combat early professionalizing in graduate students by making them apprentice teachers for two years and working scholars for a third.

In "Useful Work *versus* Useless Toil," William Morris develops his idea that the only work that is fit to be done embodies a triple hope: a hope of rest (i.e., the work should not be too much or take up most of your time); a hope of product (i.e., the work should be useful, not senseless); and a hope of pleasure (i.e., the work should engage muscle, memory, and imagination; it should be varied and be conducted in pleasant environments). Work that doesn't offer these hopes becomes useless toil, the useless toil Morris saw all around him being performed by the working class of his nineteenth-century England. He imagined a utopian future that no longer derived pleasure exclusively from consumption but predominantly from labour shared by all. The utopia didn't quite come off, but if any environment is uniquely situated to offer its workers this triple hope, it is universities. Instead, universities offer an astounding number of teachers and scholars not even the hope of entering the profession in any other capacity than that of curate of the tenured. Teaching jobs that are the least promising of the hopes of rest, product, and pleasure are outsourced to teachers who at the same time are made to understand that they are placed outside the US academy's system of just rewards precisely administered. They can wait for livings to fall free, of course, but chances for that are very slim in a system that prides itself on its abolition of preferment. The MLA, in its job search statistics, uses a "New cohort preference factor" of 10 percent to accommodate the fact that new cohorts have an advantage over older cohorts still looking for tenure-track positions. The MLA Ad Hoc Committee on the Professionalization of PhDs considers it "questionable how weighty an advantage new cohort members enjoy over members of previous cohorts. They may actually stand at some disadvantage."[29] But everyone who has been an adjunct for a few years knows that it isn't just the work, but also the worker that is being outsourced. I referred to Homer's *nani* before: adjuncts stop being seen as potential tenure-track material long before they internalize rejection and stop seeing themselves as such. If you have worked as an adjunct teacher for a couple of years, you are shop-worn rather than experienced.

-4-

Apart from hoping for a stroke of luck, the choice for adjuncts is to grin and bear it, to get out of university teaching altogether, or to leave the potato blights of domestic academia behind and exchange adjunct status at home for a full-time professorship elsewhere. This is how many adjunct teachers become gypsy scholars. Very few tenured scholars turn into gypsies; if they travel the globe it is as visiting scholars. Categories are fluid, though, and titles subject to the sort of euphemistic drift that (nominally only) turns an adjunct into a visiting scholar in no time at all. Still, by means of thumbnail phenomenology: visiting scholars aim for Harvard, Yale, Oxford, or Cambridge but will settle for lesser places (and that is where I know them from); prime destinations for gypsy scholars are the Far and Middle East. Gypsy scholars don't get removal expenses reimbursed; visiting scholars obsessively collect receipts. Visiting scholars worry about currency exchange rate fluctuations; gypsy scholars think in local currency. Visiting scholars to universities in out-of-the-way countries get to meet their consul or ambassador for wine and canapés; gypsy scholars there deal with visa problems at the Foreign Police. Visiting scholars never have been adjuncts; all gypsy scholars have. Visiting scholars highly praise all institutions they visit; gypsy scholars in their audience generally groan when they hear this. Visiting scholars are on sabbatical leave; gypsy scholars have left their country.

On the evidence of the essays in this book, grinning and bearing it is the most popular choice - if it isn't rather the default option. The stroke of luck - the just deserts of domestic tenure-track employment - came for just two of the authors, one American (Sarah Gates), one Australian (Leslie Speed). Leslie Speed landed her secure, full-time position after a stint of temporary employment away from her temporary university employment. For the rest of us it is foreign splendour.

All essays in this book offer, in different weightings and many different tones, accounts of personal experiences of being an adjunct - or having been one, or being a gypsy scholar - together with reflections on the institutional conditions one finds or found oneself in. Part I contains, with one exception, reflections by US citizens who serve or served their US institutions as adjunct teachers (the exception being Steffen Hantke, a German citizen who worked in the US as an adjunct before becoming a gypsy scholar in Korea, via Taiwan). Part II recounts experiences in non-US institutional settings. In most cases these are experiences of ex-adjuncts who have turned themselves into gypsy scholars and can look at both experiences. For two authors (Leslie Speed and Rudolphus Teeuwen), the non-US institutions they served were domestic rather than foreign, offering them adjunct employment rather than the status of gypsy scholar. James Kirwan, who fled unemployment rather than adjunct labour, and Rudolphus Teeuwen, who went on to become a gypsy scholar still, left European rather than US academic settings - settings, that is, in which professional success is linked to so many systemic vagaries besides scholarly achievement as to become typically erratic.

-5-

Sarah Gates' essay, in Part I, offers a subtle account of the psychological damage that being (and having been) an adjunct can cause. It tells of "the emotional and intellectual consequences of a long-term adjunct sentence," a sentence that is the job crisis, publication crisis, and adjunct teaching crisis all rolled into one. Being an adjunct means friendliness from tenured colleagues based on shared experiences in private life and the classroom, but not in scholarship. It is also a label that offers overwhelmed hiring committees a quick and easy desk-clearing mechanism. How to write and publish when no one thinks of you anymore as *homo scribendus*, least of all you yourself? Adjunct bitterness and *ressentiment* - that recycling and intensifying of one's blameless worthlessness - sets in and is then, unexpectedly and thankfully offset by publication success, a spectacular rescue, and a clever way of disguising one's adjunct years as years wisely and rationally devoted to one's young children.

Cynthia Nichols uses concepts from postcolonial theory to steer her anger at the way she and other long-time adjuncts at her institution have been treated toward cogent analysis. She has served since 1984 in the "non-position position of permanently temporary, integrated adjunct," and analyzes those binary markers that, remarkably, do all apply to her at the same time. Her department regards the lecturers as "'same' whenever and insofar as their labour, service, accomplishments and expertise are needed by the institution. . . . . They are 'other' and 'degenerate,' however, always and just enough to maintain the faculty's positional power, to be excluded from governance, and to save the university money." In a letter to her department, Nichols and her fellow lecturers tried to draw administrators' attention to this built-in contradiction. The utter failure to get her tenured colleagues to apply to themselves the theory they teach in their classes makes it clear to Nichols that "the designation 'lecturer' isn't just a job title or job; it's a terrifically effective hegemonic device whereby even well-meaning and caring administrators and tenured faculty can endlessly evade deep problems in their discipline and university. . . ."

In her interaction with her institution, Carla Love was luckier than Cynthia Nichols; she was able to go beyond analysis and actually improve job conditions for her and other adjuncts. Her story speaks of the potential success, even for the disenfranchised, of banding together. The substantial gains in job security and conditions she helped bring about were, in her estimation, "only possible because we are allied with other academic professionals. . . . The initial impetus for the policy changes came not from adjuncts or from faculty but from academic staff in administrative and students services positions who already had long-term contracts and wanted to broaden the scope of the job security they enjoyed to include more academic staff. . . . We owe our job security primarily to our governance connections with our non-faculty colleagues."

In their banding together with non-faculty colleagues, Carla Love and her fellow-adjuncts are doing something that, Steffen Hantke would argue, doesn't come naturally. Adjuncts who aspire to full-time, tenured positions tend to view their adjunct years as forms of paying their dues to a profession and ideology of which, although they are not, they yet *feel* part. The tenured and tenure-track are adjuncts' virtual selves. Adjuncts look up to these shimmering selves and take an advance on their aspired futures by accepting the outlook of academia as a "gift economy" where money matters are securely stowed away under the symbolic structures that determine success and achievement in full-time academic careers. This is, in current circumstances, an instance of the false consciousness that keeps adjuncts from taking steps toward improving their economic situations along the lines of, and together with, workers who live in a world of money, bottom lines, and supply-and-demand.

Janet Heller has discovered the power that part-timers, adjuncts, visiting and other non-tenured professors can gain by banding together. Having served in some non-tenured position in many institutions, Heller has found that lobbying and letter-writing helps, if there are many signatories. And if a letter to the chair doesn't help, writing to the dean might; or else to the provost. Her conclusion is that departments, colleges, and the MLA can be turned into agents for change; her essay is a 12-point plan for concrete action toward this goal.

Kathleen Thornton's experiences within her academic department are less bracing. Earlier in her 15-year career (or non-career), the atmosphere in her department was such that full-time faculty members did not automatically assume that adjuncts were intellectually or professionally defective. Now, they do. There were more full-time faculty members then, and fewer part-timers. Now, it's the other way around. And there is no united front of lecturers, adjuncts, TAs, and graduate students who have gone through their allotted years of funding: graduate students are the department's first, and cheapest, choice when part-time teaching assignments are allotted. Complain, and you get "quiet but deeply understood threats: my renewal is always at stake." The coldness with which administrators look at part-time instructors makes Thornton reflect, "We are like the mixed-race children of early American slaveholders: a constant reminder to the establishment of its inappropriate behaviour, a constant reminder of its tyranny and exploitation, a constant reminder of its injustice." Cynthia Nichols' postcolonial critique echoes through these words.

Kenneth Ryesky's essay illustrates how adjuncts in his department, although profusely used as a category of teachers, simply aren't factored in as a category of employees needing access to the IT facilities they are supposed to use in the preparation or execution of their teaching. Ryesky works at a department of Accounting and Information Systems, which makes this particular oversight on the part of the department only more unforgivable. A lawyer himself, he frames his essay as a legal brief, mixing the serious point of how adjuncts aren't given the means to partake of new technologies with hints of spoofing legal argumentation.

-6-

Are you better off as an adjunct in a foreign country? The essays collected in Part II do not give an unequivocal answer to this question. The experiences of Leslie Speed, an Australian in Australia, suggest that, unfortunately, this is not so. Australian universities do not use the term "adjunct," but their reliance, as of a series of university crises during the mid-1990s, on "casual" or "sessional" labour, Speed explains, "is merely one example of the increasing influence on Australian tertiary institutions of the American model." With the crisis in university funding growing more severe in the latter part of the 1990s and with the Australian welfare state still intact, qualifying for unemployment benefits was easier than finding even a part-time teaching job. Add to this a public backlash against universities and intellectuals probably more vicious in Australia than anywhere else, and you have a recipe for frustration and psychological exhaustion for those who cannot even achieve professional academic success.

Leslie Speed, after slipping out of academia through the service entrance at the back, eventually enters it again through the front door. Dutchman Rudolphus Teeuwen's experiences as an adjunct occurred, like Speed's, at a time when his country's government started, on the one hand, to experiment with "Anglo-Saxon" forms of budgetary discipline in the university system while on the other hand, dutifully but dispiritingly, doling out huge sums in unemployment benefits, early retirement, and sick leave payments to academics. Adjunct labour became a prominent aspect of Dutch universities' striving for "excellence" in the special sense that Bill Readings gave to that term in his book *The University in Ruins*. Still unused to adjunct teachers, though, his securely employed colleagues largely forgot to treat him like a lesser being. Still: *et in arcadia ego*. The decent treatment of adjuncts there glossed over the distinctions in remuneration and job security that come to get one in the end.

Terry Caesar came to Japan as a senior professor of American literature, hired especially to set up the new PhD programme of Mukogawa's Women's University, and oversee it for three years. But Japan turns out to be the country of third-rate universities, of professors of English petrified of speaking English, and of students who cannot be burdened with reading much more than 40 pages of light prose a week. Of the approximately two PhD students in the programme, approximately two quickly drop out. But never mind - as long as Caesar would be there, the department would have its PhD programme. Caesar quickly discovered that, to his university, he served as something in between a mascot, trophy, and a scarecrow. Once he had happily accepted this fate, he spent his Japanese years avidly reading and writing. "Japan became for me far more compelling to read and write about than to live." If English is such a ghostly, virtual presence in Japanese universities, Caesar suggested to his hosts, why not take the next step and download doctorates from the Internet? Terry Caesar is back in the US now, adjuncting at various colleges in San Antonio, Texas.

The puzzle that James Kirwan's case presents isn't Japan (although he teaches there) but his failure to translate his scholarly achievements into institutional success. Kirwan is an English philosopher who had a book out with Routledge before he was thirty. Two more books on Kant and aesthetics followed, and now a fourth one has just been published. Still, there was no job for him in all of the UK or the rest of the world. Kirwan is puzzled himself by his fate, but he relishes the independence that his Japanese job affords him. It is the independence from "professionalism" that he likes. He has stopped thinking of writing as an activity that should lead to professional preferment and is much happier considering himself someone who teaches English for a living and writes philosophy as an independent rather than a professional writer. Unfinished books will probably stay unfinished, "at least until my children are older: as a mere hobby, writing books is, for the moment, too time-consuming."

Chris O'Brien, a PhD candidate in English at a Taiwanese university and an English teacher at a technical college there, soon detected in his dealings with his employer a form of cultural mimicry at work that he dubs "the synecdochic fallacy," "the tendency to act on incomplete or erroneous data, mistaking it for complete and accurate information." His school claims "an international perspective," but all that that amounts to is the fact that he himself, a Caucasian, an *American Caucasian*, teaches there. Similar to Terry Caesar's experience with Japanese universities, O'Brien has realized that his presence makes the school's claim to English language proficiency and cosmopolitanism come true; for better or worse, he considers himself the mascot for its advertisements, the token foreigner who allows the college to remain comfortably Taiwanese. O'Brien's essay sheds light on the history of Chinese and Taiwanese synecdochic infatuation with American educational models and the ways in which it has succeeded in taking on board only some of its trappings, such as that curious zoological specimen, the American teacher.

The essays in this part of the book, mostly written by Gypsy scholars relieved not to be adjuncts anymore, offer only occasional glances at the people who take up adjunct teaching at their new universities in Asia or the Middle-East. Judith Caesar and Rudolphus Teeuwen afford us such a glimpse. Teeuwen looks at the change from foreign to domestic adjuncts at his university in Taiwan and at how foreign adjuncts there aren't frustrated scholars and grumbling PhDs but either travelling folk with (old) MAs - gypsies *and* adjuncts - or young TESOL MAs happy with the chance to practice teaching. For Taiwanese adjuncts it is also the TESOL MA that opens doors to adjunct teaching jobs that are much more fulfilling to them than to literature PhDs yearning for tenure-track recognition.

Judith Caesar, a gypsy scholar in the United Arab Emirates, segues between her US adjunct experiences and her charge to field sufficient numbers of adjunct teachers for freshman composition classes at her university in the UAE. For all the differences between universities in the USA and the UAE, she has found that they all share that bright idea that adjunct teaching is the perfect category in a department's budget to allow relatively painless savings, cuts, and indifference to pedagogical appropriateness. Students at Caesar's university in the UAE often have Arabic, Farsi, or one of the many languages of the subcontinent as their mother tongue, and yet the adjuncts that teach them are typically last-minute hires from a very limited pool: the UAE is extremely tight-fisted in giving out work permits. Looking back again at her own experiences as an adjunct, Caesar wonders whether it is really worthwhile, given institutional realities around the world, to try to be excellently qualified as an adjunct at all. "The sad truth is that throwing all your energies into teaching is not in your professional interest. Teach as well as you need to for your own self-respect, but be aware of the likelihood that no one else will know or care how well you teach. Instead of focusing all your intellectual energies on teaching, write." And, Reader, she did.

Notes

1. Donald MacLeod and Polly Curtis, "Acid Test," Special Reports: Universities in Crisis, *Education Guardian Weekly*, 7 December 2004, (26 January 2005).
<http://education.guardian.co.uk/egweekly/story/0,,1367450,00.html >.
2. John Holman, former professor of chemical education at York University, quoted in MacLeod and Curtis.
3. MacLeod and Curtis.
4. Ibid., probably paraphrasing John Holman. The MLA Committee on Professional Employment point to chemistry, mathematics, medicine, and law as disciplines reporting, in the late 1990s, some versions of a job crisis in the USA. See MLA Committee on Professional Employment, *Final Report*, submitted by Sandra M. Gilbert, December 1997, 15-16.
5. MacLeod and Curtis.
6. MLA Committee on Professional Employment, *Final Report*, 22.
7. For a succinct history of the job crisis, see MLA Committee on Professional Employment, *Final Report,* 17-22.
8. MLA Ad Hoc Committee on the Professionalization of PhDs, "Professionalization in Perspective," *Profession 2002* (New York: MLA, 2002), 187-210, pp. 186 and 206-208.
9. Robert Scholes, "Learning and Teaching" *Profession 2004* (New York: MLA, 2004), 118-127, p. 122. Scholes' envisioned guild-like system discourages early publication but this, as Cary Nelson points out, may well "infantilize graduate students" who, like anyone else in the profession, should publish "when [they] have something worthwhile to say to colleagues in a given field." See Cary Nelson, "No Wine before Its Time: The Panic over Early Professionalization," *Profession 2000* (New York: MLA, 2000), 157-163, pp. 162 and 158 respectively.
10 Jennifer Crewe, "Why Our Business Is Your Business Too," *Profession 2004* (New York: MLA, 2004). 25-31.
11. The former solution is endorsed by Lindsay Waters in his *Enemies of Promise: Publishing, Perishing, and the Eclipse of Scholarship*

(Chicago: Prickly Paradigm Press, 2004), the latter by Domna C. Stanton in her "Working through the Crises: A Plan for Action," *Profession 2004*(New York: MLA, 2004), 32-41.

12. James D. Williams, "Review: Counterstatement: Autobiography in Composition Scholarship," Review essay, *College English* 68 (2005): 209-25, p. 213.

13. The image of inside academics as Mandarins growing their fingernails I take from Maxine Hairston who, in 1985, declared the independence of composition studies from the suppression of the literature people in English departments. See: "Breaking our Bonds and Reaffirming our Connections," *CCC* 36.3 (1985): 272-82. (Also available at http://www.inventio.us/ccc/archives/hairston/36.3.pdf). This article is the subject of an interesting section entitled "Re-Visions" in *CCC* 57.3 (2006) in which two prominent compositionists reflect on the impact that this article has had on the emergence of composition as an independent academic field.

14. Eugène Delacroix, *The Journal of Eugène Delacroix*, Selected, edited, and introduced by Hubert Wellington, Translated by Lucy Norton. (1951; London: Phaidon, 1998), 44.

15 Kant obtained his *venia legendi* from the University of Königsberg in 1755 and did become professor of logic and metaphysics there in 1770, at age 46. But, no gypsy scholar, he had turned down various offers of a professorship elsewhere as well as a professorship of poetry at Königsberg six years earlier.

16. Not having access to later volumes of *GRM*, I haven't been able to check if, in some later year, Dr. Meister made further promotion from "ao. Prof." (*ausserordentlicher*, or extraordinary professor whose salary is paid by a third party and who is attached to a department in excess of its allocated formation) to ordinary professor who is properly paid by the government.

17. Joe Berry, *Reclaiming the Ivory Tower: Organizing Adjuncts to Change Higher Education* (New York: Monthly Review Press, 2005), 94.

18. Ibid., 95.

19. See the reference to this passage in *Odyssey*, XVII.322 in Longinus, *On the Sublime,*XLIV.

20. Waters, 8.

21. Ibid., 75.

22. Ibid., 51.

23. Ibid., 62.

24. Ibid., 86.

25. David Laurence, "The 1999 MLA Survey of Staffing in English and Foreign Language Departments," *Profession 2001* (New York: MLA, 2001), 211-224, p. 211.

26. Ibid., 214.

27. Ibid., 214.

28. But as if to deal with composition's potential marginality to the curriculum as merely a discipline that transfers a useful skill, composition studies in the US have developed large claims of liberation and self-discovery that they can bring to their students and practitioners. For someone like me, reared in literature, there are familiar echoes to be heard.

29. MLA Ad Hoc Committee, 206.

Bibliography

Beers, Mark H., et al., eds. *The Merck Manual of Medical Information*. 2nd Home Edition. New York: Pocket Books-Simon and Schuster, 2003.

Berry, Joe. *Reclaiming the Ivory Tower: Organizing Adjuncts to Change Higher Education*. New York: Monthly Review Press, 2005.

Crewe, Jennifer. "Why Our Business Is Your Business Too." *Profession 2004*, 25-31. New York: MLA, 2004.

Delacroix, Eugène. *The Journal of Eugène Delacroix*. Selected, edited, and introduced by Hubert Wellington. Translated by Lucy Norton. 1951. London: Phaidon, 1998.

Hairston, Maxine. "Breaking our Bonds and Reaffirming our Connections." *CCC* 36.3(1985): 272-82.

Laurence, David. "The 1999 MLA Survey of Staffing in English and Foreign Language Departments." *Profession 2001*, 211-224. New York: MLA, 2001.

MacLeod, Donald and Polly Curtis. "Acid Test." Special Reports: Universities in Crisis. *Education Guardian Weekly*, 7 December 2004. <http://education.guardian.co.uk/egweekly/story/0,,1367450,00.html>. (26 January 2005).

MLA Ad Hoc Committee on the Professionalization of PhDs. "Professionalization in Perspective." *Profession 2002*, 187-210. New York: MLA, 2002.

MLA Committee on Professional Employment. *Final Report*. Submitted by Sandra M. Gilbert. December 1997.

Morris, William. "Useful Work *versus* Useless Toil." 1884. In News from Nowhere *and Other Writings*, 285-306. Edited by Clive Wilmer. London: Penguin, 1993.

Nelson, Cary. "No Wine before Its Time: The Panic over Early Professionalization." *Profession 2000*, 157-163. New York: MLA, 2000.

Popper, Karl. "Chapter 9· Aestheticism, Perfectionism, Utopianism." In *The Open Society and Its Enemies*. Vol. 1 The Spell of Plato. 157-168. 1945. 5th revised edition 1966. London: Routledge, 1991.

Scholes, Robert. "Learning and Teaching." *Profession 2004*, 118-127. New York: MLA, 2004.

Spacks, Patricia Meyer. "The Academic Marketplace: Who Pays Its Costs?" *MLA Newsletter* 26.2 (1994): 3.

Stanton, Domna C. "Working through the Crises: A Plan for Action." *Profession 2004*, 32-41. New York: MLA, 2004.

Waters, Lindsay. *Enemies of Promise: Publishing, Perishing, and the Eclipse of Scholarship*. Chicago: Prickly Paradigm Press, 2004.

Williams, James D. "Review: Counterstatement: Autobiography in Composition Scholarship." Review essay. *College English* 68 (2005)· 209-25.

Part I

Adjunct Teaching in the USA

Shouting Down the Avalanche

Sarah Gates

This memoir (or personal essay) explores the emotional and intellectual consequences of my eleven years as an adjunct professor at a small north-eastern (USA) business college. It describes the intellectual and professional isolation that come with adjunct status; the increasingly desperate, irrational, and fruitless efforts this adjunct made to revivify her career; and her final descent into bitterness and total loss of confidence. Along the way, I describe the experience of being an internal candidate who wasn't hired, of desperate midnight submissions of old seminar papers to journals chosen at random, and finally, of some successes and the eventual re-ascent into a tenure track position, thanks to a lucky marriage. In the end, I describe life after adjunct status in my new tenure-track position and the ways that old history continues to haunt me, and I ask some questions of the profession about this random wasting of so many of its new members.

Adjunct Bitterness; Self-Confidence (loss of); Publications; CVs and Adjunct Life

> *The pharmakos [scapegoat] is neither innocent nor guilty. He is innocent in the sense that what happens to him is far greater than anything he has done provokes, like the mountaineer whose shout brings down an avalanche. He is guilty in the sense that he is a member of a guilty society, or living in a world where such injustices are an inescapable part of existence. . . . The pharmakos, in short, is in the situation of Job. Job can defend himself against the charge of having done something that makes his catastrophe morally intelligible; but the success of his defense makes it morally unintelligible.*
>
> *Northrop Frye*

> *And if you see my reflection in the snow-covered hills,*
> *Well, the landslide will bring it down - oh, the landslide will bring it down.*
>
> *Stevie Nicks*

First, my credentials. Education: PhD, 1992, English Literature (Victorian studies - dissertation on George Eliot). Graduate school GPA, 3.97. Teaching: freshman composition at a business college fall, spring, and summer for eleven years, along with ESL at another school for several summers. Mostly: handmaid in an Arts and Humanities division that is itself a handmaid to the master curriculum of "Educating tomorrow's business leaders," as the business school's stationery claims. (On black days, I used to fantasize quotation marks around the *Educating*.) The adjunct woes typical of such positions (starvation wages, lack of benefits, nomadic office arrangements, and a steady diet of remedial teaching) were all mine. But I am not here to talk about those. My circumstances in that regard were middling - worse than some and better than many. Rather, I want to try and tackle the inside of that outside, the emotional and intellectual consequences of a long-term adjunct sentence.

I started like all of us - with a dossier full of praise, a sheaf of good course evaluations, and a dissertation that my defence committee assured me should become a book rather than a series of articles. A month later, I got a job that would start in September - the part time position at the business school - and that would tide me over while I went on the job market. I had one interview at that December's MLA conference: Claremont-McKenna. They never got back to me. "Never mind. Next year will be your year," I was assured by my advisor.

*

One's full-time colleagues do not form the same attachment to the adjunct hires in their departments as they do to their full-time newcomers, or as one's professors did in graduate school. I found it very difficult, even before I was bitter, even when I was still trailing clouds of grad school glory, to approach these new colleagues as a scholar. I don't want to malign them, and I'm sure the fault lies partly with my own diffidence or pride or some such inner reluctance. They were all very friendly and welcoming in a personal way - happy to talk about children or share classroom stories. They gave me a baby shower before the birth of my second child. I felt an equal contributor during the annual pedagogy "retreats" for the rhetoric faculty while we were working out the basic premises and details for making an interconnected "freshman rhetoric programme" out of what, at the time, were separate speech and composition courses. But no one ever talked to me about scholarship or research - including the Victorianist on the staff.

And I needed that mentoring. I had never in graduate school managed to get a paper published, and because of those earlier rejections, I felt intimidated about making my dissertation into a book or sending proposals to publishers. As two and then three years went by, the feeling became more paralyzing: on one hand, I was all grown up and out of the nest and shouldn't bother my former parents from graduate school (who had new kids to take care of, after all); on the other, I would be revealing my inadequacies to, and intruding my needs or interests upon, these busy colleagues who really didn't want to spare the energy on someone who was only temporary, contingent, ad hoc, adjunct. Underneath all of it - something I can permit myself to remember now but that I didn't want to acknowledge at the time - lurked the shame: the whisper that said "Why should anyone be interested in *your* ideas, *your* projects? *You are just an obscure composition lecturer at a business school.*" (Oh, how I have come to loathe that word, *lecturer*.)

Clearly hiring committees had no interest in me. Since Claremont-McKenna, not one had even acknowledged receipt of my application materials. At some point, I stopped applying. Not for lack of response, however, but because I began to feel, as I would page through the MLA Job Information List, that I actually couldn't teach the classes the ads were describing - *not even the ones in Victorian literature*. It had been too long and I was forgetting things. In particular, I was forgetting my own qualities: the flexibility, the inventiveness, and the confidence in my own knowledge that had gotten me the PhD in the first place. And since I'd been teaching nothing but Freshman Composition since graduating, I began to feel, in the deepest regions, that it was the only thing I *could* teach. The irony in that "only"! - composition being such a difficult course to teach well, as we all know. But to me it was - and to the profession generally it is, however little anyone wants to admit it - the equivalent of being the dishwasher.

Like some kind of academic Job, I ransacked my life for sins: I shouldn't have taken the business school job in the first place. (But everyone said that such part time work would put more on my CV and might even lead to a full time position!) I bore two children. (No one advised me to do this, of course - but if not when I'm in my twenties and thirties, then when?) I wrote a dissertation on George Eliot just before the academic market for "single author studies" went sour. (But everyone said to write a dissertation on a well known canonical author, to demonstrate my seriousness and weight as a scholar!) And I combed the memories from my one MLA job interview for badly handled moments and muffed answers. Naturally, as my confidence sank lower and lower, there seemed to be more and more of those - until the whole episode came to seem like one long blunder.

But the worst sin was something I knew for certain: I wasn't publishing or coming up with new ideas. I knew there had been things to do to make the dissertation into a book, but they had become vague in the time since graduation, after "taking a little break" from the project, and then teaching year round for three years, four years, five years. More and more I told myself I was "saving it for tenure," like a pot of gold for that very rainy day. As it sat there on my bookshelf, it gradually lost any character it might have had as "work-in-progress" and hardened into a talisman, the magical repository for everything I longed to be and everything I feared most deeply about my scholarly self. I felt Victorian studies (George Eliot scholarship in particular) spinning past it while I was refining my expertise in composition pedagogy, so that everything in it was becoming hopelessly out of date. But because my confidence was so low, this feeling, instead of inspiring even the most fruitless kind of anxious surveillance over my field, just made me afraid to read anything at all - afraid, even, to reread the thing itself. What if it had flaws? Would I know how to fix them? Would I even know they were flaws? What if it was all one big disaster? Would I even recognize that? In fact, when I did try to think about it seriously and critically, all I seemed able to remember about its ideas and interpretations was that the best of them came not from me but from my advisor or the members of my dissertation group.

My copies of *PMLA* continued to arrive, faithfully reproaching my impotence six times a year. Paging through the issues (when I could face it), I found myself unable to read the articles and increasingly focused instead on the paragraphs describing the authors. They were always full-timers - from every rank (and once in a while a lucky or brilliant graduate student) - but not a *lecturer* in the bunch. And all were the authors of other articles and of books. *Who are these people? How do they do it?* I would remember from the deep past with increasing amazement that I myself had produced anywhere from four to eight seminar papers every year of graduate school. Who was that? Of course, I thought, they must have been junk - and anyway, seminar papers are not the same things as articles. It never occurred to me that graduate school is an intensely stimulating milieu, whereas teaching Freshman Composition at a business school with colleagues who don't talk about their research is an intellectual desert. I am able to understand now that this almost total intellectual isolation bears more of the blame for my barrenness than some egregious inadequacy in my character. But at the time I began to feel that everything I thought I had achieved wasn't really my own achievement. After all, look at me. Without the people who had *really* had the ideas, I hadn't a thought in my head. No wonder no one wanted to hire me. My PhD was a fluke.

I hit bottom the year the college redid its humanities core curriculum and gained two new full-time positions to help staff it. Three other adjuncts and I naturally applied for those positions. Internal candidates in general come under very close scrutiny (since we're right there, underfoot), and we were no exception. We submitted our syllabi for scrutiny, and our classes were visited several times (once by each member of the search committee), even though the external candidates were chosen for interviewing only on the strength of their letters and CVs. However, this really didn't bother me. I noted the discrepancy, but I actually thought it would work in my favour. My students tend to like me and to rise to the occasion during classroom visits, and my evaluations had always been consistently good. In fact, I felt something I hadn't experienced in a very long time: solid, realistic hope. Here at last was a job I *knew* I could do, and do well. Hadn't I been at it for half a dozen years already? At last I would be chosen as the valuable teacher and friendly colleague that I had been for all this time - by people who knew me!

One day in early November the office phone rang ten minutes before I had to teach a class. I recognized immediately the voice of the Arts and Humanities chair. This man had a low, quiet voice and a slight foreign accent that tended to continentalize his vowels and soften certain of his consonants - the letter *r* in particular - so that he sometimes seemed almost to be purring when he spoke (especially over the telephone). This lovely voice now said to me, "I have to tell you, Sarah, you're not on our short list."

I hadn't even made the first cut.

My God, I'm hopelessly deluded! I'm some kind of intellectual anorexic whose ninety-two pounds look like two hundred in the mirror! I had known I could never get or perform a job out there in the big leagues, but not even this one? *Not even an interview?*

I had to find out why I wasn't even worth interviewing by the colleagues who had been so friendly, had seen such good classes, had expressed admiration for my syllabi. I called him back later that evening (stomach in a pit of ice) and asked. He was very gentle, but he let me know firmly that I *must publish more*.

So there it was - my dirty secret, open to all. I knew he was perfectly right (and was trying to be very helpful and was fighting against his own discomfort with what he knew was very painful for me). At the same time I was seeing in perfect clarity the impossibility of following his advice. Hadn't I been trying to *publish more* for six years? (Of course I hadn't, but by then my constant awareness of *not* publishing felt oddly like attempts *to* publish—attempts to have something to publish, anyway.) I'm afraid he earned my lasting resentment, this kind man, simply because his truthful helpfulness probed my deepest, most sensitive points of self-loathing.

I think he must have sensed something of my problem because a few weeks later he suggested that I just send my dissertation off as it was - and gave me the name of his own editor. *The sacred cow.* When I thought of sending it off - just like that! - I recoiled from its two certain fates (irrationally contradictory, but who's rational in this condition?): flat rejection (*it's a piece of junk*) and acceptance (*not now - it's for "tenure"*). I dithered around in this resistant quandary for a few weeks. Once, I managed to call this editor and leave a message. He didn't get back to me. (*Why should he? You're just an obscure composition lecturer at a business school.*) Sometime in the next semester, the chairman asked if I'd talked to the editor yet. I said I had left a message, but hadn't heard back. (Thank heaven I was able to say that much.) "Well, the news isn't good anyway. He will likely tell you the same thing he just told me. No one's publishing single author studies any more, which shoots down a certain project of mine as well." The *relief*! (About my own pot of gold, that is.)

Still, I got desperate. In the next week or two I did something that I have never told anyone about. I went to my old file cabinet and exhumed the four or five papers that professors had encouraged me to "work up" into articles and reread them. Not bad! Ignoring the "work them up" clause in the deal, I printed out clean copies. Picked journals out of the *MLA Guide to Periodicals* with the highest acceptance rates. Dashed off cover letters. Enveloped, addressed, and stamped the lot, and then *fast*, before I could change my mind, dumped them into a mailbox like a marooned sailor tossing random bottled messages into the sea.

I still wince remembering that groundless, blazing, ridiculous hope - so irrational, so self-defeating. To blot it out, I added the five titles to my CV and, feeling like a thief, read the result. Wow. Here was a whole new identity, all plumped up with variety and abundance: *This is who I am!*

I don't need to say that every single one of those papers came limping home in the next few months, and I had to remove them, one by one, from that once plump and vibrant CV. I hadn't the spirit to try again, still less to try and rework any of them according to the suggestions made by the more helpful referees. Even in the most encouraging responses I was only capable of feeling the rejection, the implacable and collective professional judgment of my worthlessness. They're all junk. Even the brilliant graduate student had been a colossal fraud. Here's the real CV: lecturer. And not even good enough for an interview by your own employer. This lecturer, who only managed to give two conference papers and publish one short article in graduate school (in one of those Masterworks of Literature series for high school students), is who I am.

As it turned out, they didn't interview any of the other adjunct internal candidates either - not even the one who had a two-page list of articles on her CV and a book coming out the following year. I suppose there must have been other flaws in her candidacy, but at the time I couldn't imagine what they could be. She, too, was a warm and friendly colleague and a good teacher with good evaluations. In fact, she had left a tenured position in Puerto Rico to live near her daughter. What was wrong with her?? Later still, they denied tenure to the woman they did hire. By then I was so cynical, I could only sneer: none who work here are good enough - *because they work here*. It was the only conclusion I could come to, from my position beyond the pale.

Ah, bitterness.

When the students in one of my summer ESL classes gave me Richard Russo's novel *Straight Man* at the end of the course, I found I could hardly read it, let alone chuckle along with any of it. The main character's resentments about professorial life were too flippantly focused on just the things from which I was structurally excluded. It was like watching someone scoff at a luscious dinner from just outside the doorway, starving.

The tiniest things would get me seething. Every semester, my contract for the following semester would arrive from the associate dean addressing me as "Ms." but signing himself as "Dr." I knew this dean was utterly unconscious that he was stripping me of my credential, and that his (or his secretary's) mistake had only to do with the uniformity of adjunct contract letters which were sent to a group of individuals who didn't all have a PhD (There were graduate students and MFAs among us, as well as PhDs.) But this rational understanding of the situation did nothing to mitigate the spike of fury inspired by those letters - in fact, it produced a simultaneous spike of shame at my own pettiness. *What kind of title snob am I?* and *Intolerable affront!* surged together when my eyes would fall on that opening "Ms." and that closing "Dr." - the sign that this dean was *choosing* to use titles and had denied me mine.

I even engaged in what I would consider - did consider at the time, but didn't care - underhanded practice in the classroom. When a group of students were complaining one semester about some of the teaching methods used in another class, I broke ranks. I reinforced their complaints by pointing out the way that my own techniques were more effective. (How I needed the regard of those students! They were the only people in my professional life who gave me the identity I wanted so much.)

I loved this bitterness. It gave me gravitas. It gave me a bottomless pool of mordant wit and a thick wall of protective contempt. It kept me alive. It glowed with spectacular richness and range over not only my particular employer, but academia as a whole. No longer combing my own history for sins, I now flamed with accusations and blame. *This is ridiculous. My PhD should be just as good as anyone else's!* I began to think about "getting out."

But what else would I do? My attachment to the academy was every bit as thick and glowing as my bitterness towards it. I loved the students and I loved the literature (even though I never taught it), and I loved irrationally and extravagantly that professorial identity with which my students, at least, invested me. Bitterness and longing fed each other like fire and gasoline, and their mutual heat gave me life.

But I tried. I decided my situation was essentially an abusive marriage. To stay in was to be destroyed. So I found a psychoanalytic institute that trained its students using literary works as well as clinical cases. Thinking that I could contribute usefully to this programme while I trained in it, I enrolled. It was fascinating and exciting to be learning new ideas again, and a pleasant relief to be the student rather than the teacher in a classroom for a while. (I kept teaching at the business school, of course - adjunct pay is small, but no pay is smaller.) As I began to feel slightly more worthy, at least in my new endeavour, and very likely as a benefit of my training analysis, my passionate attachment loosened a bit - enough that I could (sort of) give up the professorial identity. (Not that I was ready to imagine myself a psychoanalyst yet. *It's too soon, I'm not ready for commitment, I'm still not over him.*) So "sort of," but not really. It was still the way I defined myself, in cynically negative terms, to my new friends and colleagues at the institute: an "escaped" or "recovering" or "lapsed" or "ex" academic.

Then I tried something truly drastic, something that would strike at the heart of the old dream, maybe kill it off at last: I took a knife to my dissertation. I carved off the *Adam Bede* chapter and sent it to *Studies in the Novel.*

By God, they accepted it! The knifing had felt like a murderous act of vengeance, but the result was revivification. I sent the Introduction to *Genre*, and their acceptance letter was so full of praise for the essay and - astonishing! - gratitude to me for sending it to them that I had to check the greeting again to make sure they hadn't mistakenly put someone else's letter in my envelope. Nope, there was my name, sure enough: Dr. Sarah Gates . . . Dear Dr. Gates . . . . Was it possible? Was my symbolic pot of gold going to be real gold after all? On a wave of audacity and euphoria, I decided to try *the top* - and sent the *Daniel Deronda* chapter to *ELH.*

Accepted!

In my euphoria, I actually dragged out the seminar paper, an essay on Tennyson's *In Memoriam*, which had gotten the most encouraging responses from its referees in that earlier desperate bid for publication. This time I gave it a fair chance. I went back into the library and *worked it up*. It was accepted at *Victorian Poetry*.

These all sound like the events of a few months as I've written them here (it's still how it feels to me in memory - a sudden rush of affirmation), but in fact they happened over the course of about three years, during which I completed the first stage of my psychoanalytic training. I had passed the fieldwork presentation and done the requisite coursework, and was now qualified to go on to a clinical internship. It was time, in other words, to make *the commitment*. And yet . . . here was my abusive spouse again, knocking at the door, offering chocolates and flowers, promising me that he loved me, that he would change, had already changed. What did I do? I left that rebound relationship flat and went back on the academic job market.

This time, I prepared better. Swallowing that "out of the nest" scruple, I met with the Director of Graduate Studies at my graduate programme. He looked over my dossier and CV to make sure everything was the best it could be and advised me that the vital thing I must achieve in my application letters was a cogent explanation for the discrepancy between my long adjunct status and my now excellent credentials. Well, my second child had turned five, and would be entering school: the perfect explanation. I had *chosen* to work part time until both children were school age and old enough for their mother to be a full-time professor. Suddenly my career looked consciously reasoned, even *planned*. (It looked so reasonable, it almost convinced me.)

And it worked. I got an interview with Bradley University.

But without therapy, abusive spouses stay abusive. I never heard from that committee after the interview.

I never got another interview.

And I had spent my gold. (I had also spent $1200, just about a full month's pay, to go to MLA for that interview - at a time when I was divorced and trying to live with two kids on child support and adjunct salary.)

*

But I was rescued. I am now a tenure-track Assistant Professor of English at St. Lawrence University. Let me explain quickly, however, that no exceedingly sharp-eyed search committee somehow spotted my small sparkle glinting in the general mud. No, what happened was a *deus ex machina* from an entirely different area of life: I fell in love with and married a man who happened to be a full professor at St. Lawrence University, and St. Lawrence had just created a new array of flexible appointment options. So we applied for, and got, a shared 2/3 – 2/3 position, tenured for him (obviously) and tenure-track for me. Thus, my rescue was just as "morally unintelligible" as my long prison term - neither one being a clear and direct result of my professional merits.[1]

As I write this, I remember so well reading or hearing accounts of other adjuncts who managed to get out of the trench by one means or another, and the mixed feelings these accounts produced: there was the hope, of course - if it happened to her, maybe it can happen to me. As time went on, though, such bits of hope hollowed, and instead of seeing comparisons between myself and the fortunate one, I saw only contrasts. Unlike me, this other person must still have ideas to publish, must still know how to interview, must have escaped the "bad smell" that I suspected my bitterness was producing, must have some quality or quirk of character or personal history that I no longer had, if I ever did. I don't want to be another holder out of hollow hopes here. How many adjuncts can possibly marry their way into tenure-track positions?

So how does it feel - to have tumbled into the greener grass after starving so long? A wonderful, wonderful relief. My colleagues feel like *colleagues*; they regard me as one of them. With some of them, I have a poetry writing group and with others, a scholarly writing group. I have a vote. I have summers off from teaching. I get travel money (now that I can *afford* to attend conferences). I can laugh with *Straight Man*: I'm in the club! I get to "resent" committee meetings, too! (Actually, it may be the psychoanalyst in me or just that I'm such a social person, but I have to admit that I enjoy meetings.) Most gratifying of all, I teach literature courses to English majors: survey, theory, intro, and, yes - Victorian literature. Last semester, I actually taught *Middlemarch*. It turns out that I *can* do this job after all.

However, as happy as this picture looks, the tapestry has its holes. On the surface, I can do this job (and how I love doing it!), but down below, in the middle of the night, lurks the angry question, *Why couldn't I get a job on my own merits?* My husband repeats to me that I did, in fact, get this job *on my own merits*. That I had to present my credentials to both the English department (who had to make the position request to the dean), and to the Professional Standards Committee (who had to approve it). That I therefore won the department's desire to include me in its ranks, and won over dean and committee, *on my own merits*. Otherwise I would not have the contract I signed a month ago. It is against the university's policy, he insists to me, to hire anyone because she is *someone's wife*. And of course, I know this is true. During the day. But in the middle of the night, I remember all those search committees who glanced at my paperwork and saw *obscure composition lecturer at a business school*, and I can't help but think that without the fortunate quirk of circumstances that brought me to the attention of this department as a whole person first (rather than as a CV), my new colleagues might have reacted the same way.

This perception steadily undercuts my efforts to shed the bitterness that still dogs me and might poison my new relationships if I'm not careful. About a semester into my new job, for example, my husband and I received an invitation to an alumni dinner at the president's house, addressed to: Dr. and Ms. This time, because the "insult" was so unexpected and so out of place in my new condition, my reaction absolutely took my breath away. I had to wait a couple of days before calling with our RSVP, so that I could mention casually and lightly enough to the secretary who had innocently addressed the invitation by hand - it wasn't in any computer programme - that I was a "Dr." as well.

Another time, a colleague was over for dinner, and the conversation turned to teaching in St. Lawrence's First Year Programme, which is team taught in the fall semester. This colleague reported her unhappy experience trying to teach with one of her partners, who was "an *adjunct*" (sour distaste) whose attitude had poisoned the whole course. I knew she was condemning this colleague not because of his adjunct status but because of his attitude or character- something individual to him. But I have felt in flesh and bone how intimately that "attitude" is forged *into* the individual adjunct's character, how impossible it is to survive adjunct status without its protection. I recognized myself in him - with all his resentment and rage. I knew all the colours and textures of his bitterness and the powerful senses of unworthiness and longing that fuelled it. And I knew exactly how painfully twisted an adjunct's relationships with full-time colleagues can become. Our rosy evening went grey. I kept quiet, unable to express a proper sympathy with her, and yet unable to begin to defend "adjuncts" because I knew my tone would quickly get out of control.

The same paralysis renders those department meetings devoted to discussing job candidates almost unbearable - the pettiness and even glee with which some candidates can be rejected! But I know I must serve on as many search committees as I can. My ideal would be to inspire my department to engage in some kind of adjunct affirmative action (which means I have to be a sterling example, myself, of the benefits of taking a risk on someone else like me - a standard I by no means feel sure I can uphold). But if I can't achieve that, at least I hope my *presence* will discourage unthinking cruelty to good teachers and scholars who have for no discernible reason been selected as unworthy of notice.

The way I got this position also gives me no help in shedding those old irrational anxieties that my PhD is a fluke, that I have spent my gold, and that no more will come - even though (and here I have to brag a bit to make my point) my Tennyson essay has now been picked up by W.W. Norton and is anthologized in their new Critical Edition of *In Memoriam*. Even though I have just completed a new article - yes! a new idea! - on *Hamlet*. Even though, as I was teaching my first real English classes to my first English majors this year, I found myself with a couple of *other* new ideas. And even though - most delightful of all - I've started getting my poems published: four came out last year. But these daytime triumphs have their midnight backlashes - doubts that flicker across my mind like tics: *the Tennyson isn't* new *work, the* Hamlet *is outside my field and will be rejected, the new ideas aren't* real *ideas, I wasn't hired as a poet . . . et cetera . . . et cetera . . . et cetera.*

Worst of all is the coming juggernaut of tenure - anxiety-provoking enough without the compounding effect of my history. *Tenure year*, says the midnight tic, *will mark the return of the obscure lecturer*: I'm ba-a-ack! I feel it coming. I recognize the signs only too well: solid, realistic hope. *Here at last is a job I* know *I can do, and do well. Haven't I been at it for half a dozen years already? At last I will be chosen as the valuable teacher and friendly colleague that I have been for all that time— by people who know me!*

*

From time to time we hear about the profoundly disturbing results of "simulated societies," sociological experiments in which one group of participants is arbitrarily designated as "inferior" and the other "superior" - Jane Elliott's blue-eyed/brown-eyed exercise, for example.[2] How much more disturbing is our profession, which is not a *simulated* society, not an experiment that comes to an end (however much it is behaving like one), but is real life - real, brutal, ruinous, and without end for the randomly chosen "inferiors"? The economic harm will persist for me until my death. What's the most I can earn, by retirement, starting now, as I am, at the bottom of the pay scale at age forty-seven? But the insidious intellectual and emotional harm will persist for all of us, for the heart of the academy, in the shredded confidence, embittered character, and wasted potential of half its younger members. How many ideas have been cut off before they could even send out their first shoots? What might I have created in all those barren years with the time, inclusion, and interest I am getting now? And how much sweeter could this new life be without the tremendous burden of anger that tempts me to lash out or to lash myself?

I was told so often during my search efforts that "people will think there's something wrong with you because you've been an adjunct for so long." Guess what? There *is* something "wrong" with me: I was an adjunct. For too long.

Notes

1. "Morally unintelligible" is the phrase Northrop Frye uses to describe the situation of the *pharmakos*, the "hero" in tragic works of the "ironic mode." *Anatomy of Criticism: Four Essays* (Princeton: Princeton University Press, 1957), 41.

2. William Peters, *A Class Divided: Then and Now* (New Haven: Yale University Press, 1987).

Bibliography

Frye, Northrop. *The Anatomy of Criticism: Four Essays*. Princeton: Princeton University Press, 1957.

Nicks, Stevie. "Landslide." *Fleetwood Mac: Fleetwood Mac*. Warner Bros-Reprise Records MS 2225.

Peters, William. *A Class Divided: Then and Now*. New Haven: Yale University Press, 1987.

Russo, Richard. *Straight Man*. New York: Random House, 1997.

Uppity Subalterns and Brazen Compositionists: Confronting Labour Abuses with Theory, Rhetoric, and the Potent Personal

Cynthia Nichols

This is a hybrid essay which mixes the scholarly, the theoretical, and the personal in an attempt to provide a fuller picture of a university adjunct's life and lot. Using postcolonial theory as a lens, and drawing on Edward Said, Gayatri Spivak, and Homi Bhabha, it interrogates the texts of neo-colonialism in the American university, and attempts to rearticulate, in a small way, the imperialist narrative of the contemporary academy and its labour practices. At the same time, the essay explores some of the daily, lived consequences of such a narrative on friends and colleagues in a small Midwestern school - the effects of neo-colonialism at the micro levels of social interaction. The essay also draws heavily on the work of such writers as James Berlin and Eileen Schnell in understanding the place of English Studies in the academy's narratives, scrutinizing real documents from a Department of English to reveal how its "subaltern" non-tenured faculty are objectified and silenced. The essay juxtaposes theoretical passages and rhetorical analyses with personal letters, and its voice ranges from scholarly/impersonal to sardonic/intimate and confrontational. Embracing such alternative, fused genres is perhaps one step we can take toward changing the contemporary university, and toward locating a space from which the academic underclass can truly speak.

Academic Labour Practices; Adjunct Labour and Postcolonial Theory; Macro and Micro Levels of Power in the Contemporary Academy; Hybrid Genres/Alternative Voices; Imperialist Narratives and the University; Academic Underclass; Women in the University; Issues in Composition/Rhetoric; Rhetorical Analysis of Institutional Documents; Voice of the Subaltern

Attending my department's World Literature conference for the first time some years ago, I was repeatedly struck by how *familiar* the concepts of postcolonial studies felt to me. I had no special education in the history of empire and diaspora, and knew very little postcolonial theory. I was a white, relatively privileged American, raised solidly middle class and with degrees from decent schools. Yet the operations of power and language, so vividly described in the conference papers I heard on colonial/postcolonial literatures and institutions, were easily recognizable to me as a long-time university adjunct. Since 1984 I had been teaching as an untenurable, need-based Lecturer at a land-grant school on the Upper Plains. By 1999, the first year of my department's World Literature conference, I was deeply entrenched in the "non-position position" of permanently temporary, integrated adjunct. Together with a sizable mob of other lecturers and graduate students, I provided the cheap, invisible labour which kept our tenured faculty and graduate programme in business. And like most of my local peers, I was only somewhat familiar with the growing literature on labour issues in higher education. We had no useful language for conceptualizing exploitation in our department, and we tended to fight mostly disconnected and ineffectual battles over relatively minor issues.

The postcolonial theory which I was absorbing, however (and ironically enough via a conference sponsored by my own department), began to suggest some useful conceptual tools. [1] In combination with a renewed focus on rhetoric and the history of academia as explored by James Berlin, such theory can help us to interrogate discourse *as* discourse and so call the bluff of centralized power. It provides a particularly apt frame for understanding exploitation in English Studies, where labour problems historically have been especially pronounced. And it can help us, perhaps most crucially, to interrogate specific local practices and discourse at the micro levels of actual documents and real person-to-person relationships in a contemporary department of English. [2]

*

One of the most persistent features of English department discourse I've been examining locally is its reliance on, and perpetuation of, "destructively decisive

Fall, 2001

Dear X,

I can imagine someone calling right now - anyone, you, one of my sisters, my in-laws - and asking what I'm doing. I'd say: "Working on my Linguistic Circle conference paper." And I assume this would mean, for just about any listener, that I'm doing some kind of academic drudge work on a nice sunny Saturday, very likely one of the last pleasant days we'll have for awhile and so "what I'm doing" will seem to the listener and even sound to me like some god-awful boring - well, some god-awful boring academic crap.

But in my defence I'll just mention that most of the stuff I write - poems, academic

oppositional categories,"[3] i.e., a belief in binary opposites, whereby one item in the pair is always honoured and the other always dishonoured: literature and rhetoric; research and teaching; study of texts and production of texts; graduate instruction and undergraduate instruction; PhD and non-PhD. Robert Scholes, James Berlin and others have written at length about how these binaries pervade and operate in the discourses of English Studies. In *Rhetorics, Poetics, and Cultures*, Berlin explores the historical formation and politics of English departments in particular, and western education in general, showing how rhetoric and poetics have alternated as dominant categories since classical Greece. Most often, he claims, rhetoric has probably been the larger category, with poetics a subcategory inside of it, although the reverse has been true since about the mid nineteenth century. He goes on to look closely at very recent, inner-disciplinary conflicts resulting from new social conditions and modes of production as well as from recent challenges to modernist-humanist views of language and knowledge. His final analysis of the contemporary English department is quite damning:

> In most publicly funded universities as well as many private ones, the first-year English requirement which the English department itself often supported by making the course (or courses) a prerequisite for literature classes. . . - enabled the English department to

papers, anything *-comes out of my feelings of connection to people I care about, and also out of sheer curiosity about the weirdness of my everyday life. Without those feelings of connection and that curiosity, I'm not sure that I'd have the energy or juice or patience to write anything at all.*

None of which is to say, of course, that I'm not enthralled by ideas in and of themselves and engaged by sometimes arcane thinking. I think I simply like to think. I take pleasure in thinking. Thinking is something to me. There are those fabulous moments in which even the body responds - the adrenaline picks up and you have to actually get up and walk around the house or the office or the coffee shop or something - because not just the mind but the body is thinking.

Ok, well, more to the point: I was trying to get going on my Linguistic Circle paper that night I called you recently with questions about teaching poems. That's how I get going on a paper or poem or whatever. I talk with someone. I blab. The conversation doesn't begin with the essay; the essay enters the conversation.

It didn't go too well on that particular occasion, however. I can't do this. Click.

generate revenue by hiring low-paid teaching adjuncts, usually women, and low-paid graduate teaching assistants. . . . Such hirings created an institutionally supported gender hierarchy, with upper division and graduate courses taught by men and lower division courses, especially composition, taught by women. . . .[4]

This newly instituted gender hierarchy, however, is only one element of what Berlin sees as the English department's shame. Its "abhorrence of the rhetorical, of political and scientific texts," he says, "does far more harm than creating a permanent underclass of department members whose putative role is the remediation of the poorly prepared."[5] By excluding rhetoric as full partner in English Studies, the department deprives students of a faculty and curriculum which would train them - as crucially now as ever- to understand any text's political agenda and historical contingency. And I'm thinking of "texts" here in a broad sense to include all forms of ancient and contemporary verbal, visual, audio, and now electronic media which so pervade and construct our students' lives and indeed their very bodies.

Excluding rhetoric as a full disciplinary, administrative, and curricular force also allows the contemporary department's literary branch to evade self-analysis, to obscure its own role in the social and political order, and thus to mystify itself as the given, the natural, and the transcendently apolitical (even as it makes the very

Maybe the mistake was mine in thinking my questions even mattered without a real conversation context. I.e., we weren't "just talking" to begin with. I was an idiot in that I tried to sort of yank you into the water - water which was nonexistent, nonexistent at least at that particular moment, the moment, the forward-into-nowhere ongoing agitation of loopy mutual engagement - which in fact is what I mean by "water," and which was, at that moment, Not.

And you were, what can I say, a bitch for failing to regard me as even a minimally respected partner in conversation. The conclusion of that phone call was especially hurtful because it suggests what I was already worried about: that you may be starting to "other" me - and all of the department lecturers - on a regular basis.

I was an idiot, you were a bitch. The more I look into the lecturers' condition and read about contingent labour in the academy, the more I find that, as an area of study, it has everything to do with idiots and bitches, doormats and bastards. In other words, with relations of power inseparably institutional and personal.

It's not surprising that the discourses of English

political choice of excluding rhetoric).[6]

Any reading of my own department, as of many departments across the country, I imagine, easily reveals the views and practices described by Berlin. Some of our literature faculty regard "English" as synonymous with "literature" (as opposed to "writing") and sometimes use the two words, English and literature, interchangeably. Literary study is sometimes identified as "deep" when compared to writing or writing studies, which is identified as "shallow."

Additionally, even though they far outnumber the literature faculty and teach far more students, and even though

departments and universities can easily be seen as imperialist ones, and that postcolonial theory makes a nicely fitting frame for analyzing those discourses as they relate to contingent labour.

What's alarming, sad, and at the same time fascinating to me is how those discourses can both potentially build and bust personal relationships E.g., ours.

More later,
Cindy

the composition/rhetoric programme keeps the graduate literature programme afloat by offering employment to its students, our rhetoric staff is a largely powerless segment of the department: historically, they have had relatively little or no voice in governance, no job security, and significantly lower salaries (in the case of graduate assistants, of course, salaries which are vastly lower). And the gender imbalance is glaring: as of this writing, 80% of the lecturers and 70% of the comp/rhet graduate teaching assistants are women, while only about 16% of the tenured or tenurable comp/rhet faculty are women. The "manual labour" of composition instruction, clearly, "has been left (almost exclusively) to the subaltern woman - the local daughter of working class roots whose Master's degree makes her the most educated member of her family, but whose opportunities for employment keep her firmly entrenched within the working class."[7] Her subsistence, paid-by-the-semester-hour position, as Karen Thompson has observed, is disturbingly similar to the piecemeal work of the needle trades so common around the turn of the century.[8] And she is of course always and firmly associated with the dishonoured half of the binaries upon which department practice is based.

I'd like to look a bit more closely, now, at these binary categories. Viewed from within the framework of postcolonial theory, the operation of (or an institution's relationship to) those categories is perhaps not as clear-cut as it appears to be at first glance. Postcolonial theory may have established these binaries as a paradigm of central interest, but it has likewise rather seriously complicated and variously challenged that paradigm.

Homi Bhabha, for instance, regards the subaltern's positionality as ambivalent and "sliding" between binary poles. "The objective of colonial discourse," he says, "is to construe the colonized as a population of degenerate types... in order to justify conquest and to establish systems of administration and instruction."[9] However, for Bhabha, such discourse never meets its objective because it assigns to the subaltern a split identity.

On one hand, the subaltern is wholly other, barbaric and inexplicable, incapable of ever attaining full assimilation. The colonizers must believe this in order to justify their positional power, the looting of foreign lands, and the imperialist project of subjecting the all to the one. On the other hand, the subaltern is at least as "same" and "educable" as necessary to fulfil the requirements of colonial labour. The subaltern is thus conveniently, variously, and illogically same *and* other, depending on the needs of the colonizers.

Where I teach, university and department texts of all kinds - verbal, written, spatial, interpersonal - are full of language which constructs the lecturer-adjunct position as ambivalent and sliding. On one hand, we are repeatedly told in a variety of terms that we are separate and contingent. Our photos hang apart from those of faculty and graduate assistants in the main department office. Our mailboxes are labelled with different colours and in a separate space. A good half of the lecturers have their offices in a completely separate building, and never share office space with faculty. Efforts have long been made to prevent us from attending meetings in which governance issues involving our courses and our jobs are discussed and deliberated. In a department memo some years back, the

Winter, 2002

Dear X,

I have to admit, it was kind of freaky to watch you hit the tenure track last year. When you arrived here many months ago, you were a vocal and passionate lecturers' advocate. Because of your background in Rhet-Comp (a discipline particularly afflicted with labour problems), because of your previous life experience as well as scholarship, your arguments for better treatment of lecturers in our school were formidable.

Now that you're experiencing the real grind of the tenure-track, however, I worry about your possible change of heart. Or about something I'll call the "hierarchy germ": that mechanism in so many institutions which, after inculcating a person with the exhaustion and stress which comes from raising her own status, subsequently encourages her to resent and objectify those "below" her as a monolithic other, even as she becomes increasingly yet chair referred to "filling in" his staffing schedule with lecturers; the vice president of academic affairs, in a recent open forum, conflated the term "lecturer" with "part-timer," distinguished lecturers as a separate category from "faculty," and referred to how he had "patched" his staffing needs that fall with lecturers. And our year-to-year contracts clearly state that there is "no expectation of routine renewal of appointment."

Nevertheless, several lecturers have been in my department for 20 years or more. When one of my lecturer colleagues objected to the vice president's conflation of "lecturer" with "part-timer," reminding him that she has been teaching here full-time for two decades, he corrected himself and publicly acknowledged her as indispensable. Lecturer numbers in my department have been over twice that of faculty, sometimes almost doubling in response to rising enrolment. That upward climb is expected only to continue, and, indeed, the current administration is aggressively committed to growth in undergraduate numbers. All of these facts are hard to reconcile with claims that we are "fill-in," "temporary," "contingent" or otherwise "adjunct."

The lecturers' position here is constructed as integrated, integral, continuing and "same" in other ways as well. We are physically in and out of the same buildings and classrooms and other spaces routinely - in fact, more so than the faculty, given our numbers and course loads. We are listed in the university directory and schedule of courses under "English Department."

resentfully proud of her own accomplishments and privileges.

This is also a germ, I believe, which aggravates psychological projection. For most of your first year here, you worked hard and truly generously to involve the lecturers in a research project which would potentially benefit them. The project fizzled for several reasons, some valid, some maybe not, and I know you were quite pissed off at the slow response and commitment of the people you were assisting. I agree that the lecturers were absolutely to blame on a number of counts.

However, it did not seem to occur to you that you were asking the underclass, in this case, to act on your terms, not theirs. You devised a project which mirrored you (the scholar) rather than most of us (what Eileen Schnell aptly calls the "mother-teachers"), and then seemed flabbergasted and disgusted when the response was minimal. You became angry at waiting a year for action on our part, forgetting that most of us have been in our positions for nearly twenty years, and forgetting or failing to imagine the debilitating effects of those years. Those effects include our

The names of NDSU lecturers have appeared on the in-house textbooks used in our freshman composition program. Our names appear on the membership lists of department committees, and we have been instructed in writing by the chair to select members from our ranks to serve on those committees. Many of the lecturers have teaching awards hanging on their office walls. Their vitae demonstrate years of publication, scholarship, and substantial service. Their university ID cards read "Faculty." They check books out of the library according to its faculty policy. Until very recently, their summer school contracts have stated that, as "faculty," they will receive less pay in the summer because their "faculty" committee and research loads are lighter then. Lecturer publications, grants, and other accomplishments are announced in the university's websites and hardcopy media. I could go on.

It is fairly evident that the discourse contradicts itself: the lecturers are "same" whenever and insofar as their labour, service, accomplishments, and expertise are needed by the institution (or, to be fair, whenever humane tenured colleagues wish to acknowledge them). They are "other" and "degenerate," however, always and just enough to maintain the faculty's positional power, to be excluded from governance, and to save the university money. It is astounding that so many tenured faculty in our college - the local keepers of the humanities torch and the pinnacles of their profession - continue to ignore this exploitation, if not in fact to actively promote it.

chronic feeling of dislocation even as our location has not actually changed; our ghostly positionlessness in the institution even as we are constantly identified with our position; the eerie quality of the discourse when it attempts, in Bhabha's terms, to "fix" us in place even as we are sliding all over the continuum and never really "anywhere" at all.

I think it's incredibly important for administrators, John Q. Public, and colleagues ranked differently from us to fully understand the dissonance experienced by the academic underclass as a result of the multi-tiered system. Remember Fanon on the psyche of the colonized? Handing back territory doesn't immediately and magically heal that psyche. You have to undo decades of psychological damage and conditioning. Most of my peers are chronically conflicted and chronically stressed, enervated, passive, and dependent, even while prone to sardonic griping.

In any case, it's almost funny, X, how much of the "benign colonial missionary" role you've played and how much of the "resistant subaltern" role we lecturers have played. I believe that the worst of last year's

*

A dramatic instance of institutional discourse which objectifies and silences the subaltern teacher is the following record of a faculty meeting. If theories of exploitation are to be at all meaningful, and if efforts toward change are to have any clarity and power, examination of specific, real-world documents is crucial. Some years ago the lecturers in my department wrote a letter to tenured faculty requesting more inclusion in department decision-making. After reminding them of some of our varied and long-time work, we said in the letter that we perceived "real disparities between our service to the department and our participation in department decision making" and we therefore requested voting privileges. A week after we presented the letter, the whole department met and we clarified that what we desired were voting privileges "where matters concerning our courses and our students are proposed, deliberated, and decided." About a week later, the faculty met to discuss our request, producing the following statement of minutes:

experience, however, is behind us. Our futures in the department are uncertain, but I hope and believe that our (and any) friendship can ultimately survive even the uniquely germy environment of the contemporary university. Perhaps wearing down the boundaries between the personal and the theoretical is one place to start.

Love,
Cindy

English Department Faculty Meeting
3:30 Conference Room
[date withheld]

The lecturers' request to be given full voting rights at faculty meetings and the open meeting with them November 2 were discussed. Discussion included the following:

- Lecturers are presently represented on the FEC and TEC - do those representatives report back to their fellow lecturers now?
- The NDSU Faculty Handbook (III, 6-7) and the HSS Handbook (II, 1-2) preclude lecturers from faculty governance.
- No other department has as great a number or proportion of lecturers as English does, some of these departments allow lecturers to vote.
- If the lecturers are a subgroup within the faculty and their role were increased would this reduce their problems?
- What is the permanence of their position given the 6-year rule?

- Whatever the nature or causes of their problems may be (anger, fear, insecurity), the problems may remain if they were to become voting members of the faculty.
- Is a university department a democracy? Is everyone equal in setting policy?
- In a hierarchical structure some may be perceived by others as being patronizing when they neither perceive themselves that way nor intend to be.
- Fear and insecurity may be caused by limited opportunities to improve job security and lack of tenure; these, in turn may emphasize for lecturers the advantage of faculty tenure.
- The lecturers' argument regarding their status may be with the University and the State Board of Higher Education. It may be an institutional problem.

After the discussion, an effort to establish a few basic principles that all faculty could agree with as a starting point for further discussion and negotiation was not immediately successful. What was successful was a proposal to establish a subcommittee comprised of three faculty and three lecturers. They would meet to study the issue, discuss it further, and then report back to their respective groups. The lecturers will be invited to select three representatives for this sub-committee in its efforts to continue our communication and community.

Submitted by [name withheld]
Distributed to English Department
[date withheld]

I'd like to look at selected passages from the above document fairly closely. *"The lecturers' request to be given full voting rights. . . ."* Our jointly signed letter did not indicate that we wanted full voting rights. Also, we explicitly stated at the department meeting that we were not asking for full voting rights. We were puzzled by this statement in the minutes.

"If the lecturers are a subgroup within the faculty and their role were increased would this reduce their

Spring, 2004
Dear X,
Given how I've scolded you in the past for succumbing to the "hierarchy germ," I thought you might be interested to hear about my recent "out of the adjunct-body experience."
As of course you well know, I was under consideration earlier this year

problems?" Our proposed solution to the inequities we perceived is here called into question; in other words, the faculty do not take it on faith that we can identity solutions to our own problems. At this point, the question seemed to me at least potentially reasonable.

"*Whatever the nature or causes of their problems may be. . . .*" The word "may," here, which is repeated later, suggests that "the nature" of our problems is somehow in question or that they don't understand the nature of those problems. This is despite the fact that those problems were clearly identified in our letter and at the department meeting. To wit: "real disparities between our service to the department and our participation in department decision making."

"*Whatever the nature or causes of their problems may be (anger, fear, insecurity). . . .*" After expressing bewilderment about our problems, or ignoring our own articulation of our problems, the faculty then proceed to guess about the causes of those problems. Their conjecture results in a list of emotional ailments, thus denying our specific grievance the force of its logic and at the same time feminizing us and our argument as emotional.

"*Whatever the nature or causes of their problems may be (anger, fear, insecurity), the problems may remain if they were to become voting members of the faculty.*" After guessing about the causes of the problems they can't define, they here go on to guess about the outcome of the solution we propose to the problems they can't define.

"*Fear and insecurity may be*

for a tenure-track position in creative writing. Despite the support of many kind people, including you, and apparently in part because of discord over the value, appropriateness, and terminal status of the MFA degree, this job prospect fell through at the level of the Vice President.

Promoting to the tenure-track a lecturer of some twenty years would certainly have been, to my knowledge, unprecedented on our campus, and I tried hard not to be too hopeful as the weeks rolled by.

Nonetheless, there were moments when it seemed like a real possibility, and I actually allowed myself to consider what happy changes might be in store for my life. John would no longer have to teach gruelling overloads on multiple campuses. We could finally buy a house and worry much less about hills. And my work life would of course become considerably more attractive: a lighter teaching load, fewer comp. courses, the right to premium department and university resources, a voice in governance, and so on.

My "near tenure experience," in other words, came with its own proverbial, bright flash of light. Or at least a small dose of euphoria. I had gone briefly "out of my caused by limited opportunities to improve job security and lack of tenure; these, in turn may emphasize for lecturers the advantage of faculty tenure." At this point, rather astonishingly, the faculty are guessing at the causes of what they guessed were the causes of the problems they admit they can't or won't identify. And those guessed-at causes of the causes are then guessed to cause an "emphasis" on faculty tenure.

Let me look at this latter item more closely still. Fear and insecurity cause lecturers to "emphasize," or assign great value to, tenure, which is job security. So fear and insecurity cause lecturers to value the conditions of fearlessness and security. This statement, of course, is circular and therefore not especially helpful. However, to be fair, I think the intended meaning is that we assign greater value to tenure than they believe it warrants. The faculty themselves perhaps feel insecure and powerless despite their tenure, and so they are puzzled that we "emphasize" their position. But this reading seems pretty weak, and of course I am now merely speculating myself. Obviously, having tenure means more security than not having tenure. All that can be clearly construed from these statements, finally, is: the lecturers suffer from insecurity because they do not have security. They are afraid and insecure because they are afraid and insecure. In other words, we have emotional problems. No grounds are ever offered for their claim (although there is an appearance, as in all circular statements, of offering claims), and no reference to any specifics of our letter or

body," as it were - out of the corpus of the underclass - and this experience of release, with all of its undeniable promise and seduction, was sweet.

Not surprisingly, I was tempted to "glance back." I.e., I began to feel some very real dissonance, even before the promotion fell through. Even as I imagined personal and professional enhancements to my daily life, I knew they would come at the expense of those lecturers who were NOT eligible for tenure - the very same lectures whose plight I have shared for two decades. For every literature or creative writing course I'd teach, a lecturer or graduate student would be needed to fill the empty spot in composition. For every cutting-edge upgrade to my office computer, there would be someone in the department whose office equipment was just as vital yet left unimproved.

My freedom and well-being, in other words, would be directly reliant upon a duplicitous system which constructs lectures as explicitly *temporary but implicitly* permanent *- and permanently necessary to the maintenance of my own would-be position.*

The events of this last year

our statements at the previous meeting are ever made.

Sandwiched between these speculations and circular remarks is evidence from university documents that dictates our exclusion; evidence from university documents which would support inclusion, however, are almost completely ignored. Guesses are made that inclusion would do us no good; guesses are not made, however, as to how inclusion might help us. The nature of department governance as democracy

have consequently magnified my awareness of adjunct exploitation. They have also, however, made more intimate my understanding of the "oppressors" and of my own potential ability - practically and psychologically to become just such an exploiter.

More Humbled at the Moment than Uppity, Cindy

is questioned; that notion is not equally explored, however, for its validity. In other words, only arguments against our inclusion are explored. Arguments *for* our inclusion are nonexistent in the document, and no evidence exists in the document that such arguments were at any point sought. It is quite clear that the faculty did not intend to seriously consider our request or even, in their discussion, to neutrally explore that request.

Their intent was to actively search out ways to deny our request. All of which makes the mention of "communication and community" at the end of the document rather glaringly disingenuous. Their flat-out denial of our request was a possibility we had prepared for. Their failure to be minimally honest with long-time colleagues, friends, and assistants - as well as with themselves, perhaps - was something else altogether, and perhaps the greatest disappointment of all.

Finally, the statement about our numbers is very telling. "*No other department has as great a number or proportion of lecturers as English does; some of these departments allow lecturers to vote.*" Aside from the revelation that some departments are apparently in violation of university policy (as referred to previously in the minutes), this statement implicitly points to the faculty's fear of our numbers. It was abundantly evident to the lecturers, when we read these minutes, that the faculty do not want us voting because we outnumber them and would therefore have considerable decision-making power. This is never acknowledged openly, however. What happens instead is that their unstated apprehensions are projected onto *us* (we are the fearful ones, we are the emotional ones), when it is they, in fact, who are anxious. And, if anyone is to be considered in any sense "emotional" here, given the questionable logic in their discussion as reported in the minutes, it would have to be them.

So what are "lecturers" then, as constructed by this document? Our ability to state our own needs and to identify solutions to those needs is unrecognized; in other words, our agency is unrecognized. Rather than subjects in our own right, we are inscrutable objects who cannot or will not be understood or reasoned with; we are feminized others with emotional problems; we are object screens onto which those with power project their fears.

The subject-object power dynamic here has been articulated by many postcolonial theorists and discourse analysts. I think this document demonstrates well what Gayatri Spivak talks about when she says that the subaltern cannot speak. We cannot speak because the colonialist subject will not hear us; has written a discourse which allows no space from which we *can* speak.

As it happened, then, as the situation that year played out, no argument we made was ever heard. And it clearly didn't matter what argument was made. Our "problems" were delegated out to an ad hoc committee, which then took them to the chair, who then took them to the faculty, who then took them to the department, who then sent them back to the ad hoc committee.

*

In my final analysis, the designation "lecturer" isn't just a job title or job; it's a terrifically effective hegemonic device whereby even well-meaning and caring administrators and tenured faculty can endlessly evade deep problems in their discipline and university, can indeed disavow any responsibility for or implication in those flaws. Even as the press trumpets the university's commitment to "people first," another mob of underpaid contingent teachers is bussed in. Even as the president speaks repeatedly of raising the university's professional status, a large portion of the university's teachers are actively discouraged from professional development. (When one of my lecturer colleagues recently mentioned to an administrator that he'd been asked to participate in a sizable grant project, he was given a lecture - no pun - on the lecturer's position: That's not in your contract. You signed your contract. You're contracted to be no one. Your signature confirms your lack of signature. Good day.

The lecturer discursive device is at the centre, and represents the locus (or one of the loci) of the current university system's untenable premises. It is one of those precise points at which the university's democratizing tendencies and traditional "moral mission" clash with its colonialist tendencies and corporate capitalist mission; where the "twin crises of morals and money" come together in mutual sharp relief. [10] Perhaps the extent to which lecturers are unrecognized is the extent to which the system's hypocrisy is unrecognized. How ingenious to devise a job designation with non-recognition built in. "Here is a position," administrators and tenured faculty seem to be saying, "not meant to be recognized," and so they go about their duties every day within the university system by not recognizing the position which is recognized every day as Lecturer. Lecturer is the name we give to our avoidance of pain. Lecturer is the name of the contradictions we will not acknowledge. Or if we do, will do nothing to remedy because the greatest accomplishment of power, as Ngugi wa Thiong'o has remarked, is to colonize the imagination and the will. Because the greatest accomplishment of power is to appear inevitable.[11]

X, you remember *The Blair Witch Project*, right? It's like that. We've been wandering in circles it seems like forever, unable to get out of the forest. At the end of a long day of walking, we find ourselves back at the same fallen tree we departed from that very morning. The stone-and-stick-and-rag semiology of the witches, hanging gruesomely from the trees all around us and stacked neatly outside of our tents, makes no sense and creeps us out. We're sick and exhausted and we fight. And now, finally, we've reached the house in the woods and at last the basement, where the witches have instructed you to turn your back. This way you can't see them kill the other children. But why would they bother to have you turn your back, you may wonder, since you know what's happening anyway? Since you, as much as anyone, are well aware of the inequities, degradations, and danger?

Answer: to keep you distracted. To keep you silent. To keep you from panicking long enough to kill us all.

Your friend,
Cindy

Notes

1. I am indebted to Elizabeth Birmingham, Assistant Professor at North Dakota State University, for the notion of postcolonial theory as a conceptual lens for academic labour issues.

2. It's important to note of course the ways in which postcolonial theory does *not* fit the subject of this paper, and care must be taken to avoid easy borrowings which obliterate real distinctions. Colonialism as a penetrating and "expansive force," a type of "self-reproduction," does not really apply to adjunct studies (see Edward Said. *Orientalism* [New York: Vintage Books, 1979]. 219.) And my white, middle-class American life of course bears little resemblance to that of third-world colonized and globally displaced peoples. It is perhaps an ugly habit of privilege that I would presume the right to claim kinship with them or to appropriate their

scholarship and critical tools. But I believe at the same time that my position as academic adjunct is part of a continuum, a global-corporate or even corporate-feudal phenomenon which includes, however distantly, postcolonial diaspora and the real colonial subaltern. Though colonialism is in numerous ways distinctly different from university labour practices, the operations of power and identity-construction in the two are related. And I tend to think that interdisciplinary scholarship and the forging of cross-cultural kinships can only be healthy in the long run, especially when it comes to resisting a persistent and omnipresent hegemony which profoundly impacts us all.

3. James A. Berlin, *Rhetorics, Poetics, and Cultures: Refiguring College English Studies* (Urbana, Illinois: National Council of Teachers of English, 1996), 13.

4. Ibid., xv.

5. Ibid., 14.

6. Ibid., 14-15.

7. Elizabeth Birmingham, interview by Cynthia Nichols, North Dakota State University, c2000.

8. Karen Thompson, "Alchemy in the Academy: Moving Part-time Faculty from Piecework to Parity," in *Will Teach for Food: Academic Labor in Crisis*, ed. Cary Nelson (Minneapolis and London: University of Minnesota Press, 1997), 278.

9. Homi K. Bhabha, *The Location of Culture* (New York and London: Routledge, 1994), 7.

10. George Dennis O'Brien, *All the Essential Half-Truths about Higher Education* (Chicago and London: The University of Chicago Press, 1998), xiv-xv and 19.

11. Some of the percentages cited in this essay will have changed by the time it goes to print. Also, credit where credit is due: adjuncting at my school is in some ways considerably better than elsewhere in the country. We do have office space with phones, we receive health and retirement benefits (if teaching at least two classes per semester), and older lecturers are permitted to teach more than just freshman composition. Also, a new department head (whose field is Rhetoric), along with the dean of our college, have recently been working admirably to promote long-time lecturers to Senior Lecturer, a position with slightly more security and pay. And our department head has strongly supported a recent move to a vertical curriculum, which will relieve long-time lecturers of the freshman composition grind and may ultimately reduce the department's reliance on adjunct labour. This kind of planning is truly commendable.

As of this writing, however, we continue to hire new adjuncts and rehire older lecturers indefinitely while still claiming the position is temporary and thus not eligible for the raises, merit pay, voting power etc. of faculty. This lack of raises has been especially damaging, and we have consequently fallen well below the cost of living. Indeed, the children of one of my colleagues, a full-time university teacher for a good decade and a half, actually qualify for government free lunches. And while the American Federation of Teachers and American Association of University Professors are present on campus, state employees here have no legal right to collectively bargain or strike, rendering unions substantially powerless.

Bibliography

Berlin, James A. *Rhetorics, Poetics, and Cultures: Refiguring College English Studies*. Urbana, Illinois: National Council of Teachers of English, 1996.

Bhabha, Homi K. *The Location of Culture*. New York and London: Routledge, 1994.

Birmingham, Elizabeth. Interview by Cynthia Nichols. North Dakota State University, c2000.

Dubson, Michael, ed. *Ghosts in the Classroom*. Boston: Camel's Back Books, 2001.

JanMohamed, Abdul R. "The Economy of Manichean Allegory." In *The Post-Colonial Studies Reader*, edited by Bill Ashcroft et al, 18-23. London and New York: Routledge, 1995.

O'Brien, George Dennis. *All the Essential Half-Truths about Higher Education*. Chicago and London: The University of Chicago Press, 1998.

Said, Edward. *Orientalism*. New York: Vintage Books, 1979.

Schell, Eileen. *Gypsy Academics and Mother-Teachers: Gender, Contingent Labor, and Writing Instruction*. Portsmouth, NH: Crosscurrents, 1998.

Spivak, Gayatri. "Can the Subaltern Speak?" In *Marxism and the Interpretation of Culture*, edited by Cary Nelson and Lawrence Grossberg. Urbana and Chicago: University of Illinois Press, 1988.

Thompson, Karen. "Alchemy in the Academy: Moving Part-time Faculty from Piecework to Parity." In *Will Teach for Food: Academic Labor in Crisis*, edited by Cary Nelson, 278-290. Minneapolis and London: University of Minnesota Press, 1997.

Adjuncts with Power: Making Policy in University Governance

Carla Love

Within their academic departments adjuncts generally lack power and status. However, when they participate in university-level governance, they not only share in the power to determine their working conditions but also develop an enhanced sense of professional identity. In my paper I focus on the governance rights granted to adjuncts by Wisconsin statute and on my experiences in shaping campus policy at my home institution, the University of Wisconsin-Madison. By working together with a diverse group of administrators, advisors, researchers, technicians, and other staff, adjuncts have been able to achieve significant policy changes in job security, appeal rights, workplace climate, and professional development, gains that make it possible to have a satisfying career as an adjunct. However, I also need to acknowledge defeats that adjuncts have met when the interests of academic staff have conflicted with those of the faculty. Still, experience at Wisconsin shows that adjuncts can successfully ally with other non-tenure-track groups to press for their rights in governance.

University, Governance, Policy, Adjuncts, Faculty

Within their academic departments, adjuncts generally lack power and status. However, when they participate in university-level governance, they not only share in the power to determine their working conditions but also develop an enhanced sense of professional identity. Here I focus on the governance rights granted to adjuncts by Wisconsin statute and on my experiences in helping to shape campus policy at my home institution, the University of Wisconsin-Madison. Based on my work in several campus-level governance bodies over the past ten years, I describe ways in which adjuncts have benefited from sharing in governance rights. I also note the limits to adjuncts' power to define our professional identity.

Before adjuncts' gains and occasional defeats in policy-making are described, a word about the campus governance structure at Wisconsin is necessary. It is an idiosyncrasy of our state university system that adjuncts are not members of the faculty. The same state statute that grants governance rights to adjuncts also places us in a category of employees separate from our tenured and tenure-track colleagues: by statute they are "faculty," while adjuncts and other professionals comprise a much larger group called "academic staff."[1] In governance practice at UW-Madison, this division means that our academic staff assembly parallels their faculty senate, each body having its own policy-making committees. While it might seem that this legislated separation of "real" faculty from academic support staff would translate into less power and prestige for adjuncts, the grouping of adjuncts with other non-tenure-track professionals in fact turns out to be a source of strength. Making up one-third of the 6,800-member academic staff, we adjuncts have profited from having an expanded power base and access to the diverse talents and policy-making skills of our non-instructional colleagues.[2]

Adjuncts and other academic staff members at UW-Madison moved into campus-level governance when a 1985 amendment to state law granted academic staff members at all state university campuses the right to be "active participants in the immediate governance of and policy development for the institution" and awarded them the primary responsibility for formulating the policies that concern their working conditions.[3] The statute specifies that academic staff members have the right to organize themselves as they see fit and to select their representatives to university-level governance bodies. At UW-Madison, academic staff members responded by constituting an assembly representing 105 districts, an executive committee elected by the academic staff at large, and five standing committees elected by the assembly. In addition, academic staff members serve alongside faculty on some forty campus-level committees.[4] To illustrate the improvements in working conditions made possible by participating in university-level governance, I will focus here on my experiences in three of these bodies - an academic staff standing committee, a joint faculty-staff committee, and the academic staff assembly - and on progress made in the areas of job security, workplace climate, and professional development.

1.   Job Security

The policies that govern the working conditions for all academic staff are written by one of the five academic staff standing committees, the Personnel Policies and Procedures Committee.[5] In my view, the policy initiatives that have had the greatest significance for adjuncts are those that have brought us access to increased job security, in the form of long-term contracts and generous notice periods. Before 1995, adjuncts usually received one-semester terminal appointments. Concerned to maintain "flexibility" by not granting long-term instructional appointments, the university rehired many adjuncts semester after semester, always on a terminal basis (the record, I believe, was held by a lecturer with 54 consecutive one-semester appointments). In 1995, the policy-making committee pushed through a change that requires departments to give renewable contracts to any academic staff member who has been employed for the past three consecutive years and is rehired for the next year. When that policy change went into effect, I and many other adjuncts received one-year contracts that renewed automatically and provided us with notice periods of up to a year.

Anyone who has taught on a semester by semester basis understands immediately what an improvement in morale and pedagogy this policy change meant for us long-term adjuncts. The anxiety of waiting until just before the beginning of a semester to learn whether we would be rehired was replaced by the security of knowing that we would be employed. Instead of receiving teaching assignments at the last minute, with inadequate time for preparation, we now learned well in advance what courses we would be teaching and had sufficient time to plan our curriculum and develop materials. There were less obvious benefits as well. If a renewable contract is terminated, the adjunct has the right file an appeal with a university-level appeals committee constituted of other academic staff members, and the university must be able to document the reason that made the termination necessary. Such appointments also bring a financial advantage: adjuncts who hold renewable contracts are eligible for merit pay increases, while those on terminal appointments are rehired each semester at the same base rate of pay.

The academic staff policy-making committee did not stop its push for job security with the mandated one-year renewable contracts, however. A more recent policy revision gives academic staff members who have held such renewable appointments for five years access to multiple-year contracts and even permanent appointments. Departments are required to review these academic staff members annually to determine whether their performance and their contribution to their department's mission merit granting them increased job security. Academic staff members who do not hold at least two-year contracts at this point are entitled to request the reasons for this in writing.[6]

The policy-making committee's efforts at providing non-tenure-track staff with improved job security extend beyond writing the policies and shepherding them through the approval process. It has also taken on the tasks of educating academic staff members about their job security rights and of monitoring the institution's progress toward granting more long-term contracts. Each year, following the mandated annual reviews described above, the committee collects job security reports from all departments and analyzes the data. When departments have not granted eligible employees longer-term appointments, they must provide the committee with a reason. If the reason for denying job security appears questionable or inappropriate, committee members follow up with the department with a phone call or personal visit. The committee also publishes the results of the job security reports on its website and in the campus newspaper, allowing adjuncts and other academic staff members to compare their job security status with that of others across the campus. We on the committee are determined to protect job security rights at the policy level and to provide individual employees with information that will encourage them to seek more secure appointments.

Thus, over the past decade, there has been a steady push to improve job security for all academic staff at UW-Madison, a trend that has especially benefited long-time adjuncts who, like me, began teaching many years ago on terminal contracts and now have permanent appointments, the adjuncts' equivalent of tenure. More have moved into renewable appointments with two- and three-year contracts. In my estimation, such substantial gains in job security for adjuncts were only possible because we are allied with other academic professionals in the UW-Madison governance structure. The initial impetus for the policy changes came from not from adjuncts or from faculty but from academic staff in administrative and students services positions who already had long-term contracts and wanted to broaden the scope of the job security they enjoyed to include more academic staff. I strongly doubt that we adjuncts would have the job security that is available to us today if we had had to rely on the faculty or the university administration to act on our behalf. We owe our job security primarily to our governance connections with our non-faculty colleagues.

Having documented the improved job security policies for adjuncts, I also need to mention the continuing resistance to their implementation in some areas of the university. As a member of the policy-making committee when the changes went into effect, I can attest to the consternation that they caused administrators who were accustomed to regarding adjuncts as last-minute hires and permanently temporary employees. Budget officers, pleading financial constraints, have repeatedly asked the committee to exempt adjuncts from the policy changes so that hiring them on terminal appointments could continue as before. Thus far, the committee has held firm against such pleas, on the principle of not dividing the academic staff into groups with and without job security. However, as the only adjunct on the nine-member committee, I have seen fellow committee members who are themselves administrators listen sympathetically to fiscal arguments, and until another adjunct is interested in joining the committee, I plan to continue to run for re-election, to try to ensure that adjuncts retain a voice in the deliberations.

While the committee remains committed to job security for all academic staff, not all adjuncts have benefited from the policy changes, as administrators in some divisions of the university have found a way to adhere to the letter of the new policies and still withhold job security. As explained above, after teaching for three consecutive years on terminal contracts, an adjunct must receive a renewable contract if rehired for a fourth year. In order to avoid having to make such a budgetary commitment, some colleges within the university have not allowed departments to employ any new adjunct for more than two consecutive years. As a result, the affected departments have resorted to hiring adjuncts to teach for two years on terminal contracts and then having them "sit out" a year before hiring the same people again on terminal contracts for another two years, and so on. Needless to say, such a practice runs counter to the spirit of the new policies, to good pedagogical practice, and to fostering staff morale. The policy-making committee and other academic staff governance bodies are still seeking an effective response to this - in our view wrongheaded - administrative practice.

2.   Workplace Climate

One of the first campus-level bodies to take on the issue of workplace climate at UW-Madison was the Committee on Women in the University, a joint-governance body with nine faculty and six academic staff members that reports to the provost. The committee's mission is to monitor, evaluate, and improve the status of women faculty and academic staff members at the university. When I joined the committee in 1996, I saw that "climate" was a recurring theme in its discussions, for example in the context of problems in recruiting and retaining women faculty members. It seemed to me that the unsupportive working environment often experienced by women faculty members was similar to that experienced by many adjuncts, both female and male. Membership on the committee provided me with an opportunity to bring adjuncts' concerns into the discussion and to work for changes that would improve our workplace climate.

The committee's earlier efforts to improve the campus climate had focused on blatant forms of discrimination such as sexual harassment and inequities in pay. During my four-year term, the committee undertook a "climate initiative. . . designed to identify and change interactions that may create a sense of personal unhappiness and professional frustration, highlight and encourage positive actions that make our campus genuinely friendly and supportive, and foster an open dialogue about how we can build a safe and productive community."[7] I believed that one first step toward such a community would be to provide adjuncts with a resource they could turn to for advice and support

The university administration had already created the position of an ombudsperson (or "ombuds" as such a person is referred to on the UW-Madison campus) for women faculty members, in response to the difficult workplace climate many of them faced. Through my experiences as an adjunct, I was able to convey to the committee that feelings of second-class status, frustration, and alienation were not limited to women faculty members and to argue that we non-faculty members also needed an ombuds to consult for mapping out strategies or seeking remedies to problems of climate in our departments. It was true that adjuncts had access to a well-staffed human resources office, but I had discovered that it was not able to respond well to climate problems: one was presented with the options of filing a grievance or simply living with an unpleasant situation. From discussions with the faculty ombuds however, I learned that more nuanced responses were available. The committee's year-long work on the ombuds issue resulted in a proposal that noted in particular the climate problems resulting from "unresolved conflicts among co-workers, perceived exclusion of individuals or groups from key activities, and lack of appropriate independence, advancement, and compensation" and that recommended the expansion ombuds services to all employees of the university as "a mechanism to facilitate the resolution of workplace problems that limit the productivity, collaboration, confidence, and creativity of faculty and staff" - language that I believed spoke directly to the experiences of my adjunct colleagues.[8]

The hoped-for response from the university administration was delayed for several years, but as the Committee on Women and other groups continued to press for universal ombuds services, the provost announced the establishment of a new ombuds office in 2003. Open to all employees, the office is staffed by four ombuds, two former faculty members and two former academic staff members, one of whom had a long career as an adjunct. The ombuds can serve the interests of adjuncts in at least two ways. First, the ombuds' office offers a confidential setting where adjuncts can voice their frustrations and talk through their options for amelioration with a knowledgeable and experienced university veteran. Since the ombuds are at work outside of the university management structure, adjuncts can rely on their impartiality. Beyond assisting individuals, the ombuds also are expected to provide objective advice to the university administration on addressing any chronic climate problems they observe. The word from the upper levels of the administration is that they are determined to provide a better workplace climate for all employees, a commitment also reflected in the appointment of a new associate vice chancellor for diversity and climate. I hope that the administration's efforts will indeed lead to a change in the university culture such that adjuncts can thrive as respected and valued members of our departments and wider campus community. Given the entrenched hierarchical structure of the institution, I surmise that the process of culture change will be a long one and that we adjuncts will continue to be confronted with climate issues. Meanwhile, the new ombuds services offer adjuncts help in making concrete changes that will improve their individual workplace climate.

3.   Professional Development

In the years I spent as a "permanently temporary" employee on a succession of terminal appointments, the matter of professional development did not figure in my thoughts; I was simply grateful to have a teaching job and to be able to do what I loved. However, when I became involved in campus-level governance, I came into contact with a broader group of academic staff members for whom professional development was a regular topic of discussion. I was able to begin exploring the question of what professional development might mean for adjuncts when I was appointed to a campus-wide "career paths task force," charged with mapping out professional development paths for academic staff members. Most of the members held administrative or student services positions; two of us were adjuncts. When we came to discuss possible career paths for adjuncts, one member voiced doubts as to whether adjuncts could actually have a career; and indeed, the general sentiment in the group was that adjuncts could not expect to be employed at the university long enough to merit professional development opportunities. It struck me as strange that a group of employees so intensely involved in the instructional mission of the university was viewed as less deserving of career development than, say, programme administrators or academic advisors. At the same time, I myself had no practical proposals to put forward.

When I became a representative in the academic staff assembly, however, I realized that something as simple as a performance review could be a powerful tool for professional development for adjuncts. When the assembly took up debate on a policy change that would make an annual written performance review mandatory for all academic staff, I spoke in favour of the measure on behalf of my constituents, some 75 adjuncts in foreign language departments, arguing that a performance review was basic to professional development. Many adjuncts, I knew, were never formally reviewed: while university policy recommended regular reviews, the lack of a requirement led to uneven practices across departments. If a review were to be required, adjuncts would gain the right to meet once a year with faculty colleagues in their departments to document their activities and accomplishments and to present ideas for further contributions they could make, whether in course development or departmental service. By means of the annual written reviews, adjuncts could build a record of their performance, initiative, and creativity to use as support when seeking a more secure appointment or a promotion to greater responsibilities.

To my surprise, representatives of other constituencies spoke out in vigorous opposition to the measure. Programme administrators with supervisory responsibilities argued against having to take on the burden of formal, written reviews when informal, day-to-day interactions were fulfilling the same role. Representatives who had difficult relationships with their own supervisors predicted that such reviews would only result in negative evaluations being placed in one's personnel file, the first step on the way to termination. Research staff in the sciences said that the faculty principal investigators for whom they worked would be unwilling to put up with yet another bureaucratic hurdle. The academic executive committee itself took the unusual step of voicing unanimous opposition to the proposal as being unnecessary: employees who wanted a performance review could always request one, without making the process mandatory for everyone.

In the end, those of us who favoured the proposal were able to persuade a majority of the assembly that a mandatory annual review represented not a threat to continued employment but rather a foundation for career development and that such an opportunity should be available to all employees as one of their rights, not as a favour granted upon a special request. A compromise was reached: the proposal to mandate an annual review for all academic staff members was approved, but without the requirement that the review be written - for adjuncts only a partial victory but an important one nevertheless. With the new policy in place since 2000, it has by now it has become routine that adjuncts meet yearly with faculty colleagues to review their accomplishments, to set goals for future semesters, and to explore further career opportunities. Since the policy also provides that employees shall participate in establishing the structure of the review, adjuncts can to a great extent determine the content and direction of the discussion.

The approval of the new policy notwithstanding, the discussions surrounding professional development in both the task force and the assembly revealed a drawback to Wisconsin's academic governance structure. The academic staff represents such a broad range of job categories that the different constituencies will not always agree on policy issues or even understand each others' positions. During the assembly debate on performance reviews, for example, I realized that I had never considered the question from the perspective of an employee working directly under an antagonistic supervisor. Nor had others probably realized the value of performance reviews to adjuncts, who are excluded from departmental structures for mentoring and reviewing tenure-track faculty.

The debates in the assembly often provide an illuminating introduction to working conditions quite different from one's own. Despite the occasional clashes, however, policy does get made. In my experience as an assembly representative, if a particular constituency was able demonstrate convincingly why a given initiative was vital to its interests, other groups were willing to support it outright or work for a mutually acceptable compromise: academic staff solidarity outweighed self-interest.

4.   Defining our Professional Identity: a Policy Defeat

While adjuncts have been able to cooperate successfully with other academic staff groups to improve our working conditions, we have been unable to prevail when our interests have conflicted with those of the faculty. The defeat that I personally found most vexing had to do with efforts to better define our professional identity through a more appropriate job title. Most adjuncts at Wisconsin are not "professors"; rather we have the title "lecturer" or "faculty associate," neither of which conveys adequately to students on campus, to colleagues at other institutions, or to granting agencies the extent of our qualifications and our responsibilities. For example, an adjunct colleague of mine who as a course supervisor had written a letter of recommendation for a graduate student was informed by the other institution that they required a letter from a supervising professor, not from a lecturer. Similarly, students of mine have been told by academic advisors not to use me as a reference, since the recommendation of someone with a lecturer title would be given less weight than a professor's recommendation. That the term "faculty associate" must be opaque to anyone other than those either awarding or holding the title scarcely needs to be mentioned.

Adjuncts' dissatisfaction with their job titles arose as a main topic of discussion at a 1999 Wisconsin-wide forum on matters of concern to adjuncts throughout the university system. The moment seemed ripe to tackle the issue on the Madison campus. With other adjuncts and a few sympathetic faculty members who had attended the forum I formed a working group to draft a proposal for a new title to submit to the governance process. Eventually our proposal to replace the titles "lecturer" and "faculty associate" with "instructional professor" was approved by both the academic staff assembly and the academic staff executive committee, which voted in June 2000 to send it on to the university system administration for implementation.

On the faculty side of our campus governance structure, the faculty senate began discussing whether an instructional professor title for adjuncts should be approved, and if so, whether it should be a true, budgeted title adhering to a position or, instead, an honorific title granted to meritorious adjuncts by the executive committees of individual departments. Faculty voiced concerns that the prestige associated with the title "professor" would be diluted by its being awarded to staff who had not faced a vetting similar to the tenure process and that adoption of the proposed title would weaken the tenure system. In February 2001 the faculty senate voted down a motion to institute an honorific instructional professor title for adjuncts.

With the academic staff and faculty governance bodies at odds over the issue, the university system administration informed the campus that departments already held the authority to create honorific, or "working," professorial titles as they saw fit. The School of Business quickly responded by granting the working title "teaching professor" to both long-time lecturers and new hires before the fall semester in 2001. That action prompted the faculty senate to revisit the job title question. Declaring the title "professor" to be an academic policy issue and thus under the purview of the faculty, the faculty senate voted to take control of the working titles "teaching professor" and "instructional professor" away from individual departments: since December 2001 the word "professor" can not be used in a title without the prior approval of that title by the faculty senate. Thus, should the School of Business wish to hire another teaching professor - or any other unit wish to give a lecturer an instructional professor title, the decision will be made by the faculty senate, a remarkable state of affairs for an institution known for its tradition of decentralized decision making. Up to now, the business school's original teaching professors remain the only adjuncts with a new title. Having listened to the sometimes virulent discussion of the job title issue in the faculty senate (for example, students were said to be "disadvantaged" when they were taught by adjuncts), I am not surprised that the faculty have not tolerated further encroachments on their professorial status. Meanwhile, the issue of professorial titles for adjuncts continues to percolate in academic staff governance committees, and strategies are being developed for a more politically savvy reintroduction of the proposal.

As the debate over job titles showed, the division of campus-level policy-making structures at UW-Madison into parallel academic staff and faculty governance bodies can result in adjuncts being pitted as adversaries against our closest institutional colleagues, the faculty. As that debate also showed, in any conflict of interest, the faculty is likely to prevail. Would adjuncts at Wisconsin fare better if we were part of the faculty rather than being defined by statute in opposition to them as "not faculty"? Based on discussions in the professional literature of adjuncts' experiences, I do not believe so. Serving in campus governance alongside other non-faculty professionals, adjuncts are respected as equal partners in academic staff policy-making, rather than being consigned to a perpetually second-class status in faculty-run governance bodies. In academic staff governance, adjuncts have access to power, recognition, and professional development opportunities that they are almost certainly lacking in their home departments, and on joint-governance committees they can raise the level of visibility of adjuncts among faculty and administrators. Most importantly, experience at Wisconsin shows that adjuncts can successfully ally with other non-tenure-track groups to take on a new identity as policy-makers and improve their working conditions.

Notes

1. In the University of Wisconsin system, non-tenure-track instructors are referred to as "instructional academic staff," with the job title "adjunct" reserved for a small subgroup whose main source of employment is outside the university. Nevertheless, for the sake of economy and consistency of usage within this volume, I use the term "adjunct" to refer to all instructional academic staff members at UW-Madison.

2. In the 2005-2006 academic year, there were a total of 7,052 academic staff members, of whom 2,222 were adjuncts (i.e., members of the instructional academic staff), 2,398 were researchers, and 2,432 were employed mainly in student services, information technology, and administration. By comparison, there were 2,053 tenured and tenure-track faculty members. See Office of Budget Planning and Analysis. University of Wisconsin-Madison. http://wiscinfo.doit.wisc.edu/obpa/whoare.htm (9 March 2006).

3. Wisconsin Statutes, Chapter 36.09(4m) reads: "The academic staff members of each institution, subject to the responsibilities and powers of the board, the president and the chancellor and faculty of the institution, shall be active participants in the immediate governance of and policy development for the institution. The academic staff members have primary responsibility for the formulation and review, and shall be represented in the development, of all policies and procedures concerning academic staff members, including academic staff personnel matters. The academic staff members of each institution shall have the right to organize themselves in a manner they determine, and to select their representatives to participate in institutional governance." Revisor of Statutes Bureau. State of Wisconsin. <http://www.legis.state.wi.us/rsb/stats.html >(9 March 2006) .

4. The assembly and its committees are described and the joint governance committees are listed on the UW-Madison academic staff website. Academic Staff. University of Wisconsin-Madison. <http://wisc infodoit.wisc.edu/acstaff/> (9 March 2006).

5. Detailed information about the Personnel Policies and Procedures

Committee can be found on the committee's website. The committee brings its policy proposals to the academic staff assembly for ratification; if passed, the proposals are sent on to the university administration for review and then to the board of regents for final approval. Personnel Policies and Procedures Committee. UW-Madison Academic Staff. University of Wisconsin-Madison. < http://wiscinfo.doit.wisc.edu/acstaff/pppc/index. htm> (9 March 2006).

6. Academic Staff Policies and Procedures. University of Wisconsin-Madison. <http://wiscinfo.doit.wisc.edu/acstaff/ASPP/ TOC. htm>. (9 March 2006) Job security provisions are found in Chapter 2.

7. Committee on Women in the University. Annual Report, 1999-2000. Secretary of the Faculty. University of Wisconsin-Madison. <http://www. secfac.wisc.edu/senate/2000/1204/1540.pdf >(9 March 2006) .

8. Committee on Women in the University. Annual Report, 1998-1999. Secretary of the Faculty. University of Wisconsin-Madison.

Bibliography

Academic Staff. University of Wisconsin-Madison. <http://wiscinfo.doit. wisc.edu/acstaff/> (9 March 2006).

Academic Staff Policies and Procedures. University of Wisconsin-Madison. <http://wiscinfo.doit.wisc.edu/acstaff/ASPP/TOC.htm>. (9 March 2006).

Committee on Women in the University. Annual Report, 1998-1999. Secretary of the Faculty. University of Wisconsin-Madison.

___. Annual Report, 1999-2000. Secretary of the Faculty. University of Wisconsin-Madison. http://www.secfac.wisc.edu/senate/2000/ 1204/ 1540.pdf (9 March 2006).

Office of Budget Planning and Analysis. University of Wisconsin-Madison. <http://wiscinfo.doit.wisc.edu/obpa/whoare.htm> (9 March 2006).

Personnel Policies and Procedures Committee. UW-Madison Academic Staff. University of Wisconsin-Madison. <http://wiscinfo.doit.wisc. edu/acstaff/pppc/index.htm> (9 March 2006).

Revisor of Statutes Bureau. State of Wisconsin. <http://www.legis.state. wi.us/rsb/stats.html> (9 March 2006).

Academia as a Gift Economy: Adjunct Labour and False Consciousness

Steffen Hantke

Confronted with the question from his father, an academic outsider, as to why he did not get paid for the work he put in for a conference presentation, the author considers the notion of labour in an academic setting. Inspired by neo-Marxism, he develops a theoretical frame for a new way of looking at academia as a specific economic form and the place of adjunct work in it. Academic life functions according to the principle of a "gift economy," and what that economy exploits in adjunct teachers is their "false consciousness," their willingness to embrace an ideologically formulated position that in fact excludes them.

Adjunct Labour and False Consciousness; Gift Economy; Dues Paying and Symbolic Returns; Marxism

A few years ago, I submitted a proposal to a conference that was to take place in a city within driving distance from where I lived. During the time it took the conference organizers to inform me that my proposal had been accepted, I moved halfway across the country. This meant that the costs of attending the conference would triple compared to my initial calculation. I would have to fly instead of being able to drive, and without a car, I would have to stay in one of the downtown hotels close to the conference that charged about triple of what one of the motels would have cost that would have been within my range had I taken the car. Would attending the conference be worth it under these circumstances? As I deliberated about this question, my father made this suggestion: "Why don't you just spend the money that they're paying you for giving a paper and use it to pay the expenses for the trip?"

Before his retirement a few years ago, my father had worked as an engineer for the auto industry. During his forty years of drawing a regular pay check, he had come home from work every day at four in the afternoon, had taken his family on four-week summer vacations to Italy and Spain every year, and during his working life had changed companies exactly once in order to improve his chances of professional advancement. Though he would have preferred to see me "get a real job," he accepted my decision to go to college, major in literature, and pursue a career in academia. He had admitted to me that, asked what exactly his son did for a living, he had to keep his answers vague. That was fine with me, since I myself could not have explained much better what my father had done during the eight hours every day that preceded his return from the office.

This suggestion of his, however, on how to finance my attending of an academic conference, was an eye-opener for me of sorts. Once past the initial reflex of groaning and rolling my eyes at his cluelessness about how academia did in fact work - there was no speaker's fee; in fact, you paid *them* to be allowed to attend, and your reward would consist of your right to add two lines to your CV, making you, hopefully, more attractive to prospective employers - I thought about my father's comment some more. I admitted to myself that, from his point of view, the suggestion made perfect sense. Working meant that you either performed a service or produced something which someone else valued sufficiently to pay you for it. You were paid either for your time or for the finished product. He had seen me work on my conference presentation. He knew that, for the better part of a month, I had written and polished the presentation, had selected film clips and cued them up on a videotape. He had seen the effort, the genuine labour, which had gone into this presentation. Was it not perfectly logical that I would be paid for it?

To the degree that I could reconstruct my father's train of thought with such ease, the alarming implication of this question for myself was to ask myself why I, with equal ease, had been so ready to set it aside as irrelevant for my own work. Well, the answer was, I was properly socialized into my profession. Trained as an academic, I accepted the common professional practice that had me travel halfway across the American continent, foot the bill out of my own pocket, pay half of a month's salary for registration, and then speak for eighteen to twenty minutes to a handful of moderately interested people, who would be in the room because they had done exactly the same thing. Until my father made that very sensible suggestion, it had never occurred to me to wonder why I did what I did. Or how all of this, from a sober-minded economic point of view, made no sense at all, or was downright bizarre.

Once I had started trying to look at my own chosen profession from my father's point of view, there were other details about academic life that struck me, upon second thought, as odd. Daily life constantly demands from us that we say one thing and do another - cartoons like *Dilbert* and films like Mike Judge's *Office Space* have shrewdly exploited this gap between reality and cultural orthodoxy for laughs. But academic life seemed rife with these contradictions: everybody knew that you attended conferences not to present papers but to hang out with colleagues over lunch because this was where the real career decisions were made; that university presses were non-profit organizations and yet constantly talked about making a profit out of the scholarly books they did or did not deign to publish; and that, rumour had it, tenured faculty, as soon as they had the freedom to pursue any kind of scholarly endeavour they wished, would immediately fall into a kind of intellectual stupor that ended their prolific writing and publishing.

To the dubious extent that any of this is actually true, perhaps none of it is really that unusual; every profession depends, to one degree or another, on informal procedure. Was there backroom dealing? Well, even if there were, did it always lever petty, incompetent, and arrogant jerks into positions of power, or did it sometimes help good people to catch a break and get a start? Were there ironclad general rules launched to safeguard objectivity and the functioning of the meritocracy? Yes, but there were also human beings involved, who were doing favours, taking likes and dislikes, and grinding axes. It would have been foolish (or fascist) to dismiss this human element. In the back of my mind, I even had a more scholarly cultural explanation for all of this.

Academic life functions according to a principle akin to what Lewis Hyde has called a "gift economy."[1] As a member of this professional subculture, you were not getting paid directly for your labour. You "contributed" to scholarship, which meant, in essence, that you gave the fruits of your labour away for free, or even facilitated this gift-giving by paying money to the receivers of your gift. That is, you received no fee in direct payment for writing an essay or book or presenting a paper at a conference, and, in addition, you subscribed to the journal that published your essay or paid registration fees to the conference that listed your presentation. While your side of the equation could be measured in cold, hard cash, the return for your gift would, in the first instance, be largely symbolic: you would receive three contributor's copies of the journal your essay was published in, for example, or be served a chicken dinner during the keynote address at the conference you attended. In the final instance, however, you awaited the arrival of the grand payoff - the job interview that would lead to the tenure-track position, that position itself, and finally, tenure. This was the moment when the world of symbolic and economic exchange would finally dovetail: you had proven your worth as an aspiring member of the community and were now finally accepted to the club with full membership privileges.[2]

Conscientiously, I had been paying my dues for years while I was awaiting the invitation into the club. My applicant status consisted of years of working as an academic adjunct, performing the same scholarly tasks as those who were already enjoying full membership (writing and publishing, serving as referee and member of the editorial boards of scholarly journals), exceeding their workload in some respects (as with the size of my teaching load) while being spared other aspects of that workload (administrative responsibilities). I never complained . . . well, I pissed and moaned a little, like everyone else. But in the strict sense of the word, I never complained. In my mind, I was "working on my CV," padding and streamlining it, getting it ready for that invitation to the club.

Between this period of "getting ready" and the arrival of the invitation to the club, years went by. During these years, I worked within higher education, most of the time employed at one or several universities on a semester-to-semester basis, sometimes with a contract for one year. During all this time, I had health insurance exactly once, when my year contract put me at the status of "visiting professor," and never received retirement benefits. Over the years, my highest salary had been $3500, my lowest $900 per class - that is, $3500 or barely a quarter of that for teaching three credit hours a week from September to December, or January to May. Summers I survived on my savings.

This was my situation at the time when I told my dad about the conference and what it would cost me to attend. Obviously, had I been tenured, or even just tenure-track at that moment, to attend the conference would have been less of a problem, since, most likely, my institution would have paid a substantial portion of the bill. I was only pinching pennies because I was operating without such institutional support. But this was the Catch-22: had I been tenured, I would have been less urgently in need of those two lines on my CV. But as an adjunct waiting for his break into the next higher level of the profession, I needed those two lines desperately. Hence, I would have to grin and bear it, and pay my own way.

To the degree that adjuncts aspiring to real careers within their field think of themselves as "paying their dues" or "waiting for their moment to ascend," the social contract that underlies the gift economy of academia remains intact. Both sides honour their respective contractual obligations, as the moment of payoffs is merely delayed and not altogether cancelled. As long as this logic of postponement determines the work situation of adjuncts, they have no substantial reason to complain. They may grumble, though - about bad working conditions, underpay, and degrees of economic exploitation. To move beyond grumbling and question the contract itself only becomes a possibility when financial remuneration for academic labour is no longer postponed, or rerouted first through complex mechanisms that transform symbolic into economic value, but when the economic is uncoupled from the symbolic value. Is this the case with academic adjuncts? Is it accurate to include adjunct labour in the logic of the gift economy that describes the professional subculture of academia so well? To answer this question, let's first look at the economic side of academic adjuncting.

The economic logic of adjunct labour is simple and compelling. As long as the job market is as well-stocked with highly qualified candidates as it is right now, and has been for the last twenty years, part-time and full-time faculty will deliver the same quality of teaching. Part-timers come with the added advantage over full-timers of being paid on a lower pay scale, and enjoying none of the legal prerogatives regarding job security that full-timers do. Without contract negotiation, their number can be adjusted up or down depending on the variation in the institution's enrolment numbers from one year or semester to the next. Their status of relative job insecurity also inclines them toward a certain degree of what I would call economic and political docility; that is, they are less likely to organize, unionize, or even just assert themselves against the institutions employing them because they perceive their position, and rightfully so, as precarious. Consequently, hiring practices, first, in US universities, and then, following this model, in those of other countries around the world, have gradually but steadily moved from favouring full-time to favouring part-time faculty. This quantitative shift has been accompanied by a restructuring of hierarchical boundaries within the profession that, in effect, more deeply entrenched the distinction between the full-time and part-time labour pools by limiting mobility between them.

Because the economic structures of adjunct labour have become increasingly uncoupled from the symbolic structures that determine full-time academic careers, achievements and accomplishments are measured differently for adjuncts and full-timers. Clearly, economic conditions determine social standards, because, obviously, there are no intrinsic differences between scholarship generated by part-timers and full-timers. Since the structures that determine the accumulation of symbolic professional capital deny adjunct labour the status of cumulative gain - since one year of adjunct teaching is like the next, and so on - adjuncts can transform their job experience into professional capital only with great difficulty.[3] Even worse, years of adjunct teaching might be taken not as a sign of professional accomplishment but a sign of failure to make the transition to full-time status. Success at the adjunct level might prohibit one's transition to full-time status within the same institution, and so forth.

The academy as a functioning gift economy produces an ideology that serves its members well. Most scholars in the humanities operate within paradigms that, in one way or another, provide legitimizations for the existence of the discipline that generates or employs them. The uselessness of the humanities, which seems to permeate so much of the thinking within their surrounding culture, is countered by attitudes prone to different types of scepticism - you regard the larger culture with disdain; you declare the larger culture significant only in all those of its aspects that it values the least about itself; you declare yourself as being of crucial importance for the larger culture exactly because you operate outside of it.[4] In almost all of these discursive situations, I am struck by the relatively insignificant position that is attributed to money. Economics may matter greatly *within* the discourses of individual schools of thought and disciplines, pre-eminently of course in Marxism and its contemporary variants, but it hardly ever matters in the discourse *about* these same disciplines. The conclusion I would draw from this gap is that the more secure your economic position is, the less you need to talk about economics. The security that comes with a regular pay check makes you susceptible to not thinking about yourself in terms of how much you make.

Conversely, this would mean that the scholarly work produced by those who work in adjunct positions is marked by a keen critical attention to, and understanding of, the power of cold hard cash. Adjunct labour should provide the majority of Marxist critics in the academy. Of course, this is not the case. For one, I found that adjuncts like myself also subscribe to the ideology of the gift economy. They grant their subscription to this ideology as a token of their willingness to submit to the social and symbolic codes of the professional subculture they wish to join. Publicly assenting to this ideology is a signal for all those who care to listen that one already *is*, at least in spirit, a member of the community; one only awaits the official reciprocation of this commitment, which should arrive any minute now. This signal function might explain why anyone would submit to an ideology that so obviously fails to describe his or her own situation. I have little sympathy for that earlier version of myself who lived through a decade of adjuncting by telling himself that my failure to get a tenure-track job was the result of a silly or tragic oversight, an aberration, an accident that fate would surely remedy some time soon.

As long as adjuncts subscribe to the ideology of the gift economy as a matter of social convention, i.e. as a primarily pragmatic gesture toward reaffirming the symbolic structures organizing the professional subculture, there is no problem. We all submit to social rules we know are pragmatically absurd - like wearing a tie to a job interview or eating your dessert with a different spoon than your soup - because we acknowledge their symbolic function. But then nobody is economically disadvantaged by wearing a tie to a job interview. Adjuncts, meanwhile, might be dissuaded from taking concrete steps toward improving their economic situation as long as they subscribe to an ideology that tells them that no need for such practical steps exists.

The term that much vulgar Marxist discourse has for this phenomenon is "false consciousness," a willingness to state an ideologically formulated position while being besieged on all sides by irrefutable evidence to the opposite. In the case of academic adjuncts, it would manifest itself, for example, in adjuncts asserting their essential importance for an institution which, in its treatment of these adjuncts, is providing ample proof that it considers them expendable, replaceable, and marginal. To be precise, their marginality is exactly *not* a matter of consideration, a question of perspective - how the institution "looks at" its employees. If this were so, then strategies would make sense that aim at changing the institution's mind, convincing it that its view is erroneous and that a view exists that is somehow more attuned to empirical reality.

It is obvious, I think, that adjuncts will not succeed in improving their job situation if they try simply to talk their institutions out of exploiting them, trying to make them see the error of their ways. Other measures are called for, measures that draw the discussion from the realm of the symbolic to that of the economic. The disenfranchisement of adjuncts is no coincidence or derailment of the system. But neither is making conferences prohibitively expensive for those who, in order to accumulate professional capital, need to attend them most urgently; or forcing adjuncts, through low salaries, into accepting teaching loads that, as a matter of simple economic survival, prevent them from spending their time on the scholarship that would gain them access to tenure-track positions.

I am not presenting a grand conspiratorial explanation for the oppression of adjunct labour in academia. As hesitant as full-time academics are to surrender any of their professional prerogatives, I believe them to be genuine when they express sympathy for the plight of part-timers. As much as we all realize that there will never be full-time positions for all those hopeful students who graduate every year with degrees in the humanities, we do all wish them satisfying careers in their chosen fields. But we also know that institutions of higher education, whatever messages are delivered within the classroom, do operate within a larger culture that asks primarily for their economic feasibility and efficiency. This means that the interests of employer and employee are distributed roughly in the same manner as they are elsewhere within capitalist economies - for one group to make a profit with as little expense as possible, and for the other to make a living. Whatever shared interests may otherwise exist between those two groups, in this fundamental aspect of their relationship their interests are opposed, and hence their interactions must be adversarial. To point out this very simple fact, to challenge the idea that academic adjunct labour participates in the cultural logic of the gift economy, and to raise the question what strategies for negotiation follow from this for academic adjuncts, has been the main goal of my discussion in the previous pages.

Notes

1. Lewis Hyde, *The Gift: Imagination and the Erotic Life of Property*. (New York: Vintage, 1979), 74-87.

2 . Hyde accounts for the existence of what he called "double economies" (77-8), among which he counts the literary and the scientific communities. Within the group, they reward their members with the symbolic gift of communal recognition, but they also reward them, for their membership in communities in the realm outside the professional community, with money for their accomplishments. Hyde sees problems with those who violate the rules of one community by playing by the rules of the other - e.g. scientists who sell their research to corporations - but does not further discuss the mechanisms by which the professional subculture is integrated within the larger culture.

3 . I am using the term "professional capital" analogous to Pierre Bourdieu's concept of "cultural capital" in its broader sense, suggesting similar mechanisms determine social and hierarchical positioning on the macroscopic level of society at large and the microscopic level of individual professional subcultures embedded in it.

4 See Terry Eagleton's recent work, e.g. *After Theory* (Cambridge: Basic Books, 2003), as well as Eagleton's review of Frank Furedi's *Where Have All the Intellectuals Gone*, in which he writes: "The spooky music of *Mastermind* says it all. Intellectuals are weird, creepy creatures, akin to aliens in their clinical detachment from the everyday human world. Yet you can also see them as just the opposite. If they are feared as sinisterly cerebral, they are also pitied as bumbling figures who wear their underpants back to front, harmless eccentrics who know the value of everything and the price of nothing" (*New Statesman*).

Bibliography

Eagleton, Terry. Review of Frank Furedi, *Where Have All the Intellectuals Gone? New Statesman*, November 21, 2004.
    <www.newstatesman.com/site.php3?newTemplate=NSReview_Bshop &newDisplayURN=300000088090>.
Hyde, Lewis. *The Gift: Imagination and the Erotic Life of Property*. New York: Vintage, 1979.

Franchising the Disenfranchised: Improving the Lot of Visiting Faculty and Adjuncts

Janet Ruth Heller

This essay defines some problems that adjuncts and visiting faculty share at academic institutions and suggests concrete ways that departments, colleges, and national faculty organizations like the MLA and AAUP can help non-tenured instructors and professors. Due to sexism in academia, women predominate in both job categories. Adjuncts and visiting faculty often lack job security, health insurance, retirement benefits, living wages, and voting rights. Non-tenured faculty can band together to press for better working conditions. However, colleges and universities should commit themselves to provide all employees equitable working conditions and fair consideration for job openings. Unions and professional organizations for faculty should support adjuncts and visiting professors; these organizations should also publicly criticize institutions of higher learning that exploit untenured faculty. Finally, unions and other faculty organizations need to lobby state governments and the federal government and its agencies to increase understanding of and funding for higher education.

Adjunct; Evaluation; Fringe Benefits; Grievance; Job Security; Salaries; Sexism; Visiting Faculty; Voting Rights; Women

I have held many non-tenured jobs, including stints as a writing tutor, lecturer, full- and part-time instructor, coordinator of a writing tutor program, and visiting assistant professor. I had a tenure-line job at Nazareth College of Kalamazoo for a year and a half, but I got laid off in 1990 due to the institution's financial problems. In 1992, Nazareth College closed completely. I am currently a visiting assistant professor at Western Michigan University. Because the job market is so tight in writing and English literature, many of us visiting faculty have been "visiting" for a long time. For example, I served for seven years as a visiting assistant professor at Grand Valley State University. In this essay, I will define some problems that adjuncts and visiting faculty share at academic institutions and suggest concrete ways that departments, colleges, and national faculty organizations like the MLA can help non-tenured instructors and professors.

While visiting faculty are paid better than most adjuncts, the two categories have much in common. Universities and colleges hire both adjuncts and visiting faculty to fill temporary and permanent needs. Temporary needs include covering sections for a tenure-line faculty member who is on sabbatical or medical leave or who is briefly serving in an administrative position. Permanent needs include teaching introductory or freshman courses that tenure-line faculty avoid whenever possible. Both adjuncts and visiting professors get hired on a semester or yearly basis and rarely have multi-year contracts. Thus, people in both types of positions have no job security. Some visiting professor slots come with health insurance, retirement accounts, and other benefits, but many such positions, like the jobs of adjuncts, do not. Visiting faculty with PhD degrees usually earn about half of what they would be paid with the same credentials in a tenure-line job. So colleges and universities with visiting faculty essentially get a PhD for the price of an MA. A 1999 Conference on College Composition and Communication survey finds that compensation for contingent faculty is low and that it is "difficult to maintain a minimum lifestyle relying on this type of employment."[1] When visiting faculty and adjuncts do committee work for their departments, engage in major public service, participate in conferences, or publish scholarly or creative work, these efforts do not help them to get higher salaries, merit pay, or promotions. Finally, a large percentage of contingent faculty are women: this is true at both the adjunct and visiting professor levels and reflects academic sexism.

Furthermore, visiting faculty and adjuncts often have no voting rights and are excluded from any department or division meetings that focus on personnel issues, even when these issues concern us. This exclusion also means that we miss important discussions that could affect our careers and the future of our institutions. Contingent faculty thus inhabit a no-person's land. However, I have discovered that while individual non-tenured faculty are almost powerless, we can gain power and recognition by banding together. Colleges and universities can steamroller over one person, but they cannot ignore *groups* of instructors. When I was at Northern Illinois University, I tried alone to get a more interesting teaching load and a change in my title, to no avail. However, at Grand Valley State University, seven visiting faculty members in the English Department, including me, worked together to improve working conditions and to overturn our dean's decision to limit our positions to three years. We began by asking our department to endorse a statement to suspend the three-year limit rule. After a massive lobbying effort on our part, several letters to the department, and two faculty meetings, we were successful. We then met with the dean, who was rude and turned down our request with no explanation for his policy. This angered us enough to appeal above his head to the provost and then to the president, who decided to reverse the dean's decision. We did research to prove to the provost and the president that no other division on campus had the three-year rule for visiting faculty. We also presented him with our impressive résumés. When the department tried to punish three of us by not renewing our contracts, we appealed to the president and the English Department for reconsideration, and we did get our contracts renewed. We also saved other visiting professors who had served for three years in the Division of Arts and Humanities from losing their jobs.

We discovered that many members of the University Academic Senate and other deans supported us and helped us reach our goals. We empowered ourselves and were successful. Also, a sympathetic new chair helped four visiting faculty to attain tenure-line jobs in our department.

The Conference on College Composition and Communication, Modern Language Association, and the American Association of University Professors have issued statements urging colleges and universities to treat adjuncts and visiting faculty more equitably. In 1989, the CCCC issued its "Statement of Principles and Standards for the Postsecondary Teaching of Writing." This document deplores the exploitation of non-tenure track faculty and recommends that all faculty teaching writing be full-time and tenure-track employees. Furthermore, it suggests that most writing classes be capped at 20 students and that basic writing classes be capped at 15 students. The CCCC statement insists that adjuncts and visiting faculty "deserve special consideration in matters of governance, job security, and incentives for professional development." Specifically, the document calls for compensation and fringe benefits comparable to those given to tenure-line faculty with similar credentials and responsibilities.[2]

The *MLA Newsletter* of summer, 1994, contains the "MLA Statement on the Use of Part-Time and Full-Time Adjunct Faculty" (formulated in February, 1994). This document urges colleges and universities "to improve employment conditions for essential adjunct faculty members." Specifically, it urges departments to open up more tenure-line jobs, instead of adjunct/visiting slots. The statement also insists that adjunct/visiting faculty should "be hired, reviewed, and given teaching assignments according to processes comparable to those established for the tenured or tenure-track faculty members" and that adjunct/visiting faculty should "be paid equitable prorated salaries and should receive basic benefits such as health insurance." Furthermore, the MLA guidelines argue that non-tenure-line faculty "should be eligible for incentives that foster professional development, including merit raises and funds for research and travel" and "should participate in determining departmental and institutional policies."[3]

However, college departments, the MLA, and the AAUP could do more to help adjuncts and visiting faculty members. Non-tenured faculty are important but undervalued members of academia and should be treated and paid like professionals and colleagues, not like second-class citizens. However, most colleges and universities make it difficult for adjuncts and visiting faculty to have the power to change their circumstances. This results in frustration and humiliation for many untenured faculty. Students also suffer when their professors become embittered or depressed. Here are some suggestions to improve academia for all members of the community.

1. Stop setting up committees to study the problems. This just delays action. Instead, meet with adjuncts and visiting faculty to determine their needs and then take concrete steps to help them finish their theses, get promotions, improve working conditions, and get tenure-line jobs. For example, untenured faculty should not have heavier teaching loads than other professors. Such inequality makes it difficult for adjuncts and visiting faculty to get any work done on dissertations, articles, books, or creative work. Another problem is overcrowded offices. Untenured faculty often share an office with up to a dozen other instructors. This makes it hard to meet with students in privacy and to grade papers or do research in peace and quiet. Some universities do not give non-tenured faculty access to computers or library carrels and even may deny library or parking privileges during semesters when the adjunct or visiting faculty members do not teach. Administrations, unions, and non-tenured faculty should push for equitable working conditions for all employees.

2. Departments need to help adjuncts and visiting faculty find better jobs. Offer to look at letters of application and résumés to make helpful comments. Offer to visit instructors' classes and write them letters of recommendation for their placement files. Let non-tenured faculty teach some courses in their area of specialization so that they have more varied teaching experience.

3. Give instructors the same support that other faculty receive for attending conferences and doing research. This will increase the creativity and productivity of all faculty members. Such equity will also lead to greater job satisfaction for adjuncts and visiting

professors. Failure to do so results in untenured faculty becoming a permanent lower caste.

4. When departments have openings, instructors and visiting professors should be given full consideration. Departments often hire someone from another state because that individual seems exciting and exotic. Adjuncts and visiting faculty are taken for granted and become part of the woodwork. Most tenure-line faculty are unaware of the research interests of their department's instructors. Women and minority contingent faculty need better access to information about openings, and search committees need to take them more seriously as candidates for tenure-line jobs.

5. Concerned departments and the MLA should lobby colleges and universities to make salaries, health insurance, and retirement benefits for non-tenured faculty equitable. Factors such as years of teaching experience, publications, and public service need to get taken into account for adjuncts and visiting faculty.

6. Give untenured faculty full voting rights in their departments and divisions and representation on all major department committees, university committees, and faculty senates. This will insure that adjuncts' and visiting professors' concerns will be heard and discussed.

7. Establish fair and consistent written policies for the evaluation of non-tenured faculty and a grievance policy. This will protect instructors from arbitrary chairs and deans. Faculty ombudspeople need to take an interest in adjuncts and visitors, helping them to be treated equitably.

8. Pressure college administrators to pay adjuncts and visiting faculty higher salaries. Wages should adequately reflect an instructor's years of education, teaching experience, publications, department service, etc. Untenured faculty should also be eligible for merit pay.

9. The MLA, AAUP, NCTE, and CCCC should publish lists of colleges and universities that exploit untenured faculty and should not carry job vacancy announcements for these institutions or allow them to recruit candidates at conventions.

10. All four organizations could do more to make sure that their delegate assemblies, committees, meetings, and conventions are open to untenured faculty. Special membership rates for adjuncts/visiting faculty would help. Reserving slots for untenured faculty on important committees and delegate assemblies would show interest in the most vulnerable faculty and their concerns. The MLA, AAUP, NCTE, and CCCC need reasonable registration and hotel rates and should urge chairs of panels to include more adjunct/visiting faculty members and topics of interest to untenured faculty. These organizations could also urge colleges and universities who interview candidates at conventions to help defray the expenses of any candidates who are adjuncts or visiting faculty.

11. I agree with Cary Nelson's proposals in the 1996 issue of *Profession* that the MLA needs to "lobby far more widely and aggressively on behalf of higher education" on both the state and national levels.[4] This effort should be led by the MLA president and Executive Council.

12. Untenured faculty need to work together to push for reforms. Individual action is difficult and often ineffective. I have drawn strength from the shared concerns and encouragement of other visiting professors and adjuncts. Academic unions need to cover untenured faculty.

Notes

1. "CCCC Reports on Survey of Freestanding Writing Programs," *The Council Chronicle* (NCTE) 11.3 (February 2002): 1.

2. Committee on Professional Standards for Quality Education, "Statement of Principles and Standards for the Postsecondary Teaching of Writing," Conference on College Composition and Communication, 1989.

3. Modern Language Association, "MLA Statement on the Use of Part-Time and Full-Time Adjunct Faculty," *MLA Newsletter* (Summer 1994): 17.

4. Nelson, Cary, "How to Reform the MLA: An Opening Proposal," *Profession 1996* (1996): 45.

Bibliography

Berver, Kitty, Don Kurtz, and Eliot Orton. "Off the Track, but in the Fold." *Academe* (November December 1992): 27 29.

"CCCC Reports on Survey of Freestanding Writing Programs." *The Council Chronicle* (NCTE) 11.3 (February 2002): 1- 6.

Committee on Professional Standards for Quality Education. "Statement of Principles and Standards for the Postsecondary Teaching of Writing." Conference on College Composition and Communication. 1989.

Farrell, Thomas J. "How to Kill Higher Education." *Academe* (November-December 1992): 30-33.

Kiefson, Ruth. "The Politics and Economics of the Super-Exploitation of Adjuncts." In *Tenured Bosses and Disposable Teachers: Writing Instruction in the Managed University*, edited by Mark Bousquet, Tony Scott, and Leo Parescondola, 143-149. Carbondale: Southern Illinois University Press, 2004.

Kolb, Katherine. "Adjuncts in Academe: No Place Called Home." *Profession 1997* (1997): 93-103.

"Minutes of the MLA Delegate Assembly." *PMLA* 119.3 (May 2004): 606-14.

Modern Language Association. "MLA Statement on the Use of Part-Time and Full-Time Adjunct Faculty." *MLA Newsletter* (Summer 1994): 17.

Nelson, Cary. "How to Reform the MLA: An Opening Proposal." *Profession 1996* (1996): 44-49.

Papp, James. "Gleaning in Academe: Personal Decisions for Adjuncts and Graduate Students." *College English* 64.6 (July 2002): 696-709.

Wilson, Robin. "Scholars Off the Tenure Track Wonder If They'll Ever Get On." *The Chronicle of Higher Education* 14 June 1996: A12-13.

"Fair is Foul and Foul is fair": Schizophrenia in the Academy

Kathleen K. Thornton

The situation in American universities of professional academics who are classified as non-tenured teaching faculty or part-timers is paradoxical and exploitive. On the one hand such faculty members may have served their departments and the university for long periods of time without the perks or recognition rewarded to those who are on tenure lines. They have taught thousands of undergraduate students, served on hundreds of committees, written an equal number of letters of recommendation and perhaps have written books. On the other hand, they are deemed expendable by the university they have served and are classified as "less" than their colleagues and certainly less than the junior faculty who are hired to take on the tenure lines, sometimes in the very fields such part-timers have been teaching for upwards of 15 years. They are cheap labour who are necessary but a liability in times of budget crisis and who are looked upon as second class citizens who, it seems, ought to be grateful to be hired to teach, even if it is for approximately one tenth the salary of the junior tenure-track faculty. They exist in an environment fraught with anxiety about their financial futures and constantly have their self-worth devalued by the institutions they serve. Theirs is a no-win situation: if they wish to continue in the profession they love, they must suffer such indignities. To suffer such indignities is to reinforce their second class status.

Non-tenured; Part-time; Academics; Exploitation; Paradox; Employment; scholars

The University at Albany has a distinguished teaching faculty. It is a faculty that is made up not only of tenured and tenure-track faculty but also of a cohort of "part-time" faculty lines. That is, faculty who work "full-time," but are paid out of "part-time" money and who lack the job security, perks, and recognition guaranteed to "full-time" faculty. In this dichotomy we have a first glimpse of the multiple perceptions applied to part-timers: lecturers, adjuncts, and graduate students who had previously been on teaching fellowships but who have now exhausted their funding and teach part-time as they attempt to finish their dissertations. Over the years, we have been variously labelled "part-time," "adjunct," "gypsy scholars," "migrant workers," or "lecturers." The labels suggest the low status we are afforded and are demeaning, especially when used to describe the group of highly educated, hard-working individuals who make up this class.

I am one of those individuals. In preparing to write this piece, I had approached one of my colleagues, a fellow lecturer whose work with the union has brought about the end to some of the university's more draconian policies. I asked her to co-author this piece, since she has been here even longer than I and could shed light on the differences between our experiences. I waited for her draft, emailing her several times to ask about her progress. Finally, we sat down together. After some attempts, she told me, she simply was unable to write the piece. She explained it this way: "Every time I sat down to put on paper my experiences as a part-liner, I found ways to avoid confronting the experience. To write it out would make the situation real in a way that just thinking about it doesn't." She insisted that it was simply too painful to re-envision the last 18½ years, years of her service to the English Department and to the institution and thereby to acknowledge the humiliation of being denigrated as a part-time employee with a year to year contract renewal. I agreed. Thinking about our situation stirred up a cauldron of emotions, reminiscent of those misshapen and grotesque ingredients the three witches of *Macbeth* simmered in their obscene brew.

I knew exactly how she felt. After serving my department for sixteen years, and, after a series of negotiations and strong-minded department chairs who argued my importance to the middle managers of the university, I had finally been given a contract of three years with a scheduled review and the potential for renewal for another three years. However, it soon became obvious that such agreements were not binding; at least not in the same way as agreements were for those hired on tenure-track lines.

"That was then, this is now." Words similar to those came to me early in 2003 when, without a review and without warning, my three-year renewal was reduced to a one-year appointment. When I first learned of the change, it was because the three-year renewal term on my appointment papers had been "whited out" and the change handwritten in. Our administrative assistant immediately notified the chair and then called to see if there had been some mistake. She was told there was not. Then, she told me. I was stunned into silence and when the words finally imbedded themselves in my brain, I felt as if I were going to be ill. I couldn't breathe and I couldn't speak. It was as if I had been kicked in the stomach.

A few days later, I expressed my deep dismay and outrage at the way I had been treated. I alternately choked back tears and fought to keep my anger in check, since raging at the injustice would accomplish nothing other than momentary relief and might do a great deal of damage. I could not, and still cannot, believe the insensitivity and ingratitude and cavalier dismissive treatment this "penny-wise, pound-foolish" managerial decision conveyed.

My department chair listened sympathetically, wrote emails to those whom he thought were in a position to right the wrong only to meet with the despicable language explaining that the policy had been implemented because "we need fiscal flexibility in these troubled economic times."

Flexibility?? Those of us who are lecturers teach two classes each semester and bear heavy administrative responsibilities in addition to serving on departmental committees. I teach two classes each semester and I serve as the Director of English Undergraduate Advisement, overseeing the progress of our 760 majors! In essence, I was doing two full-time jobs for the price of one. And I am not alone. My lecturer-colleagues perform similarly. In addition to teaching their two classes each semester, other "part-time" full-timers run the University at Albany Writing Centre, administer the English Undergraduate Internship Programme and sponsor Sigma Tau Delta, and direct the Centre for Humanities, Arts, and TechnoSciences. We also serve on committees, oversee independent study projects, write letters of reference, and participate in scholarship by attending conferences, writing books, articles, grants, and poetry. Yet, despite this, and despite our titles of lecturers with an academic year appointment, we are considered "part-time" because our salaries are paid from "soft" or "part-line" monies.

When my chair tried to point out the illogic of a position that tried to maintain the pretence that at any time in the near future the department or the university could do without the services and expertise I and other colleagues who had been treated with equal callous disregard brought to the program, he received a one-line reply. Essentially, it read: Thank you for your input but we are following college policy in these renewals.

College policy is not the same as university policy but when you are in the field of humanities instead of the sciences, the money and support is simply not there. Short of having a bake sale, what are the humanities to do? In the upcoming year, we will be attempting to reduce millions of dollars of shortfall. What this means to my position or the position of the other lecturers is anyone's guess.

"That was then, this is now." Sixteen years ago, my department was at what we would call full strength. To be hired to teach at the University at Albany full-time faculty were expected to be ABD or have degree in hand. To be considered as a part-time faculty member, applicants had a doctorate or MFA in hand. Even then, we were assigned classes at the lower level. All these classes appealed to the general population or were classes that addressed our areas of expertise. Only rarely were we assigned upper-level classes and then not until we had been part of the teaching cohort for some years.

Our colleagues valued us for having successfully completed our education. It was understood that our status as lecturers or part-timers was not necessarily a reflection on our abilities. It was understood that we might not have had the luxury of moving out of the area or conducting a full-blown search, that we may have had spouses whose positions locked us into the area, etc. We weren't exactly "family," but we were not the stepchildren confined to sweep the ash pile, either. Still, the administration hired us semester by semester for the paltry sum of $2,500 per class, a class usually of 40 students. When one computes the number of hours the "part-timer" spent in the classroom, meeting students during office hours, and preparing the materials to teach, it is painfully obvious that our degrees and scholarship were not valued.

Recently, too, we endured an inquiry of whether or not lecturers were "appropriate" faculty to write letters of reference for our students. I listened to full-time faculty insisting that student applications were weightier when accompanied by a letter of reference from a "recognized" scholar. While this might be true for students applying to PhD programs at Harvard, Yale, and the other Ivies, it is not true for the bulk of students the University at Albany graduates with English degrees each year. It was indeed a paradox. On the one hand, we argued that if we were not "substantive" enough to write the letters for the number of students who asked, it would definitely lessen our burden since many of us were asked to write between fifteen and twenty letters a semester. On the other hand, if our assessments of our students didn't matter, why were we teaching them and evaluating them in the classroom? We asked if we were supposed to announce at the beginning of the semester that we were not tenured or tenure track faculty and were, therefore, without authority or worth and any recommendation we would write would not be valuable to the student. My blood pressure usually registers low but I felt my blood boiling. We are good enough to teach undergraduates in large number and across a wide spectrum of courses but we aren't good enough to be hired on lines or to write letters of recommendation! And mind you, the four lecturers about whom I have been writing are those with administrative and programmatic responsibilities and who have approximately 90 years combined service to the English Department.

A colleague of mine who had learned of my situation offered this scenario as a means of placating me. I know she meant to make me feel better but she didn't. She argued that if I were working at one of the private colleges in the area, I would have more work (teaching 4 classes each semester instead of two), would still have to advise students, and would still have to serve on committees for about the same salary I was currently earning. What she failed to mention is that at one of those institutions after sixteen years of continuous service, I would have tenure and most likely the rank of associate or full professor rather than to continually face the uncertainty of being employed.

As far as graduate students are concerned, times have changed as well. Sixteen years ago, graduate teaching assistants were restricted to teaching 100-level classes (Reading Literature, Reading Prose Fiction, Reading Drama, or Reading Poetry) and every so often, one of us had the plum assignment of teaching "Reading Shakespeare" or "Science Fiction," or "The Short Story." After all, we were a four-year university and our students and their parents had every expectation that their tuition dollars would insure that classes were taught by academics who had earned their degrees.

That was then, this is now. The configuration of the department and the teaching terrain sixteen years later is vastly different in the Department of English. We have had our ranks decimated and have lost faculty to institutions that could pay them better than we could. We have had faculty retire and had their lines disappear while more and more part-time faculty and graduate students are slotted into their place. We exploit graduate students while they are studying for their exams or trying to write their dissertations when we turn them into part-time faculty when their funding runs out. And, as is clear, part-liners are exploited.

No longer is there an understanding of the mitigating circumstances that may have kept us here. Instead, there is a coldness and deliberate effort to see part-liners as a budgetary burden rather than as individuals. We are classified, categorized, and deliberately set apart from other members of the department. The university does not value those lecturers who have dedicated their careers to undergraduate teaching; instead, it holds a sword over their heads, threatening their livelihood, despite the fact that they are some of the most industrious and dedicated members of the department.

These changes are to the detriment of the undergraduate student and to the integrity of the English Department and the university itself. Such changes provide a way for the academic community to create yet another tier in its fascination with hierarchy, control, exploitation and cheap labour. It provides for the perpetuation of a class system of "haves" and "have nots," "us" and "them." While faculty promotions have always had to do with scholarship, service, and teaching, linking accomplishments with salary and prestige, the lecturers and part-line employees benefit not at all from any commitment they make to those same activities. In fact, the current economic system encourages a two or even three-tiered labour force: the first, one of privilege that distinguishes itself by its commitment to its own research and graduate education; the second, those on a three-year appointment who have some stability, who teach a bulk of the undergraduate population; and the third, those hired either annually or semester by semester. For lecturers and part-timers, it provides for a system of intellectual and economic indentured servitude, insecurity and humiliation while relegating qualified teachers and scholars to second or even third class citizenship in the intellectual community of which they are a part and in which they perform the majority of tasks. We have become, as one of my colleagues noted, the "bottom-feeders" in the system.

Here's who we are: one of my fellow lecturers has written four books. Her teaching ranges from James Joyce and 20th Century writers to film theory and psychoanalytical criticism; another lecturer has written two books and has filmed an award-winning documentary with the grant money she received. She teaches writing, American literature and the literature of Hawaii. A third teaches creative writing, the Beat Poets, and science fiction. In the past two academic years, I have had four papers published and delivered ten different conference papers, the topics of which ranged from Hawthorne's *Blithedale Romance* to Shakespeare's *Measure for Measure* and *Macbeth* to film adaptation, practices of teaching, and cultural studies. I was recently told that the only reward there was in my giving such papers had to be personal satisfaction, since it made no difference in the terms of my renewal.

What is the message here? It's easy enough to decipher. Don't bother to be engaged intellectually in the discourses of your profession because no one cares. Moreover, were you producing work of any significance, you'd have a "real job." Therein is the schizophrenia of which this title speaks. I thought I did have a real job - at least I have for the last sixteen years. Were I not active in the discipline, however, I would reaffirm the hierarchy established by my being a part-timer since part-timers are not expected to engage in research, someone along the line determining that there is no intellectual curiosity attached to part-line work and since part-timers are expendable, why would they care about doing research? And since they don't care and since they do not participate in the discourses of the discipline, they are expendable! I get dizzy when I try to track the "logic" of such suppositions. It's as convoluted a system of logic as suggesting that teaching two classes and putting in 15-20 hours of advising each week constitutes part-time labour.

In a series of equally bold logical gymnastics that make one feel as if she has truly fallen down the rabbit hole or eaten on "the insane root that takes the reason prisoner," the powers that be have persuaded the tenured faculty that our graduate students *should* teach upper-level English undergraduate courses when they are on teaching fellowships or when they have exhausted their funding. This latter group is thrown a bone of $2,500 to teach a 40-seat class. I am talking about grad students who have not finished their exams and have not started their dissertations. Somehow, we have drunk from the cauldron and the apparitions that appear allow us to convince ourselves that they have the necessary expertise to teach on the three or four hundred level, courses that should be taught by our marquee-named faculty - the ones whose names are listed in the undergraduate bulletin. So, like Macbeth believing in his own invincibility, we allow ourselves to be persuaded that our department is vital so long as we have grad students and part liners to take the teaching responsibilities.

At the same time, there is an assumption that lecturers or part-timers who not only have degree in hand but who also have worked for the university for up to 20 years may not be intellectually sophisticated enough to teach upper-level classes themselves or can teach them when there is no one else available to do so but who would be "unthinkable" as hires when a search in the very area in which they currently teach is being conducted! So, we are good enough to teach 300 and 400-level courses year after year, but we aren't good enough to be hired when positions in those areas open. Similarly, graduate students who have barely cut their teeth on course work are somehow more "expert" in the areas we have spent our lives examining - until, perhaps, they are unable to complete their course work or exams or dissertations in a timely fashion and must seek part-time work. Then, they become us.

What is the message these practices send to the graduate students themselves, then and now? At one point, when they are teaching assistants, they are "qualified," but the moment their funding expires, they are not? What does it say to those with degrees? You *were* acceptable but you are now less acceptable than these graduate students who must be "cutting edge" even if they cannot perform a close reading of the text or think that because they once read a Shakespeare play, they are qualified to teach the author!

And here is the monetary value for your work: $2,500 per course. Not even minimum wage, by my calculations.

What, too, is the message sent to our undergraduates and their parents? What has their undergraduate experience come to mean to the university at large? What is their tuition really buying them?

I recently heard an argument put forward by an associate dean that high school teachers could teach the introductory reading and writing classes because they knew how to teach and they had master's degrees. I have taught high school English. There is a vast difference between the intellectual challenges of a high school classroom and a college classroom - at least there should be, especially a college classroom at a university. What wasn't stated in his comments but was embedded in his observations was that high school teachers could be hired at $2,500 a course, have their egos flattered as they were named adjunct faculty of the University at Albany, and would save the College of Arts and Sciences a great deal of money.

I have also listened to my colleagues argue that it is more important to give the work to our graduate students who have exceeded their funding without finishing their degrees than to give the work to those of us who have been with the university for years - almost as if we are an embarrassment to them for not leaving and for tolerating the type of treatment we have been subjected to. We are like the mixed-race children of early American slaveholders: a constant reminder to the establishment of its inappropriate behaviour, a constant reminder of its tyranny and exploitation, a constant reminder of its injustice.

One year, we were all "fired" because there was a budget shortfall. Our health insurance was cancelled and we had no idea if we were going to have work again. Although we were all rehired, thereafter, it was more or less understood, that we were never sure we would be asked to teach. These actions accomplished two things: to remind us that the power over our financial security was in the hands of administration, and to make us grateful for any terms by which we would be rehired. It was, and is, humiliating.

No one in this profession aspires to the bottom rung of the ladder of academic hierarchy that is embedded in the structure of the corporate university. No one willingly embraces an academic life that teeters on the precipice of despair and financial ruin. No one willingly undergoes the whips and scorns of outrageous fortune, constantly having to prove her worth to people whose understanding of loyalty is wedded to the $ sign at the bottom line. No one aspires to sell her worth and knowledge for $2,500 a course or the $40,000 or so a year lecturers earn.

I have earned a doctorate, have delivered numerous conference papers, have published articles, have organized a regional conference for NYCEA, serve on the board of directors for NYCEA, organized a symposium in honour of Judith Fetterley, and have done service on the Undergraduate Advisory Committee, the UG Curriculum Revision Committee, and the Honours Committee. My service is "voluntary," but my status makes my response involuntary. I am literally between the hammer and the anvil. Were I to decline, claiming there is no reward for my service (I get no leaves, no promotions, no classes off), I would be labelled obstructionist since I have a wealth of knowledge about requirements and policies of the university that others in the department lack but need in order to perform some of their jobs. When I remind people that what they are asking me is outside of the job I have, I am told that I shouldn't be so negative and that cooperative problem solving is what makes the system work. Whose system? I wonder.

If I comply, then I perpetuate a system of exploitation and prove myself to be either a fool or dedicated to a code of behaviour that is neither rewarded nor appreciated by the organization for which I work. I have heard others receive praise for the work I produced behind the scenes. I have watched others being given or take credit for the information I have provided them, as well as being appointed or promoted or tenured. And the bitterness grows with each passing year. My attempts to rebel have been met over the years with quiet but deeply understood threats: my renewal is always at stake.

I can teach and have taught everything from literature (Shakespeare, Poe & Hawthorne, 19th Century American Writers, Modern American Drama, Modern World Drama, Reading Literature, the Short Story, Reading Drama, Reading Prose Fiction) to writing (Expository Writing and Critical Writing) to film (Shakespeare on film) to public speaking. When someone retires or leaves the university for "greener pastures," more often than not, it is my schedule or the schedule of one of the other lecturers that undergoes a transformation: not that my department is mistreating me. It just seems as if my versatility allows me to plug holes in the schedule that would otherwise require courses to be cancelled.

I used to be flattered. That is, until I watched younger candidates come to apply for positions for which I had more experience and expertise but without the requisite book in print or the marquee names in my reference folder. In the "new" university, where the concern is the "bottom line" economically, we pay "lip service" to academic quality. While administrators agree in principle to hiring fewer part liners, providing long-term part-timers with the stability of three-year contracts, and providing recognition for part-time teaching excellence, it is only to the public ceremonial aspects that administration takes heed. We honour our part-time teachers of excellence with a reception and a modest salary increase but we neither appoint them to three-year contracts nor to full-time positions that become available. To be once a part-time employee or a lecturer is to live with the mark of Cain. We are forever outsiders, we are forever living on borrowed time, and we are forever looking over our shoulders wondering when and who will deliver the coup de grace. That was then, this is now. As for tomorrow, unlike Scarlet O'Hara, we cannot put off the unpleasant and hope for a better future. All we can do is try to survive, put our egos away in a drawer, swallow our pride, work as hard as we always have, complain not a whit and take no ethical stand or draw any controversy to ourselves and maybe, just maybe, there will be a tomorrow, even if it creeps in this petty pace from day to day.

Bringing Adjunct Faculty into the Fold of Information and Instructional Technology

Kenneth H. Ryesky

With few exceptions, colleges and universities claim initiatives to bring modern instructional and information technologies into the classroom. Adjunct faculty members teach a significant percentage of college courses. Part-time employment circumstances and workplace conditions often differ from those of full-time faculty, thus posing many challenges and impediments to facilitating the new and emerging technologies in adjunct-taught courses. Using "case method" discussion of several illustrative scenarios derived from actual situations and experiences of the author and his fellow adjuncts, this essay highlights various issues inherent in bringing technological currency to adjunct-instructed courses, and spotlights several dysfunctions encountered by various colleges of the City University of New York ("CUNY") system in putting CUNY's grand information technology scheme into practice. Issues include, but are not limited to, availability of technological resources to the adjunct; providing support for the adjunct by CUNY; specialized information technologies and databases for certain courses; remuneration and compensation policies for adjunct faculty; the social and professional interactions between adjunct faculty and other University social groups; and prevailing professional, institutional and personal biases against adjuncts. The aforementioned issues, and others, pose challenges to CUNY's strategic plans for instructional technological currency, and have broad application at institutions other than CUNY.

Adjunct; Adjunct Bashing; Computer; Disparity; Human factor; Faculty; Part-time; Professional; Social; Technology

> *Mere powder, guns and bullets,*
> *we scarce can get at all;*
> *Their price was spent in merriment*
> *and revel at Whitehall,*
> *While we in tattered doublets*
> *from ship to ship must row,*
> *Beseeching friends for odds and ends*
> *- And this the Dutchmen know!*[1]

1.   Introduction

On 14 November 2003, the City University of New York ("CUNY") held a Conference entitled "Instructional/Information Technology in CUNY: Issues, Innovations, Integration." This essay is based upon the author's presentation at that Conference. As a large and diversified institution, CUNY serves in many respects as a model for other colleges and universities. The ongoing CUNY experience with instructional technology and information technology ("IT")[2] is certainly no exception.

The employment of adjunct faculty[3] has been a definitive and growing trend in American academia.[4] The trend has certainly affected CUNY, where, in 1998, the percentage of undergraduate courses taught by adjunct faculty was 48% at the senior colleges and 49% at the community colleges.[5] Though this essay spotlights the author's personal experiences at Queens College CUNY, the observations are largely applicable to other institutions as well.

Adjunct faculty employment conditions and circumstances are quite diverse from college to college, department to department, and individual to individual, and quite often differ markedly from those of full-time faculty. Access to campus computer systems or other types of IT is a key area of great disparity.[6] "Contingent faculty are fortunate to share an office space or computer access and are unlikely to be eligible for professional development grants, research support, or even participation in collegial meetings either to benefit from peer evaluation or to share information about student learning and adapt curricula to student needs."[7]

The need to manage the human factor has long been recognized as a critical issue in technologically-intensive operations, good and evil,[8] especially where new technologies and new applications are in a state of development or flux.[9]

A significant percentage of CUNY instruction is in fact being done by adjuncts. Moreover, currency in the information technologies is well recognized, implicitly and explicitly, for student and faculty alike, as a priority throughout CUNY, where "Expanding the Use of Technology in Teaching and Learning" is a stated objective.[10] Regardless of one's views regarding adjunct faculty, it therefore is quite vital to facilitate the use of IT among CUNY adjuncts.[11]

This essay will explore various issues that need to be addressed in facilitating IT currency and use among adjunct faculty. Several illustrative cases will be presented, the relevant issues exemplified by the cases will be explored, and, where relevant, possible remedies to the problems will be discussed.

2.   Illustrative Cases

The illustrative cases that follow are derived from the experience of the author and/or other CUNY adjuncts. Each case will be presented, and then used as a basis for identification and discussion of the issues exemplified by the case. The cases will begin with a simple adjunct office lacking IT amenities, and then progress to further scenarios involving adjunct faculty, in order to demonstrate and discuss relevant issues which must be addressed in order to avail IT to the adjunct-instructed course.

Funding, of course, is always a salient matter in bringing about any technological change. Real life efforts to address adjunct faculty participation in any technological revolution at CUNY or elsewhere will certainly need to be mindful of the costs of the initiative and how they are to be underwritten. The superficial attention given to the financial factors in the discussion to follow is in no way intended to diminish or invalidate the great importance of the purse. At such time and to such extent as the adjunct faculty members are embraced by any IT currency initiative at CUNY, the fiscal factors will, no doubt, be accorded their due regard by all concerned.

2. A. Case 1: The Converted Closet Office

2. A. 1 The Problem

Unlike their full-time colleagues, the adjuncts in this office had no desktop computers upon which basic hardware and software was available for preparing lectures, exams and assignments (*e.g.*, word processing, spreadsheet, printing capabilities, etc.). The adjuncts in this Case had the mutually exclusive choice of being in their office or using the campus IT; they could not do both.

Another problem was that, all IT issues notwithstanding, the two adjuncts were physically removed from the Department office, and therefore attenuated from the social interactions that serve as an informal but nevertheless effective communication and information system.

Figure 1: The Converted Closet Office (1)

Due to lack of space, the author and a colleague had been assigned office space in a building across the parking lot from the Department offices, in an out-of-the-way 8' x 10' room formerly used as a closet to store old books. The room had barely enough space for two desks, chairs, and some filing cabinets. There was no computer equipment, and indeed, neither the data jacks nor the telephone jacks were operative. This situation lasted approximately three and one half years, pending reconstruction of the building in which the Department is normally located.

Figure 2: The Converted Closet Office (2)

2. A. 2 Discussion
Install a computer terminal in the room:

The prospect of installing a computer terminal in the room has various issues. In addition to the omnipresent budgetary matters, there are security issues. With multiple individuals having access to a computer terminal, the security of the files may be at issue, though a spirit of interdepartmental collegiality and congeniality, if present, would tend to minimize this factor. Password access to the files and programmes can tailor the computer facilities to the needs of the respective computer users and provide a degree of security. Of greater concern is the security of the room, physically set apart from the main Departmental offices and therefore not subject to the informal monitoring services provided by the other Departmental faculty, and the supporting secretaries and clerks.

For computer terminals in a remote room such as the one described in this Case, maintenance and support may become relevant concerns. Even when the computers are in a functional mode, there should be some sort of defined responsibility for maintenance tasks such as virus scanning, updating software, deleting extraneous and obsolete files from the hard drives, etc.

Once the physical hardware is in place, there would need to be some sort of regimen or protocol for the enforcement of cyber-hygienic practices so that the system not be infected by viruses as a result of activities such as swapping of floppy disks. And the potential for problems along these lines increases exponentially as the numbers of adjuncts using the office increase from the two adjuncts in this particular room, as, for example, a situation in which "[o]ver 50 adjunct faculty share the 3 adjunct offices available to the [Sciences] Department making the offering of office hours unpredictable. Most adjunct faculty have no discernable work areas."[12]

And if there be peripheral devices such as printers and scanners, their maintenance must likewise be attended to, if only to replenish paper and ink.

Adjuncts use portable laptop or notebook type computers:

A matter that needs to be determined early on is whether adjuncts are to be given the portable computers by CUNY, or whether they are to supply their own. Back in the days of chalk and slate blackboards, CUNY provided the adjuncts (and other faculty) with the relevant information media teaching tools, namely, chalk and erasers (the blackboards generally being securely installed in the classrooms). The thousand-fold cost differential between a notebook computer and a box of chalk[13] would impose obvious budgetary barriers upon any plan to similarly provide the adjunct faculty members with individual computers. Even if such budgetary obstacles could be surmounted, there surely would be the matters of accountability for the laptop computers on the part of the adjunct who has been issued one.

If, on the other hand, the adjuncts were required to provide their own laptop computers, there would be, in addition to the inevitable and justifiable demands from the adjuncts for some sort of reimbursement, issues of technical compatibility between the laptop computers and the CUNY system. If, as in the illustrated Case, there is no available connection to the campus computer network, then issuing laptops to adjuncts would have limited results; adjuncts would be able to work with documents with word processing or spreadsheet software, but would have no ability to access real time information or central databases often essential to maintaining currency the courses and subjects taught. Moreover, if there be no available computer network connection via the wires or otherwise, but ordinary telephone system jacks are operative, then the adjunct might be (and indeed, at least one has been) tempted or compelled to use the campus telephone system to dial up to his or her personal Internet Service Provider, a practice with obvious diseconomies for adjunct and CUNY alike.

Additionally, theft of computers, laptops or otherwise, is a persistent problem on college campuses.[14] Adjuncts frequently use their assigned rooms as places to temporarily store their personal belongings. Accordingly, physical security remains an issue if laptops are used to avail IT resources to adjuncts, regardless of whether the laptops are CUNY-owned or adjunct-owned.

Allowing Adjuncts to use computers in other locations on campus:

[N.B. The issues involved in accommodating the adjuncts in student computer labs are further discussed in Case 3 below.]

In addition to the other security concerns previously mentioned, there is the potential for conflict between the adjuncts' computer activity and the host computer users' normal routines where adjuncts are given computer privileges in other campus offices. As an example, there is potential for unacceptable disruption in the Department office if the computer intended for use by the Department secretary were to be fair game for access by the Department's adjunct faculty. Indeed, such disruption prompted the author's Department Chair to issue a pronouncement banning the use of secretarial computers by faculty, adjunct or otherwise. Where the host computer is intended for use by a different Department or office altogether, the disruption potential is increased, as is the potential for interdepartmental territorial conflict.

The illustrated Case demonstrates another complicating factor at CUNY. The operative labour contract has an Adjunct Professional Hour provision[15] which has been interpreted by some to be a specified time period for which affected adjunct faculty members are being paid an hour's salary, and during which time they are to be in their offices. If the adjuncts in the illustrated Case are at a student computer laboratory or at a computer elsewhere on campus, then they are not in their office, and thus, the time spent accessing the computer system might technically be viewed by some as not applicable towards the Professional Hour.[16] There accordingly arises the issue of the manner of interpretation, application and enforcement of this Professional Hour provision by the union, Department and CUNY Administration. Adjunct remuneration policies and issues are thus quite relevant to bringing IT to adjunct-taught courses.[17]

Physical attenuation of the Adjuncts from the Department Office:

Though not per se an IT issue, the dynamics of the informal information transmitted through social interaction play a vital part in any organization.[18] Moreover, informal communication plays a significant role in shaping the cohesion of any work group.[19] Any degree of exclusion of individuals from the informal communication pipelines will in some way affect group cohesiveness. Group performance is impacted in no small way by social dynamics, and the social interactions cannot be ignored in successfully implementing any strategic objective, including the implementation of IT.

2. B. Case 2: The Library Laptop Loan Programme

> *The Reserve Desk of the campus library has laptop computers available for sign-out by students.[20] The computers are available to students only; faculty members, adjunct or otherwise, may not participate in the program. The rationale for excluding faculty is "[s]ince laptops were purchased with the technology fees paid for by students ONLY (not staff, not Adjuncts,) and since we could only afford a minimal number of laptops, it was decided that for the time being only students should benefit from this new purchase paid by them.[21]*

2. B. 1 The Problem

Just who shall be responsible for ensuring that adjuncts are availed IT resources? Is it appropriate – or fair – that a programme or office within a university, whose specific mission is to facilitate student needs, be compelled to expend its resources toward matters unrelated to its mission such as facilitating adjunct faculty members?

2. B. 2 Discussion

Resources intended for student benefit should be availed to students, and resources intended for faculty benefit should be availed to faculty. Administrators of such programmes must ensure that their programmes operate as intended. If, for example, doing good for an adjunct would work to the detriment of the students intended to be helped by a venture such as the Library Laptop Loan programme in this Case, then the programme administrator, duty-bound to ensure that the programme serves its intended constituency, is appropriately compelled to deny access to adjuncts.

There are several possible approaches to assigning responsibility to ensure that adjunct faculty members can access IT resources. The "point person" might be centralized in the IT bureaucracy, or might be decentralized in the individual Departments. While local circumstances may well dictate that the specific schemes for facilitating adjunct IT access vary from college to college, it is important that a specific policy at in fact exist at each college, and that such policy identify with specificity just where and in whom some defined responsibility is reposed.

Where such policy does not exist, there runs the risk that enterprising adjuncts might look to sources on campus that are neither geared to nor appropriate for connecting the adjunct with the campus IT. The adjunct is thus placed into a bind: He or she can proactively seek out IT empowerment by beseeching friends for resources and thus benefit the students but in doing so cause the disruption of orderly campus organizational functioning; or else he/she can avoid the conflict inherent in bucking the system, but in doing so, not have access to IT resources, to the detriment of the students. The system is ill served by such a condition. There needs to be policy and procedure to avail IT resources to adjuncts.

2. C. Case 3: The Student Computer Lab

The author, upon inquiring as to his use of a student computer lab on campus, was informed by the student assistant on duty that the lab was for students, and that he was to use the computer terminals in his own Department (there were none in the Department available to adjuncts). A few days later, upon further inquiry to a higher-up administrator, the author was given an account to enable his access to any student computer lab on campus.

2. C 1. The Problem

The operative campus policy on adjunct access to IT did not formally exist or, if it existed, was not adequately communicated to all relevant personnel.

2. C. 2. Discussion

It is axiomatic that promulgated organizational policies must be communicated to all concerned personnel within the organization. Policies regarding adjunct access to IT resources need to be communicated to the IT purveyors down to and including the student assistants in the campus computer laboratories, and to the adjuncts themselves, which effectively means that Department Chairs and Department Secretaries must also become cognizant of such policies.

If, in the instant Case, no formal policy indeed existed for adjunct access to student computer labs, then the bringing of the matter to the attention of the cognizant administrator was a signal that such policy ought be promulgated, instead of having to deal with each adjunct on an ad hoc basis. Where no policy has been promulgated, a situation can easily arise where all functional departments disclaim responsibility for connecting adjuncts with IT resources, to the long-term big-picture detriment of college and student alike.[22]

This Case now presents a convenient juncture for excursus, to briefly discuss availing IT to adjunct faculty through the use of campus computer laboratories. There are several acceptable approaches to doing so, any or all of which may be appropriate to a given CUNY campus. These include (1) a computer lab reserved for faculty only; (2) particular terminals in a student computer lab reserved for faculty (or for faculty and graduate students); (3) priority terminals which students may use, but must yield to faculty members when so requested; and even, as typified by the instant Case, (4) issuing faculty computer accounts which enable the adjunct to use any campus computer lab on same basis as the students. What is *not* acceptable is a situation where, taking into consideration the totality of circumstances, adjunct access to computer facilities is *inferior* to that of the students. Such indeed was the situation that temporarily existed in the instant Case when the author, having no computer facilities in his office, was denied access to the student computer lab.

There is much to be said for using campus computer labs as a means to avail IT to adjuncts. Problems can crop up on the opposite extreme, however. If, for example, the adjunct is using an ordinary computer in the computer lab, and is seated next to a student, then privacy issues may be implicated if the adjunct is working on grades or other personal student data, or is composing an exam paper for the class. And, depending upon factors such as the IT resource needs of others, the bounds of reasonableness may be tested in situations where the adjunct spends all of his or her "office hours" in a computer lab, even to the point using the lab as a venue for meeting with students. Sensible and appropriate rules and protocols, whether formally specified or otherwise, must be followed in such regard.

2. D. Case 4: Weekend College

2. D. 1 The Problem

IT is not made available to students or instructors at times when weekend or evening classes are held.

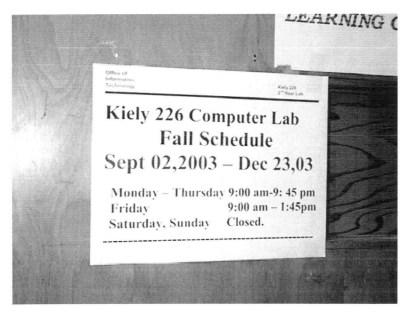

Figure 3: Lab Closed
*The author's Sunday morning class was scheduled from 8:30 AM to 12:15
PM. The campus Library did not open until 12:00 Noon. The one campus
computer lab open on Sundays did not open until 10:00 AM. The one campus
computer lab with projection screen facilities was closed Sundays. Data
projectors and other audio-visual equipment were unavailable for faculty
sign-out before 10:00 AM.*

2. D. 2 Discussion

Evening and weekend classes are more likely than not to be taught
by adjunct faculty; therefore, any issue involving evening or weekend classes
implicitly concerns adjuncts. The limited availability of IT for evening and
weekend classes is thus a matter that affects adjuncts at least as adversely as
it affects students.

Here, the author and other adjuncts whose designated office space
lacks computer access cannot do something so simple as check out something
on the Internet when prepping for class; access to the student computer labs is
meaningless if the labs are not open during and before scheduled classes.

Some colleges have support services for faculty who teach weekend
and evening classes.[23] Such support services need to include Internet and IT
access for faculty at meaningful times for class preparation and instruction.
Where no such support services are present, even an enterprising adjunct

such as the one in Case 3 above would have difficulty beseeching a cognizant administrator if the administrator's regular office hours did not coincide with the hours the adjunct is normally present on campus.

If the classrooms are wired with network connections for computers, then availing laptop computers and data projectors to adjunct faculty who teach evening and weekend classes might be one element in the resolution of this problem. But, as mentioned earlier, such is not without its own issues. In this case, if the audio-visual (AV) personnel are not available to deliver the equipment to the classroom and the instructor therefore must personally obtain it, then there is, at the very least, a class disruption while the instructor goes to the AV office (which might be at a campus location remote from the classroom).

Nor are adjuncts the only ones adversely affected by the unavailability of IT resources during scheduled class times. Many academic disciplines and professions have become very dependent upon particular databases and/or technologies for accessing and searching such databases. The field of Law, for example, has become dependent upon on-line databases such as LEXIS-NEXIS, which is available CUNY-wide.[24] Students whose classrooms lack IT connections to such databases at the time of the class session are no less disadvantaged than their instructor, particularly where a real time interactive database accession is appropriate or desired for the lesson.

It has long been taken for granted that a classroom will have an operative blackboard, and that the instructor will either find be issued chalk, find chalk in the classroom or will otherwise have chalk available. If the familiar slate and chalk technologies are to be supplanted with the new IT, then such IT must likewise be expeditiously available to the adjunct (with due regard for the relevant budgetary, operability and security factors).

2. E. Case 5: The Grant

Several years ago, I won a very large 3-year federal grant from The Fund for Improvement in Post Secondary Education (FIPSE) for development of an online forum for ESL teachers. The feds knew I was an adjunct and had no problem with it. In fact, they gave me the largest CUNY FIPSE grant at Hunter during those years. But CUNY has a rule that adjuncts can't be directors of grants, so I was required to find a full-timer who would put their name to it (to help get tenure) as director. I did all the work, but the "director's" name was on it. At the end of the first year, my full-timer left the university . . . . I had to find another full-timer. This time, the Dean appointed someone without my input, someone who had absolutely NO knowledge of the field, someone who had never even been in the classroom. At the end of the year, that person decided she didn't want to sign my time cards anymore, and quit. So another person was appointed . . . and so on. I wrote the grant proposal, ran the project, did all the paperwork, hired employees, but nowhere at CUNY is there any record of this. I am sure that this is repeated often, but we don't know about it because adjuncts are not allowed to put their names on grants at CUNY.[25]

2. E. 1 The Problem

The operative CUNY regulations impose restrictions upon adjuncts handling funded research projects.[26] Such restrictions, in addition to having a repressive effect upon the egos of adjuncts who secure grants, can actually serve to impede the quality of the research through misadministration of the grant.

2.E.2 Discussion

It is, of course, necessary to have rules and regulations with respect to funded research. It is also necessary that responsible and accountable people exercise meaningful control over the expenditure of the grant funds, particularly where such funding is from an instrumentality of the Federal Government.[27] Nevertheless, there is no logical reason why, under the appropriate circumstances, an adjunct cannot direct a grant.

If indeed it is CUNY's intent and objective to develop and expand IT resources and applications, then adjuncts clearly have much to offer towards such an end. It was recognized comparatively early in the Computer Age that "[i]nnovation must become a way of life... Creativity must be encouraged and rewarded in an environment where risk is accepted as a calculated policy of corporate action."[28]

The role of adjunct faculty in academia has shifted dramatically over the past few decades. Adjuncts now have a major presence, and play a major role, at CUNY and other educational institutions. In light of such changes, the rules that restrict adjuncts from directing grants need to be revisited and reconsidered, so that responsible and qualified individuals who happen to be adjuncts can, without impairing the research efforts of full-timers, optimize their contributions to, and use of, campus IT, to the betterment of all concerned.

2. F. Case 6: The Loading Dock:

Figure 4: The Loading Dock
14 October 2003: A big pile of discarded computers, monitors, printers and other equipment cluttered the loading dock of the Queens College "I" Building.

2.F. 1 The Problem

      Adjuncts perceive that while CUNY regards computers as cheap discardable junk, CUNY regards adjuncts as not worthy of having computers in their offices.

2. F. 2 Discussion

      At the very least, a problem of perception has been created. It is, of course, necessary to discard obsolete and non-functional computer hardware from time to time. But the unexplained sight of computers, which might otherwise be put to good use in offices, lying in a junk heap on the rear dock sends a powerful and negative message to the adjuncts (and such messages are surely amplified by the sight, a few days later, of discarded packing crates from the new high end equipment that replaced the discarded hardware). Adjuncts whose offices lack even the most basic computer facilities can easily interpret the sight of computers, keyboards and monitors cast onto the rubbish pile as a proclamation that CUNY does not care about adjuncts' IT needs. It is very unrealistic for CUNY to expect to motivate adjuncts to use IT when CUNY is concurrently telling the same adjuncts that their IT needs are irrelevant.

Adjuncts need to know that they are included in CUNY's grand scheme for IT in the classroom. Credible plans to connect the adjuncts to campus IT need to be clearly communicated to the adjunct faculty members. Even where budgetary or technical factors preclude the immediate installation of necessary computer hardware in adjunct offices, the promulgation of, dissemination of and substantial adherence to reasonable timetables for implementation, together with reasonable interim measures for availing IT to adjunct faculty members, can go a long way towards preserving the Administration's credibility and cultivating the adjuncts' goodwill.

2. G. 1 Case 7: The Discussion Group Posting

The current trend of adjuncts and part-timers trying to take over the faculty union is scary. We have a group of individuals who for one reason or another could not make it. Nobody has a childhood dream of becoming an adjunct faculty. You become one because you were unsuccessful in the competition and you have no other choice. Now, these individuals who could not make their way to the main lobby through the street entrance and were able only to get to the basement through the side door are trying to force themselves to the main elevator in order to get to higher floors. When we hire a new full time faculty, we open the competition to young individuals who proved themselves and are promising. We will never agree to treat years of adjunct teaching as a criterion for natural advancement to full time lines. [29]

2. G. 1 The Problem
Negative views of Adjunct faculty.

2. G. 2 Discussion

As demonstrated by this posting, adjunctcy itself is the basis for stigmatization in the eyes of some in academia.[30] Adjuncts are frequently viewed with disdain and scorn by many individual full-time faculty and administrators, and indeed, this personal and institutional view of adjuncts as inferior *Untermenschen* frequently facilitates, in a self-feeding cycle, the unprofessional treatment of adjuncts by their employers, including the unavailability of such basic office supplies and services as the full-time faculty implicitly view as necessities for teaching.[31]

During the 2002 contract negotiations between the CUNY and the Professional Staff Congress, the CUNY Association of Scholars ("CUNYAS") issued a detestation of specific union proposals to allow "the time spent handling e-mail related to the course taught" as a valid activity to be performed in the compensable professional hour;[32] to "[provide] adjuncts with office space . . . and with desk, chair, telephone, file cabinets, bookshelves and *computers* [emphasis added];"[33] and to provide for adjuncts "eligibility for participation in faculty development opportunities."[34] Inasmuch many IT technologies require some degree of training, specialized skills, and participation in discussions relating to reasons and techniques,[35] the latter objection should be no less disturbing than CUNYAS's objection to availing computer access to adjuncts.

The bias against adjunct faculty, then, corrupts the thought processes of many in academia, even to the point where adjuncts are thought so unworthy as to not be deserving of access to IT resources, notwithstanding the inescapable rational conclusion that such availment would far serve the better interests of the University and the students.

Moreover, administrators and Department chairs who condone adjunct-bashing (let alone participate in it) cannot then expect enthusiastic cooperation in *any* initiative or effort, IT or otherwise, from the adjuncts in their charge.

Negative attitudes towards adjunct faculty are a further impediment to facilitating IT in adjunct-instructed courses. Effective leadership towards, and implementation of, the lofty IT objectives espoused by CUNY is materially undermined by a CUNY academic culture that espouses anti-adjunct attitudes.

3.   Conclusion

Like any other organization, CUNY is both a technical system and a social system; and the growing complexities of the technical and social aspects have impacted their interaction and integration with one another. Accordingly, implementing technology at CUNY or any other college or university requires attention to social issues; and vice versa.[36]

The need to manage and give due regard to the sociological aspects of technology has oft been demonstrated throughout history, including the case of the decisive and pivotal British victory over the allied French-Spanish naval forces at the Battle of Trafalgar in 1805. There, in developing and implementing the signal flag communications system that would facilitate his fleet's win over an enemy having more ships, men and guns, Admiral Nelson was quite mindful of the social interactions among the users of the signal system. [37] What held true for the state-of-the-art IT in Nelson's day is surely no less applicable to IT at CUNY in our own day.

It is clear, then, that technology alone cannot and will not successfully bring adjunct faculty into the IT fold at a university. The social issues need to be addressed along with the technological issues if IT is to become the norm in the classroom, adjunct-taught or otherwise. [38]

Barriers and impediments to integrating adjunct faculty into IT include, but are not limited to:

- Limited or lacking availability of relevant technological resources to the adjunct.
- Exclusion and attenuation of the adjunct from cohesive faculty groups.
- Inconvenience of technological training and assistance for the adjunct.
- Compatibility issues between the campus technology and the adjunct's personal technology.
- Unrealistic Administration and Departmental expectations of and support for the adjunct.
- Specialized information and IT needs of some courses taught by adjuncts.
- Communications gaps between the adjunct and the campus technology administrators.
- Remuneration policies for services rendered and expenses outlaid by the adjunct.
- Professional and personal bias against the adjunct in academic and administrative circles.

Adjunct faculty have been referred to as "higher education's replaceable parts,"[39] "the least secure, most underpaid, and most exploited academic workers,"[40] and as "higher education's best-kept dirty little secret."[41] As discussed above, negative and demeaning attitudes towards adjuncts abound in American academia, and certainly are to be found at CUNY.

But regardless of one's sentiments regarding adjunct faculty, it is obvious that excluding IT from adjunct-taught courses serves the legitimate interests of neither full-time faculty, CUNY administration, the CUNY system itself, nor the students. The imperative to involve "broad representation from the campus community" in the IT planning processes[42] must also encompass adjunct faculty members.

Legislation such as the Civil Rights Act,[43] the Freedom of Information Act,[44] the Small Business Act,[45] and the Competition in Contracting Act of 1984[46] are all based upon the proposition that restricted access to vital rights and resources causes unfairness and inefficiency in society. Indeed, the very existence of CUNY is based upon such legislative sentiments favouring equal accessibility to educational resources.[47] Unfortunately, equality of access to IT resources is severely wanting for CUNY's adjunct faculty, to the detriment and inefficiency of the CUNY system as a whole.

It is necessary to fine-tune and clarify IT policy and procedure at the various CUNY colleges, but this alone will not bring IT to adjuncts' classrooms. CUNY's success in dealing with IT (and indeed, all other challenges of our changing educational world) requires system-wide cultural change in the perceptions of and attitudes towards adjunct faculty members.[48] And, as with other systemic cultural changes in an organization, such is best facilitated by definitive and unequivocal words and actions from the upper layers of the organizational chart.[49]

Notes

1. Rudyard Kipling, "The Dutch in the Medway," from *Songs Written for C. R. L. Fletcher's* A History of England (1911), *Complete Verse*, Definitive ed. (New York: Doubleday, 1940): 727.

2. "IT" is used simultaneously and interchangeably in this essay as an acronym for "Instructional Technology" and/or "Information Technology," unless the sense otherwise demands the use of one to the exclusion of the other.

3. This essay will use the terms "adjunct" or "adjunct faculty" to refer to teaching faculty who are employed on a basis other than the full-time tenure track. Such individuals are sometimes referred to by titles such as "part-time faculty," "contingent faculty," "Special lecturers" or the like. See Jane Buck, "Full-time Students, Part-time Faculty" (remarks at 87th Annual Meeting, American Association of University Professors), 9 June 2001, (12 March 2006). <http://www.aaup.org/statements/archives/Speeches/2001/01ambuck.htm>; American Federation of Teachers, Higher Educ. Program and Policy Council Task Force on Part-Time Faculty, *Statement on Part-Time Faculty Employment* (hereinafter cited as *Task Force Report*) (1996), (12 March 2006): I(B).

<http://wa.aft.org/index.cfm?action=article&articleID=ddb468ab-019c-418d-9383-d6415f1420b9>.

4 Valerie Martin Conley, *Part-time Instructional Faculty and Staff: Who They Are, What They Do, and What They Think.* National Center for Education Statistics, Report No. NCES 2002-163, March 2002, (12 March 2006). <http://nces.ed.gov/pubs2002/2002163.pdf> (hereinafter cited as *NCES 2002-163*).

5. City University of New York, *CUNY Master Plan 2000, Part II*, 20 November 2002, (12 March 2006).
<http://portalsearch.cuny.edu/cms/id/cuny/documents/informationpage/00 0834.htm> (hereinafter cited as *CUNY Master Plan*).

6. *NCES 2002-163*; Conference on the Growing Use of Part-Time and Adjunct Faculty, *Conference Statement* (Washington, D.C., 26 - 28 September 1997) (12 March 2006).
<http://www.oah.org/reports/ptfaculty.html>.

7. Ernst Benjamin, "How Over Reliance on Contingent Appointments Diminishes Faculty Involvement in Student Learning," *Peer Review*, 5(1) (Fall 2002): 4 (8 March 2006).
<http://www.aacu.org/peerreview/pr-fa02/pr-fa02feature1.cfm>.

8. George F. Viehmeyer, Jr., "Systems Engineering Methodology," in *A Forum on Systems Management*, ed. Ingrid H. Rima, (Philadelphia: Temple University Press 1969): 20 - 41. *Cf.* Simon Wiesenthal, *The Murderers Among Us* (New York: Bantam/McGraw Hill, 1968): 316 - 317:

> Once Himmler was present when experiments using exhaust gases from submarine engines for extermination had proved highly unsatisfactory. Himmler had been furious, and there had been draconian punishment. Machines broke down, but the people handling them never did. How could it be that the people operating the gas chambers and ovens were more reliable than the machines? Had they been trained mechanically *and* psychologically to stand the terrific strain? The question bothered me for years. . . . All facts pointed toward the conclusion that special cadres of technically skilled and emotionally hardened executioners were trained somewhere. Castle Hartheim and other euthanasia centers were the answer [emphasis in original].

9. *See, e.g.* James D. Thompson, *Organizations in Action* (New York: McGraw-Hill 1965): 51 - 65 & 132 - 143.

10. *CUNY Master Plan*; Queens College CUNY, *Periodic Review Report for the Middle States Commission on Higher Education*, 1 June 2002, (12 March 2006). §§ 3.7.1 at 49 - 51 and 4.9.3 at 109.

< http://qcpages.qc.edu/provost/Full%20Report%2009.pdf>.

11. CUNY Task Force for Educational Technology, "Faculty Workload and Support," *Report of the University-Wide Task Force for Educational Technology*, May 2001, (12 March 2006) (hereinafter cited as *CUNY Task Force Report*): <http://www.core.cuny.edu/TFETrpt8.PDF>.

12. John Jay College CUNY, Dept. of Sciences Comprehensive Planning Committee, *Report to the College Comprehensive Planning Committee on Phase II Space Requirements for the Dept. of Sciences,* Spring 2000, (12 March 2006).
< http://web.jjay.cuny.edu/~phase2/asmentrep/cpcreport.html>.

13. At the time this essay was written, one nationally well known supplier, Staples, listed the price of a box of chalk at $.69 (Item No. 662775), and a Hewlett-Packard Pavilion DV5020US with AMD™ Turion™ 64 Processor at $1,049.98 (Item No. 632073). Author's search of Staples.com website <http://www.staples.com >, 12 March 2006.

14. Ric Kahn, "The Thieves of Academe: Colleges Wage War on Campus Theft," *Boston Globe*, 21 January 2001, City Weekly, p. 1.

15. City University of New York and The Professional Staff Congress/CUNY, *Memorandum of Economic Agreement for a Successor Agreement (1 August 2000–31 October 2002)*, 4(h), initialed 3 March 2002: Published in *Clarion*, Contract Special, May 2002: 4. The provisions of the Memorandum remain in force as this essay is written, pending negotiation of a new contract to cover periods after 31 October 2002.

16. Evangelos Gizos, Provost, Queens College CUNY, Memorandum to Department Chairs, "Guidelines on New Contract Provisions on Duties of Adjuncts Entitled to One Additional Hour," 5 November 2002 (12 March 2002). <http://qcpages.qc.cuny.edu/provost/Fac_staff/Duties% 20of% 20Adjuncts%20with%20Additional%20Hour%20-20memo.htm>.

17. This essay does not deal with the issue of adequacy of adjunct remuneration (though the author, in other contexts, unabashedly advocates higher salaries for adjuncts). The salience of the remuneration issue necessarily grows in proportion to the out-of-classroom time required of an adjunct to use or prepare IT for the course taught.

18. Keith Davis, *Human Behavior at Work*, 4th ed. (New York: McGraw-Hill, 1972): 261- 270.

19. David R Hampton, et al., *Organizational Behavior and the Practice of Management*, 3rd ed. (Glenview: Scott Foresman & Co. 1978): 195-197.

20. Queens College Libraries, *Library Laptops for Loan to QC Students*, June 2004, (12 March 2004).

<http://qcpages.qc.edu/Library/info/laptop.html>.

21. Izabella Taler, Rosenthal Library, Queens College CUNY to Kenneth H. Ryesky (e-mail), 9 December 2002 (on file with author).

22. Cf. *In re Lillibridge*, *N.Y.Law Journal*, 28 October 1994, p. 29, at p. 30 (N.Y. Ct. Cl. 1994):

> County Line Road is aptly named for it divided Monroe and Orleans Counties, each of which had separate DOT [Department of Transportation] units responsible for maintenance. In the words of a DOT employee assigned to Orleans County, the responsibility for removing the foliage was "not mine," while, according to employees assigned to Monroe County West that responsibility "was within the jurisdiction of Orleans County."

23. See Adelphi University, *Adjunct Faculty Handbook*, 2005-2006, (12 March 2006): 10.
<http://www.adelphi.edu/faculty/pdfs/adjfac_handbook.pdf>.

24. CUNY Office of Library Services, *E-Journals & Reference Databases*, <http://libraries.cuny.edu/resource.htm> (no date) (12 March 2006). Indeed, accessibility of the judicial opinions databases has a major impact upon the court systems and the law profession itself, see Kenneth H. Ryesky, "From Pens to Pixels: Text-Media Issues in Promulgating Archiving and Using Judicial Opinions," *Journal of Appellate Practice & Process* 4(2) (2002): 353, 366 - 397.

25. Anthea Tillyer to PTCUNY Yahoo discussion group (listserve posting) (29 September 2003).

26. Research Foundation of the City University of New York, *PSC-CUNY Research Awards: Guidelines: Eligibility* (2006) (12 March 2006). <http://www.rfcuny.org/PSCCUNY/Guidelines/PSCEligibilty.html> ("Since the Program was specifically designed for those permanent faculty where research is a condition of their employment, applications from Visiting Professors, Substitutes, or Adjuncts cannot be accepted."); ibid., *CUNY Collaborative Incentive Research Grants Program*, 2006 (12 March 2006). <http://www.rfcuny.org/r&dweb/collab.html> ("Only full time faculty at the campuses of CUNY are eligible to apply.").

27. Misusing Federal funds carries potentially serious consequences. See *False Claims Act*, U.S. Public Law 97-258 (1982).

28. William Karp, "Management in the Computer Age," in *MIS: Management Dimensions*, ed. Raymond J. Coleman and M. J. Riley (San Francisco: Holden-Day, Inc., 1973): 246, 248 - 249.

29. "Anonymous233702" to a discussion list formerly posted on the Internet, 17 June 2001, (7 June 2002).

<http://academic.brooklyn.cuny.edu/history/johnson/pscdues.htm>, now archived in *Internet Archive, Wayback Machine.* <http://web.archive.org/web/20020618234535/http://academic.brooklyn.c uny.edu/history/johnson/pscdues.htm>, 18 July 2002, (12 March 2006). The original posting was on a web page formerly maintained by Professor Robert "KC" Johnson, History Department, Brooklyn College. Prof. Johnson's experience in obtaining tenure stirred a controversy of national proportions, *see, e.g.* Karen W. Arenson, "CUNY Chief Gives Tenure To Professor In Brooklyn," *N.Y. Times*, 25 February 2003, § B, p. 6, col. 6; Scott Smallwood, "Tenure Madness," *Chronicle of Higher Education*, 23 May 2003, p. A10. As reported by Anderson and Smallwood, assertions to the effect that Prof. Johnson lacks collegiality were put forth during the course of his tenure controversy. Prof. Johnson's failure to even respond to the author's e-mail inquiry regarding the subject web page is not inconsistent with such assertions.

The issue of whether and to what extent the statement regarding the opening of the hiring competition to "young individuals" constitutes an admission that CUNY violates the *Age Discrimination in Employment Act*, U.S. Public Law 90-202 (1967), is beyond the scope of this essay, and is left for discussion in the context of the appropriate conference, symposium or lawsuit.

30. See, e.g., Robert E. Roemer and James E. Schnitz, "Academic Employment as Day Labor: The Dual Labor Market in Higher Education," *J. Higher Educ.*, v. 53 (1982): 514, 527-528; George Roche, The Fall of the Ivory Tower 214 (Washington: Regnery Publ. Co., 1994) ("Additional 'slave labor' is provided by thousands of part-time faculty with full Ph.D.s, who work for low salaries and benefits *and are treated with scant respect*" [emphasis added]).

31, See, e.g., Michael Murphy, "Adjuncts Should Not Just Be Visitors In The Academic Promised Land," *Chronicle of Higher Education*, 29 March 2002, p. B-14:

> But, at the same time, the rhetoric of crisis that characterizes so much of the part-timer discussion has also created a very dangerous and widespread misrepresentation: that the use of instructors necessarily produces *inferior* instruction, that students paying ever-rising tuition bills are "short-changed" when they work with "pretend" professors. It is all too easy these days to universalize the economic urgency of the much-proclaimed "*adjunct* problem" and thus, even quite inadvertently, to reinforce the prevailing bargain-basement mythology about part-time

faculty members that both popular and academic newspapers disseminate widely."

See also George Van Arsdale, "De-Professionalizing a Part-Time Teaching Faculty: How Many, Feeling Small, Seeming Few, Getting Less, Dream of More," *American Sociologist* 14(4), p. 195 (November 1978).

32. CUNY Association of Scholars, *Parity for Adjuncts? The New Threat to Academic Standards* (hereinafter cited as *CUNYAS Report*), 6 May 2002, (12 March 2006): ¶ I(5)(B) <http://www.nas.org/affiliates/cunyas/parity.html>. There is no evidence that time spent by any CUNY full-time faculty in handling course-related e-mail correspondence requires a pro rata docking of money from their pay checks, nor that such time must be compensated in order to fulfil the full-time faculty office hour requirements. Indeed, at least one Department of Education report notes that e-mail is a "logical" form of communication between instructional faculty and their students. *NCES 2002 161*: 17 & 31.

33. *CUNYAS Report*: I(5)(E).

34. Ibid, I(5)(F).

35. *CUNY Task Force Report*: 4-5 ("Sustainability" recommendations).

36. See, e.g. John V. Murray and Frank A. Stickney, "The Human Factor in Matrix Management" in *Matrix Management Systems Handbook*, ed. David I. Cleland (New York: Van Nostrand Reinhold Co., 1984): 231-254.

37. John Keegan, *The Price of Admiralty* (New York: Viking-Penguin, 1989): 48-52; David H. Zook, Jr. and Robin Higham, *A Short History of Warfare* (New York: Twayne Publishers, 1966): 115.

Signal flags had long been used in military battles. Sun Tzu, *The Art of War*, trans. by Samuel B. Griffith (London: Oxford U. Press, 1971): 90-91 (Commentary on Sun Tzu by Chang Yü (12th-13th cent.): "Therefore officers and men are ordered to advance or retreat by observing the flags and banners . . . ."). However, Nelson's hands-down defeat of the French-Spanish naval forces at Trafalgar was facilitated by a newly perfected interactive "talking flag" signal communications system which allowed Admiral Nelson's ship crews to effectively communicate with one another, and to adjust their formations and battle plans, even after the battle had commenced. *Zook & Higham*.

Prior to Nelson's successful use of "real time" flag communications at Trafalgar, the British rules for naval battle engagement necessarily required fastidious adherence to predetermined ship line formations; and those rules had been so strictly enforced that Admiral John Byng was court-martialled and shot in 1757 for deviating from them, *id.* The widespread reluctance of British naval officers during the Revolutionary War to take certain risks against the less inhibited American patriots was attributable in no small part to the example that had been made of Byng two decades earlier. Mark M. Boatner III, *Encyclopedia of the American Revolution* (Mechanicsburg: Stackpole Books, 1994): 153-54.

38. *CUNY Task Force Report*: 3-4 ("Community-Building").

39. David L. Kirp, "How Much for That Professor?" *N.Y. Times*, 27 October 2003, § A, p. 21, col. 2.

40 Henry Steck, "Corporatization of the University: Seeking Conceptual Clarity," *Annals of the Amemrican Academy of Political and Social Sciences.* 588 (2003): 66, 79.

41. John C. Duncan, Jr., "The Indentured Servants of Academia: The Adjunct Faculty Dilemma and Their Limited Legal Remedies," *Indiana Law Journal*, vol. 74 (1999): 513, 516.

42. *CUNY Task Force Report*: 3 ("Setting and Achieving Goals," Recommendations 3 & 4).

43. *Civil Rights Act,* U.S. Public Law 88-352 (1964).

44. *Freedom of Information Act*, U.S. Public Law 89-554. (1966).

45. *Small Business Act,* U.S. Public Law 85-53 (1958).

46. *Competition in Contracting Act*, U.S. Public Law 98-369, div. B, title VII, subtitle D (1984).

47. *N.Y. State Educ. Law*, § 6201.

48. *See* Barbara A. Wyles, "Adjunct Faculty in the Community College: Realities and Challenges," *New Directions for Higher Education* 89 (Winter 1998).

49. There are, of course, factors beyond the direct control or cognizance of CUNY's top administration, including, but not limited to, the tax disadvantages for adjuncts who, finding college-provided office facilities inadequate, choose to do their work at home. *Cf. Matter of Sylvester L. Tuohy*, New York State Tax Tribunal, Docket DTA No. 818430, 13 February 2003, (12 March 2006). < http://www.nysdta.org/Decisions/818430.dec.htm>.

Bibliography

A. General

Adelphi University, *Adjunct Faculty Handbook*, 2005 - 2006.
    <http://www.adelphi.edu/faculty/pdfshttp://www.adelphi.edu/faculty/p
    dfs/adjfac_handbook.pdf/adjfac_handbook.pdf > (12 March 2006).
American Federation of Teachers, Higher Educ. Program and Policy
    Council Task Force on Part-Time Faculty, *Statement on Part-Time
    Faculty Employment*. 1996.
    <http://wa.aft.org/index.cfm?action=article&articleID=ddb468ab-
    019c-418d-9383-d6415f1420b9 > (12 March 2006).
Anonymous233702. Posting to discussion list, 17 June, 2001. To a
    discussion list formerly posted on the Internet, 17 June 2001.
    <http://academic.brooklyn.cuny.edu/history/johnson/pscdues.htm>, (7
    June 2002). Archived in *Internet Archive, Wayback Machine*, 18 July
    2002.
    <http://web.archive.org/web/20020618234535/http://academic.brookly
    n.cuny.edu/history/johnson/pscdues.htm> (12 March 2006).
Arenson, Karen W. "CUNY Chief Gives Tenure to Professor In
    Brooklyn." *N.Y. Times*, 25 February 2003, § B, p. 6, col. 6.
Benjamin, Ernst. "How Over-Reliance on Contingent Appointments
    Diminishes Faculty Involvement in Student Learning." *Peer Review*, 5(1)
    (Fall 2002).
    <http://www.aacu.org/peerreview/pr-fa02/pr-fa02feature1.cfm> (12
    March 2006).
Boatner, Mark M., III. *Encyclopedia of the American Revolution*.
    Mechanicsburg: Stackpole Books, 1994.
Buck, Jane. "Full-time Students, Part-time Faculty" (remarks at 87th
    Annual Meeting, American Association of University Professors). 9
    June 2001.
    <http://www.aaup.org/statements/archives/Speeches/2001/01ambuck.h
    tm> (12 March 2006).
City University of New York. *CUNY Master Plan 2000, Part II*, 20
    November 2002.
    <http://portalsearch.cuny.edu/cms/id/cuny/documents/informationpage
    /000834.htm> (12 March 2006).
_____, Task Force for Educational Technology, *Report of the University-
    Wide Task Force for Educational Technology*, May 2001.
    <http://www.core.cuny.edu/TFETrpt8.PDF> (12 March 2006).

____, Office of Library Services, *E-Journals & Reference Databases* (no date). <http://libraries.cuny.edu/resource.htm> (10 March 2006).

City University of New York and The Professional Staff Congress/CUNY. *Memorandum of Economic Agreement for a Successor Agreement (1 August 2000–31 October 2002)*, ¶ 4(h), initialed 3 March 2002. Published in *Clarion*, Contract Special, May 2002.

Conference on the Growing Use of Part-Time and Adjunct Faculty. *Conference Statement* Washington, D.C., 26-28 September 1997. <http://www.oah.org/reports/ptfaculty.html> (12 March 2006).

Conley, Valerie Martin. *Part-time Instructional Faculty and Staff: Who They Are, What They Do, and What They Think*. National Center for Education Statistics, Report No. NCES 2002-163, March 2002. <http://nces.ed.gov/pubs2002/2002163.pdf> (12 March 2006).

CUNY Association of Scholars. *Parity for Adjuncts? The New Threat to Academic Standards*, 6 May 2002 <http://www.nas.org/affiliates/cunyas/parity.html>.(12 March 2006).

Davis, Keith. *Human Behavior at Work*, 4th ed. New York: McGraw-Hill, 1972.

Duncan, John C., Jr. "The Indentured Servants of Academia: The Adjunct Faculty Dilemma and Their Limited Legal Remedies." *Indiana Law Journal*, vol. 74 (1999), 513, 516.

Gizos, Evangelos. Memorandum to Department Chairs, "Guidelines on New Contract Provisions on Duties of Adjuncts Entitled to One Additional Hour," 5 November 2002. <http://qcpages.qc.cuny.edu/provost/Fac_staff/Duties%20of%20Adjuncts%20with%20Additional%20Hour%20-%20memo.htm> (12 March 2002).

Hampton, David R. *et al.*, *Organizational Behavior and the Practice of Management*, 3rd ed. Glenview: Scott Foresman & Co. 1978.

John Jay College CUNY, Dept. of Sciences Comprehensive Planning Committee. *Report to the College Comprehensive Planning Committee on Phase II Space Requirements for the Dept. of Sciences,* Spring 2000.<http://web.jjay.cuny.edu/~phase2/asmentrep/cpcreport.html> (12 March 2006).

Kahn, Ric. "The Thieves of Academe: Colleges Wage War on Campus Theft," *Boston Globe*, 21 January 2001, City Weekly, p. 1.

Karp, William. "Management in the Computer Age," in *MIS: Management Dimensions*, ed. Raymond J. Coleman and M. J. Riley. San Francisco: Holden-Day, Inc., 1973.

Keegan, John. *The Price of Admiralty*. New York: Viking-Penguin, 1989.

Kipling, Rudyard. "The Dutch in the Medway," from *Songs Written for C. R. L. Fletcher's* A History of England (1911). In Rudyard Kipling, *Complete Verse*, Definitive ed. New York: Doubleday, 1940.

Kirp, David L. "How Much for That Professor?" *N.Y. Times*, 27 October 2003, § A, p. 21, col. 2.

Murphy, Michael. "Adjuncts Should Not Just Be Visitors In The Academic Promised Land," *Chronicle of Higher Education*, 29 March 2002, p. B-14

Murray, John V. and Frank A. Stickney, "The Human Factor in Matrix Management." In *Matrix Management Systems Handbook*, ed. David I. Cleland. New York: Van Nostrand Reinhold Co., 1984.

Queens College CUNY. *Periodic Review Report for the Middle States Commission on Higher Education*, 1 June 2002.
< http://qcpages.qc.edu/provost/Full%20Report%2009.pdf> (12 March 2006).

_____. Queens College Libraries. *Library Laptops for Loan to QC Students*, June 2004 <http://qcpages.qc.edu/Library/info/laptop.html> (9 March 2004).

Research Foundation of the City University of New York. *CUNY Collaborative Incentive Research Grants Program*, 2006. <http://www.rfcuny.org/r&dweb/collab.html> (12 March 2006).

_____. *PSC-CUNY Research Awards: Guidelines: Eligibility* (2006). <http://www.rfcuny.org/PSCCUNY/Guidelines/PSCEligibilty.html> (11 March 2006).

Roche, George. *The Fall of the Ivory Tower*. Washington: Regnery Publication Company, 1994.

Roemer, Robert E. and James E. Schnitz. "Academic Employment as Day Labor: The Dual Labor Market in Higher Education." *Journal of Higher Education*, 53 (1982), pp. 514, 527-528.

Ryesky, Kenneth H. "From Pens to Pixels: Text-Media Issues in Promulgating Archiving and Using Judicial Opinions," *Journal of Appellate Practice & Process* 4(2) (2002).

Smallwood, Scott. "Tenure Madness," *Chronicle of Higher Education*, 23 May 2003, p. A10.

Staples.com. < http://www.staples.com > (12 March 2006).

Steck, Henry. "Corporatization of the University: Seeking Conceptual Clarity." *Annals of the American. Academy of Political and Social Sciences* 588 (2003): 66, 79.

Sun Tzu. *The Art of War*, trans. Samuel B. Griffith. (London: Oxford University Press, 1971).

Taler, Izabella. E-mail to Kenneth H. Ryesky, 9 December 2002.

Thompson, James D. *Organizations in Action*. New York: McGraw-Hill, 1965.

Tillyer, Anthea. Listserve posting to PTCUNY Yahoo discussion group (29 September 2003).

Van Arsdale, George. "De-Professionalizing a Part-Time Teaching Faculty: How Many, Feeling Small, Seeming Few, Getting Less, Dream of More," *American Sociologist* 14(4) (November 1978): 195.

Viehmeyer, George F., Jr. "Systems Engineering Methodology." In *A Forum on Systems Management*, ed. Ingrid H. Rima. Philadelphia: Temple University Press, 1969.

Wiesenthal, Simon. *The Murderers Among Us*. New York: Bantam/McGraw Hill, 1968.

Wyles, Barbara A. "Adjunct Faculty in the Community College: Realities and Challenges," *New Directions for Higher Education* 89 (Winter 1998).

Zook, David H., Jr. and Robin Higham, *A Short History of Warfare*. New York: Twayne Publishers, 1966.

B. Statutes and Tribunal Decisions (in Bluebook order)

Competition in Contracting Act, U.S. Public Law 98-369, div. B, title VII, subtitle D (1984).

False Claims Act, U.S. Public Law 97-258 (1982).

Age Discrimination in Employment Act, U.S. Public Law 90-202 (1967).

Freedom of Information Act, U.S. Public Law 89-554. (1966).

Civil Rights Act, U.S. Public Law 88-352 (1964).

Small Business Act, U.S. Public Law 85-53 (1958).

N.Y. State Educ. Law, § 6201. *In re Lillibridge*, *N.Y.Law Journal*, 28 October 1994, p. 29, at p. 30 (N.Y. Ct. Cl. 1994).

Matter of Sylvester L. Tuohy. New York State Tax Tribunal, Docket DTA No. 818430, 13 February 2003. <http://www.nysdta.org/Decisions/818430.dec.htm> (12 March 2006).

Part II

Adjunct Teaching outside of the USA

Out of the Frying Pan:
From Casual Teaching to Temp Work

Lesley Speed

This autobiographical essay recounts the experiences of a casual university teacher in Melbourne, Australia, during the Australian university crisis of the late 1990s. The chapter situates the author's experiences in a social context by addressing larger repercussions of the Australian university crisis and drawing on sociological research. The Australian university crisis resulted from the drastic reduction of Federal funding to Australian universities under the conservative government of Prime Minister John Howard, which came to power in 1996. This crisis was accompanied by an anti-intellectual backlash against academics and resulted in the author's long-term reliance on casual and short-term university teaching work, as a result of which she experienced considerable hardship. The author consequently chose to give up teaching and become a full-time office temp, a role that not only proved more lucrative than casual teaching but also provided unexpected insights into such issues as workplace politics and Australian anti-intellectualism. This autobiographical essay argues that casual teaching employment provides an inadequate financial and psychological basis for dealing with misfortune within or outside academe.

University Teachers; Casual Employment; Autobiography; Academic Life; Graduate Teachers; Anti-intellectualism; Universities; Australia

"Things can *always* get worse": the implications of these words were to resonate for me on many occasions after I heard them. The focus of the telephone conversation in which my doctoral supervisor made this pronouncement during the late 1990s was the Federal government's recent, drastic cuts to Australian tertiary institutions. The betrayals, conspiracies, retrenchments, abusive tirades and nervous breakdowns that issued from the subsequent national university crisis were indelibly to mark my experiences as a casual university film studies teacher in Melbourne, Australia. My reliance on short-term teaching jobs during an industry-wide crisis emerged as a blueprint for financial, psychological and personal disaster. The ensuing succession of traumatic events ended only when I decided to break the cycle of dependence on casual teaching jobs and make a living from temporary administrative work. Ironically, the notoriously unstable occupation of office temp enabled me to return from the brink of a nervous breakdown. I write this chapter to demonstrate how reliance on casual university teaching can exacerbate the effects of unforeseen misfortune.

Although some of the terminology used in Australian universities differs from that used in the United States, casual teaching labour is as fundamental to tertiary institutions in Australia as in other countries. The term "adjunct labour" is not used widely in Australia, where casual university teaching jobs are usually referred to as "sessional" or sometimes as "casual." In these jobs, teachers are appointed on a semester-by-semester basis and are paid by the hour. Sessional teaching work provides no formal incentive to undertake research. It also has few summer school positions, relegating many sessional teachers to poverty during the non-teaching period that extends from early December to late February, the antipodean equivalent of North America's summer break. In Australia, sessional university teachers are generally referred to either as lecturers or tutors, not professors. Indeed, the title of professor is applied more freely in the United States than in Australia, where this title is reserved for the most senior academics. In this respect, Australia derives its terminology from the United Kingdom. Such differences aside, I believe my experiences will touch a chord with those of university teachers in other countries.

Although sessional university teaching requires higher intellectual credentials than most casual jobs, it bears fundamental similarities to the casual and part-time jobs that have proliferated in other fields in recent decades. As Stanley Aronowitz and William DiFazio observed in the mid-1990s, many citizens

> who are classified in official statistics as 'employed' actually work at casual and part-time jobs, the number of which has grown dramatically over the past fifteen years. This phenomenon, once confined to freelance writers and artists, labourers and clerical workers, today cuts across all occupations, including the professions.[1]

This is the context in which I came to situate universities' reliance on casual teachers, an example of North America's increasing influence on Australian tertiary institutions. When I was first employed as a casual academic, however, I lacked a larger socio-economic perspective in which to situate my role. My first experiences as a sessional teacher in the humanities involved being seduced into an academic lifestyle in which my colleagues rarely, if ever, discussed the social dimensions of casual teaching work. While this aspect of the culture can be attributed partly to the relative plenitude of sessional teaching jobs in Australian universities in the mid-1990s, I believe it was also fuelled by a wishful tendency among inexperienced academics to consider themselves above identifying with casual employees of, for instance, supermarkets and fast food chains. In subsequent years, I found this culture of self-absorption to be a woefully inadequate basis for surviving university employment.

1.   The Lure of Casual Teaching

Given that remuneration for sessional teaching is neither generous in relation to the hours involved nor constant throughout the year, I was one of many who embark on this type of work for other reasons. I became a university teacher as a PhD candidate because I was encouraged by academics to gain some teaching experience. In my first teaching semester, I was entranced by the sense of belonging to an academic community, the relief from the isolation of pure research, the intellectual stimulation and spontaneity of teaching, the opportunities to engage with people of various backgrounds, the sense of privilege and prized knowledge, the encouragement I received from established academics, and the occasional opportunities to teach in my own research area. I discovered in university teaching a career path that attracted me far more than any other I had known. Accordingly, I took further teaching jobs to gain more experience. Being young, energetic and willing to piece together an income from part-time jobs and other sources until I obtained a more secure position, I found many attractions in being a university teacher.

At that time, before the university crisis, recruitment of casual tertiary teachers involved a heady interplay of ingratiation and exploitation. Since some sessional teachers had a casual attitude to the job, established academics were perpetually engaged in recruiting sessional teachers. Experienced casual staff were sometimes retained through flattering, yet vague, allusions to possible future long-term employment. There was, however, little discussion of the actual degree of competition that existed for the tenured academic jobs to which many casual teachers aspired. In this context, I was told that my youth (and more youthful appearance) enhanced my interaction with undergraduates and that my enthusiasm rendered my lectures and tutorials more engaging than those of some older, jaded academics. Only later did I realize that flattery of this type also served to reinforce the flatterer's authority, bolstering his or her attempts to accrue protégés that could serve as political allies against other academics. Indeed, some established academics regularly held court amid a circle of deferential sessional employees.

In this apparently collegial atmosphere, however, many sessional teachers struggled with their workloads. As some worked nights and held multiple part-time jobs, a few of my fellow sessional teachers failed to complete their PhDs. It was even more difficult to notch up a list of refereed publications with which to impress a prospective employer. For a casual teacher in a course run by someone other than their mentor, research was and is rarely discussed in relation to teaching. Against these odds, I made research the axis of my academic activities, defying anyone who gave me career advice based on a proportionate relationship of hours worked to payment received. I took on a limited teaching workload while working on my PhD, an option that was facilitated by an academic scholarship. After receiving my degree, I doggedly adhered to a programme of steady research production. This largely self-driven regimen helped to bolster my morale when periods of unemployment undermined my sense of having institutional support, but was strained during times of acute stress.

When I received my PhD at the age of twenty-eight, I was told I didn't have enough teaching experience to be likely to get a tenured teaching position. Yet a PhD was also widely believed to be the main requirement for a tenured job. I consequently found myself being buffeted by contradictory floods of advice. A sessional tutor with a PhD was almost unheard of in Australia in 1996, but within five years the university funding crisis would wreak such havoc that a doctorate would become a prerequisite for obtaining sessional teaching work at any major university. With a newly minted PhD but no steady job, I was ridiculed by even those academics who purported to be my friends. Nobody was willing to view my situation as an early symptom of an industry-wide trend that could ultimately affect his or her own job. Among the changes that later took place, some tenured academics were made redundant. Australian universities ceased to offer tenured jobs, replacing tenure with a less secure "permanency" that is termed continuing employment. Before the changes, however, I experienced an isolating sense that I was somehow out of time with the university system. When interviewed for academic jobs, for example, I perceived that some of the grey-haired interviewers were shocked by my youthful appearance. Believing that the weight given to this first impression reflected the prejudices of jaded academics whose involvement in day-to-day teaching was minimal, I learned that gaining a PhD at a relatively young age is less advantageous than many people assumed.

Moreover, in successive short-term teaching jobs I was forced to expend considerable energy on proving myself to unfamiliar and sometimes condescending staff. I also wondered if my energy was wasted, after I found myself teaching courses that other academics seemed to have abandoned. In one teaching job that I held on a short-term, part-time contract, most of the existing curriculum was more than a decade out of date. With insufficient time to revise the course, I incorporated more up-to-date material into my lectures, to the mild confusion of some students. While the institution acknowledged that financial resources prevented the appointment of a full-time staff member who could teach and maintain such a course, the incident was symptomatic of an already widespread reliance on casual and short-term teachers to hold together shaky curricula. Accordingly, some casual teachers saw no reason to exert themselves in jobs in which they perceived little future. One tutor with whom I worked was absent so often that I had to field enquiries from her students as well as from mine. Another tutor left the country before the end of the course, leaving behind incompletely assessed student work. This apparent irresponsibility mirrors the fact that these teachers were being paid poorly and on a piecemeal basis for work requiring considerable and specialized knowledge.

Yet these situations now seem relatively insignificant in comparison to the repercussions of the subsequent industry-wide crisis. In the late 1990s, Australia's thirty-seven public universities, hitherto heavily dependent on government grants, were propelled into crisis by major funding cuts that were implemented by Prime Minister John Howard's newly elected conservative government. Between 1996 and 2001, the proportional funding of Australian universities by the Federal government shrunk to "about half" of the total AU$9 billion cost of running the universities.[2] The changes wrought by the Howard government came to be viewed as a major stage in the implementation of free-market economic practices within the Australian tertiary education sector. Despite some people's hopes that these changes would be merely a temporary measure, in time the cuts forced a lasting overhaul of Australian universities.

This progression had been foreshadowed in 1989 by the introduction of fees for Australian tertiary education, under then Prime Minister Bob Hawke's Labour government. Although modest by American standards, at then less than AU$1000 a semester, these fees were immediately recognized as a manifestation of economic rationalism's encroaching influence on Australian politics and society. The Hawke government's changes to higher education also signalled the erasure of the last traces of social reforms implemented in the early 1970s by another Labour Prime Minister, Gough Whitlam. The latter is so admired among

Australian artists, intellectuals and left-wing voters that his name and face were celebrated in the 1990s by a successful rock band, The Whitlams. Central to the Whitlam government's reforms had been the abolition of university fees, resulting in the expansion of Australian tertiary education. The changes to university funding in the late 1990s meant that older academics, who benefited from the Whitlam years, now faced a future that bore no resemblance to that which they had known.

The broad repercussions of the 1990s funding crisis included higher fees for all students, more international students, a closer association between wealth and tertiary education, downsizing and restructuring of academic departments, loss of high-profile academics to overseas posts, increased competition for research funding, and the undermining of universities' intellectual and organisational independence. On a smaller scale, but of no less significance for those working in universities, the funding crisis created larger workloads, larger class sizes, more bizarre attempts to teach international students who had inadequate English, increased pressure on the humanities to justify their existence, increasingly desperate behaviour among academics whose jobs were under threat, and escalating competition for long-term jobs. Whereas the completion of a PhD is traditionally perceived as a milestone that signifies personal achievement and facilitates new opportunities, within three years of completing my doctorate I descended into a nightmare from which escape would prove to be a major feat in its own right.

2.   Casual Teaching and Crisis

The university crisis precipitated my recognition that protracted casual teaching work provides a poor basis for encountering life's hardships. The following account of my experiences includes references to events external to my work, of necessity to demonstrate how the instability of casual teaching tends to exacerbate the effects of complex unforeseen events. As the debilitating repercussions of prolonged casual employment can pervade a teacher's life outside the workplace, I believe universities hold significant moral responsibility for problems experienced by casual teachers. Not only does sessional teaching's unsteady income limit an employee's access to financial goals that people in permanent jobs take for granted, but casual teaching work also fails to provide an adequate degree of psychological or physical wellbeing to serve as a buffer against misfortune.

The first consequence of the university crisis, for me, was prolonged reliance on sessional teaching jobs. Over several years, this predicament took an insidious financial and psychological toll, particularly on my ability to sustain a professional demeanour and stable domestic life.

As a casual teacher I had no way of predicting where, what or whether I would be teaching one semester later. The level of morale that I needed to fulfil my role as a teacher was annually undermined by a three-month, unpaid non-teaching summer period. My confidence was also fraught by the struggle to survive on paltry unemployment benefits between teaching jobs. Australia's system of unemployment benefits is government-funded and places no limit on the length of time a person may receive benefits, but requires the unemployed to complete tasks in return for the latter. These tasks commence with completing a jobseeker diary and progress to mandatory part-time or volunteer work.

Throughout most of my sessional teaching jobs, I was registered as unemployed and received benefits (reduced in proportion to my earnings) because my teaching income was so irregular as to be considered inadequate. I discovered that having a PhD made it far more difficult to obtain even a part-time, menial job than to qualify for unemployment benefits. My ability to survive alternately on benefits and casual teaching income was facilitated by careful budgeting and the fact that I lived in a low-rent, shared house. However, my home had walls that were paper-thin and the toilet was in the back yard. The academics who served as my mentors never mentioned that having a back-up occupation might be a good idea, just in case my plans didn't work out. As I had therefore established no alternative occupation, I gained experience by accepting teaching jobs even if they entailed a two-hour commute or required knowledge that was outside my experience.

My resolve suffered a crucial blow with the loss of the support of most of my friends. My housemate and childhood friend, Stevie, informed me that she had "a problem" with the fact that I was an intellectual. She suggested that I get a job in a video rental store. Before long, she also recruited her boyfriend, Adam, and our housemate, Andrew, to deride me in the presence of people I had believed to be our mutual friends. On alternate occasions, Stevie's betrayal seemed to stem from: her perception that I betrayed her social class, her aversion to feminism, her low self-esteem, her alcoholism, her belief that I'd "sold out," her disappointment that I couldn't afford to buy property with her, her perception that I'd become a yuppie, and her desire to placate Adam's concern that her university degree highlighted his lesser education. I eventually concluded that her behaviour stemmed primarily from a refusal to accept change, an impulse that seemed ironically to be exacerbated by the harm she caused to our friendship. The worst consequence of this development was the fact that I had to continue to coexist with Stevie, Adam and Andrew because I couldn't afford to move out of the house. My only recourse was to hide my true feelings from further ridicule.

A separate circle of girlfriends also responded to my chosen career as a personal betrayal. Their antipathy emerged in their alternate assumptions that teaching was a contemptible occupation and that I was inadequate to the job. One of my girlfriends informed me that I wasn't "really lecturing," when I was actually employed as a university lecturer. Another shook her finger scoldingly and said to me, "Your opinion is shit." Some friends developed a habit of firing questions in my direction and then interrupting me, undermining my right to speak for myself. Since we'd all been raised in upwardly mobile suburbs of Melbourne (not far from the locations used for the soap opera *Neighbours*), I was disconcerted to discover such a disparity between my friends' perceptions of their identities and mine. My friends seemed to identify my ambition with social barriers that I didn't see. Although some of my girlfriends' lives were circumscribed by their status as second-generation Australians of Mediterranean or Asian background, their resentment contradicted the fact that they had relatives and friends with good jobs as lawyers, doctors, or accountants. I was encountering at first hand a bitter undercurrent of Australian society.

In contrast to the class systems of the United Kingdom and Europe, Australian class identity is often underestimated, unrecognized or unacknowledged. As in the United States, Australia's lack of "a . . . system of inherited titles, ranks, and honors" means that a person "can be puzzled about where, in the society, he [or she] stands."[3] Such confusion was manifested in the contradiction between my friends' purported loyalty and their frank disapproval of my life's direction. Moreover, such negativity was encouraged by the Australian university funding crisis, which was now front-page news. Public antipathy to the nation's tertiary institutions had been stirred up by the Howard government's self-serving criticisms of the university sector. This backlash served for some of my acquaintances and so-called friends as an excuse to ridicule academics in general and me in particular. Thus, the Howard government drew upon existing anti-intellectualism to rationalize the severity of its economic reforms.

At any time, Australian society's emphasis on sporting achievement is inclined to favour anti-intellectualism, which is manifested in this country as a tendency to blame academics for anything from graffiti to income tax. Unsurprisingly, this aspect of Australian society has also attracted the attention of foreign visitors. For instance, an American industrialist wrote in the 1990s of his discovery, during a recent first visit to Australia, of "an anti-intellectual bias even greater" than that of his country.[4] The origins of Australian anti-intellectualism can be attributed at least partly to the influence of the British working classes, to which many

Australians can trace their ancestry. Even today, many Australians believe that the most authentic Australian identities are those of rural manual workers, such as farmers and miners.

As in working-class environments, anti-intellectualism in Australia is linked to a tendency to regard "ambiguously" those who "take up some educational activity."[5] This attitude is often also evident among Australians of non-British backgrounds, many of whom originate from peasant cultures and assimilate the ways of the Anglo-Australian majority to their own class origins. In contemporary Australia, any evidence of old-fashioned "respect for the 'scholar'"[6] tends to be overshadowed by the fact that most Australians experience difficulty in relating to intellectuals. Yet Australians' overwhelming failure to articulate this tension in class terms perpetuates the majority's estrangement from intellectuals, who thus have few opportunities for meaningful engagement with the general public. It was in this context that, in the 1990s, some sections of the Australian media circulated particularly unfavourable portrayals of academics, aggravating the damage caused by the Howard government's reforms.

While many of my friends and acquaintances were caught up in this backlash, as a casual employee I had little authority with which to defend myself. In addition to being treated as though intellectuals are scarcely superior to paedophiles, I was in the contradictory predicament of struggling to gain a career foothold while being viewed by my friends as an élitist traitor. The people who attacked my aspirations had apparently been seized by a pre-emptive version of the "tall poppy syndrome," an Australian impulse to denigrate as un-Australian those who are perceived to have achieved great success. Being confronted with a persistent and often malicious lack of support prompted me to reconsider friendships and be guarded among strangers.

Around this time, I also began to have trouble falling asleep at night. When I did sleep, I was woken by vivid nightmares. I dreamt that gigantic green and red insects were crawling on my bed sheets. I also dreamt that intruders were climbing up the outside of my house. Once when I awoke from such a nightmare, Stevie appeared at my bedroom door and asked if I was the person who had been screaming. I remembered having heard screams, but found it hard to believe that they had issued from me. I also couldn't confide in her, since I believed that her betrayal was one of the reasons for my suddenly disturbed sleep patterns. Gestures of concern from those who attacked me accentuated my sense that I was under surveillance by enemies.

The disjunction between my private life and my work became increasingly wild. Weeks into my first full-time university teaching position, a one-semester contract, my housemate Andrew's sister was murdered by a serial killer. As when any person dies suddenly and at a young age, bereavement can prompt erratic behaviour and thereby destroy relationships. Since I was new to my job and not a relative or close friend of the victim, I felt obliged to show up for work the next day. I woke at five am to make my weekly two-hour drive to the small-town campus where I was working. There, I would complete the week's teaching before returning to the city. Yet the vicarious trauma that I suffered through sustained proximity to the victim's family made it difficult to concentrate on my job, particularly on days when I worked at home on class preparation and assessment. Although I trusted some of the academics to whom I reported, the pace of commuting and teaching provided no real opportunity to discuss the tragedy with anyone at work. I was also acutely aware that competition for academic jobs meant absences from a one-semester job could be taken to suggest I was less than completely dedicated.

My work subsequently became a means of dissociating myself from the tensions at home. Our household was eventually driven apart by Andrew, who proceeded to behave in ways more arrogant and deceitful than seemed to be justified by mourning. More than ever, my home felt like a psychological prison, of which the boundaries were being enforced by my failure to achieve the economic stability that would have enabled me to advance my life. I benefited from developing new friendships with academics, including older, more resilient people. Yet, at work, my exhilaration at being a full-time (if temporary) academic was tempered by the discovery that I held a position subordinate to someone who was patently unsuited to teaching. I taught at a campus where I previously applied for a job and had failed to get an interview. Now, I found that the person employed was an inept teacher whose research didn't seem to justify the appointment. Students voiced objections to this person's teaching but I was not at liberty to concur. This was my first encounter with the expectation that casual and short-term teachers compensate, unquestioningly and without recognition, for inadequacies of long-term staff.

I was also confused to learn that a comfortable salary and office provided no protection against randomly and gratuitously insulting encounters. When one of my students fainted during class, a teacher from a nearby classroom barged in, looked past me and asked a female student if she was the teacher. On two occasions, union representatives walked into my lectures and addressed the students without even acknowledging my presence. In another instance, an academic who was not of my acquaintance berated me without provocation because I hadn't attended a lunchtime protest meeting (I'd been teaching a class at the time). While some of these encounters clearly issued from tensions created by the university crisis, as a temporary employee I lacked access to the senses of security and familiarity that seemed to cushion long-term academics. The resilience that I needed to function successfully as a temporary academic was repeatedly undermined by the role's requirement that I venture into unfamiliar institutional contexts amid an industry-wide crisis.

The crisis' reduction of job opportunities and escalation of competition led to my term as a full-time lecturer being succeeded by a recurrence of poverty. I was back doing sessional teaching work, of which there was now less because universities had increased the workloads of full-time teachers to reduce spending on casual staff. The money I'd made as a temporary, full-time lecturer was used to pay for car repairs and a one-month trip to the United States for my brother's wedding; I'd already missed my other brother's foreign wedding because the teaching job I held at the time provided no practical opportunity for taking leave during semester. At one point, teaching jobs were so scarce that I had practically to beg for a few weekly sessional hours. The work was now also complicated by the difficulties of collaborating with established academics who were reluctant to tighten their own belts as the universities demanded: some lecturers were being asked to either increase their workloads or pay for sessional assistance out of their teaching salaries. While established academics complained about this situation, casual teachers had more to lose because they had no job security and were paid less.

Another disaster occurred when one of my casual co-workers was charged with possession and production of child pornography. This person, Robin, had already offended people with his smug demeanour and prejudiced remarks against Jewish and overweight students. Behind the flaxen hair and blue contact lenses, however, there lurked even greater corruption. Robin and I were working in the same team of tutors when a newspaper report of his criminal charges reached the university. With Robin's immediate suspension, the lecturer responsible for the course departed for an overseas conference, leaving me in charge of two inexperienced tutors. Bound by the institution's decision not to make an official statement about the case, we tried to teach Robin's classes but found ourselves the targets of confused and angry accusations from his students. In one class, the students were appeased only after I explained that the university had forbidden us to discuss the case. In the end, justice was served through Robin's conviction and banishment by the university, which apologized for leaving me to field student abuse. Yet the larger issue of the degree of responsibility held by casual teachers remains one of the most problematic aspects of adjunct university labour.

In Australia, a lecturer who is employed on a sessional basis by a single institution for a prolonged period may take action through the National Tertiary Education Union to have the university formalize a long-term employment contract. Yet universities now tend to employ sessional lecturers on a single-semester basis only, thus preventing such a situation from arising. Moreover, it is widely believed that a sessional teacher who takes union action is likely to have difficulty gaining future academic employment. Few stake their futures on testing this theory. Concurrently, casual teaching staff are liable to become pawns in the political schemes of established academics.

The ruthless political climate of the university crisis led to rumours of increased nervous breakdowns among academics. I experienced indirectly the effects of a nervous breakdown when a tenured lecturer with whom I worked underwent such a crisis, which nearly ended her career. Her breakdown was precipitated by a fraught relationship to the politics of her academic department, a situation fed by years of corrosive and underhand factional behaviour. When her mental state reached a point at which she could not teach, I found myself experiencing her political situation at second degree through being called upon to serve as her teaching substitute. In turn, my already complex situation was detrimentally affected by the barely concealed glee that some of her - my - colleagues emitted when her breakdown occurred. Indeed, my experiences as a sessional university teacher were greatly soured by academic politics.

When my colleague's breakdown occurred, I was a tutor in a course of which she was supposed to be in charge. As her friend, however, I had also taken on parts of her job to cover her growing incompetence. I was handling student enquiries that would ordinarily be referred to a tenured academic, and I was supervising other tutors. I also found myself called upon to provide explanations for why the course co-ordinator was hardly ever there. When I indicated these problems to a senior academic, however, he was evidently oblivious to the real extent of her problem. He accused me of failing to appreciate the training and experience I had received through her. By the time her nervous breakdown was later diagnosed and made public, I was close to having a personal crisis of my own. For casual teachers, the ability to work under pressure is paradoxically both a prerequisite for the job and a potentially dangerous behavioural pattern, in which a heightened ability to face challenges can lead to failure to perceive warnings of impending potential disaster.

My own crisis accelerated with a succession of incidents that collectively strained my financial situation, my domestic arrangement and my career prospects. In one month, I had a minor car accident, my home was robbed, and my housemates and I were notified that we had to vacate our home. As my financial situation was now dire and my new accommodation entailed an unavoidable rent increase, I had to borrow several hundred dollars from my parents. One December, my financial resources were so reduced by Christmas shopping that I tried to pay for a carton of milk with small change, only to be scolded by the shop assistant because she was inconvenienced by having to count it. This and accumulated other incidents gave me first-hand experience of how poverty renders a person more susceptible to a range of secondary problems, including low confidence, poor resistance to ailments, and an unfulfilling social life. Yet my career as a sessional university teacher was to end not through poverty alone, but through another experience of the callousness that now prevailed in Australian universities.

I was approached by a high-profile academic named Basil. His plan was to launch a major new research project that would earn him kudos in the eyes of his superiors; it would also include a secondary yet integral role for me. Only later did I discover that the proposed research project was an ill-conceived amalgam of fads that was unlikely to receive funding and had few definite participants. Basil's bid for my participation was so vacuous that he hadn't bothered to read any of my research. I also learned that Basil's scheme was driven less by reality than by his fantasy of becoming the type of big-name researcher who would employ a youthful female assistant, the role that he presumably envisaged for me. Despite the project's flaws, however, my need for a job left me with little choice but to agree to participate.

I also accepted Basil's support when he encouraged me to apply for a continuing teaching position in his department. In an effort to promote myself in the most professional way possible, I concealed the extent of my financial problems from all but my closest friends. Indeed, I was embarrassed by the fact that my long-term receipt of unemployment benefits required me to participate in a government programme that popularly bore the degrading title, "Work for the Dole". For Basil's part, he told me that he didn't want to know what I did for money when I wasn't teaching. In hindsight, this was troubling because it enabled him to avoid considering consequences of my possible failure to get the job. Basil openly supported my application and gave his colleagues clear indications that I was the preferred candidate. In the interview, however, there were signs that something had changed without warning. The head of the panel ignored me, another panel member spoke to me in a manner in which one might address a twelve-year-old, and Basil himself avoided eye contact.

Even so, I didn't bargain for the extent of Basil's ineptitude. When I phoned to inquire about the outcome of the selection, he insisted that we speak in his office. I wondered why he couldn't talk over the phone, but had no alternative other than to meet him. I didn't get the job. I believe the reason Basil asked me to come to his office was to let him see if I was wearing something attractive. He proceeded bluntly to itemize negative aspects of my job application, failing to acknowledge its strengths or the fact that competition for academic jobs had escalated because of the university crisis. Although he hadn't read my research, he stated tactlessly that it was "not enough." This statement devastated me to the extent that I nearly stopped producing research, a decision that would have been self-destructive in the competitive employment market. My research had been the primary means by which I buoyed my morale through four years of intermittent unemployment, poverty and humiliation. The full extent of Basil's stupidity became evident, however, when he advised that I improve my job prospects by obtaining a large competitive external research grant. As Basil himself had recently informed me, sessional employees were ineligible to apply for such funding because we lacked an institutional affiliation. Being insulted by an idiot in a position of responsibility exacerbated the low morale and sense of exclusion with which I already struggled.

This rejection nearly ended my academic career. Basil's withdrawal of his earlier support reinforced my existing belief that older academics were prejudiced against younger ones. He wasn't the only academic I encountered who thought nothing of brutally slapping down early career academics. Indeed, I later learned that my chances of getting the job had been undermined by gossip disseminated by Basil's rival, with whom I had worked and whom I had considered an ally. Meanwhile, the new university climate was emerging as one in which some humanities doctoral graduates were forced to consider seeking alternative careers, in such areas as education administration. In light of this trend, I was losing hope of gaining long-term academic employment and concluded that knowing people in the field was no advantage. In a quest to use my experiences to effect change, I wrote a letter to Basil's boss in which I warned that Australian universities were likely to experience a crisis of generational succession. I also resolved to apply for no further academic jobs until I recovered fully from the ordeal. My recovery eventually took more than two and a half years.

Discouraged, humiliated, and faced with widespread assumptions that my failure was entirely my own fault, I withdrew almost entirely from the academic world. I didn't think I'd be able to climb out of the abyss into which the last rejection had propelled me. I finished teaching the semester by presenting a falsely serene demeanour. The difficulty of this was exacerbated by my sense that my life had spun out of my control. I'd become convinced that I had no ability to prevent myself from being harmed. Months before the events of September 11, 2001 introduced many people to the real meaning of horror, I was living in a psychological hell composed of successive encounters with bullying, murder, paedophilia, exploitation, bad career advice, institutional crisis, unwanted interventions, poverty and nervous breakdown. At its worst point, my sense of imminent catastrophe was so strong that I was scared to drive my car or to cross the street. I instinctively knew that an overhaul of my life was necessary to escape this hell.

Not coincidentally, my reassessment of my career was paralleled by my decision to expel false friends from my life. I realized that my hesitation in rejecting the friends who vilified me had been linked to a desire to guard myself against Australian anti-intellectualism by eschewing behaviour that could be characterized as elitist. Now I dismissed that scruple as a waste of time and acted ruthlessly and strategically. I distanced myself from Andrew and found another housemate. I sent Stevie an email in which I told her exactly what I thought of her, indicating that I no longer considered her a friend. After further thought, over the next few years I ejected other people from my life. I eventually banished dozens of people who had been apathetically passing themselves off as my friends. Indeed, I didn't fully recover my self-esteem until I was sure I had discarded all the people who turned against me.

I also considered doing office work to raise money until I got a long-term academic job. I reasoned that I could explain my true situation to a temp agency and then present myself to host employers as someone without an academic background who normally does administrative work. Having applied for university administrative jobs without any success, I now needed money more urgently than ever. On the one occasion when I was interviewed for a university administrative job, I'd been told by an academic member of the interview panel that I should go back to doing sessional university teaching and live on unemployment benefits for the remaining months of each year. Astounded by the irresponsibility of an educated person who would recommend that a woman in her thirties with a PhD plan to subsist on unemployment benefits, I resolved not to take any more career advice from academics. I also conceded that I could get money more quickly by being willing to work in industries in which I hadn't previously been employed, and in which the extent of my academic experience might be less likely to emerge as a barrier. Taking the advice of friends and relatives who were familiar with the requirements of temp work, I turned to this occupation for money and an attractively predictable routine.

3.   The Double Life of a Temp

I embarked on a double life when I became a temp. Having been warned that most temp work is menial, I didn't expect the job to excite me. Instead, I planned to position my after-hours academic research activities as my main source of intellectual stimulation. However, I did expect the transition from sessional teaching to temporary administrative work to provide new experiences and insight into the culture of the business world, which for me was almost as unfamiliar as a foreign country. The schedule that I planned was inordinately demanding by almost any standard. I would do administrative work from nine to five and use my weekends to conduct research and write research papers. On the tram to and from work, I would read academic books. My social life would contract only slightly, since it had already been decimated by my friends' betrayals. As a blueprint for surviving the duration of the Australian university crisis while maintaining the option of a future academic career, my plan was more sustainable than subsisting on sessional teaching and unemployment benefits.

The opportunity to use university facilities after I stopped teaching was provided by Maryanne Dever of Monash University, who came to my rescue with the offer of an honorary research position. This provided the institutional link that no film studies department had ever offered me. I also received moral support from other academics and film-related personages, including David Hanan, Rose Capp, Rolando Caputo, Adrian Danks and members of the Melbourne International Film Festival. Yet I couldn't face another academic interview panel. I knew, nevertheless, that I had to continue to be research-active because I might never find another job as satisfying as teaching. My enquiries about arts jobs outside universities indicated that these positions were as highly sought after and political as the teaching jobs I'd already been pursuing. In the event that I wasn't able to get an academic job and was too old for a graduate job in another field, I'd try to build an administrative career on my temporary employment experience. Indeed, administrative work now seemed appealingly attainable and tranquil.

Whereas many temps hope temporary work will lead to permanent employment, I came to the role from an altogether different angle. I was attracted to temp work's frequent banality and had no trouble adapting to new workplaces. Although temps can experience periods of unemployment between jobs, as a temp I had no shortage of work. For a while, the opportunity to work every day of the week, pay my debts and save money made me happy to stuff envelopes, enter data, send faxes, and perform mail merges. Yet I felt I had no immediate need for a permanent job. I had no mortgage and loathed the idea of stuffing envelopes on a permanent basis. When a company at which I worked underwent downsizing, I thrived on the changes, whereas other temps feared losing their jobs. As time passed, the increasing strength of my aversion to a permanent administrative job helped to indicate to me the extent of my recovery.

I never discussed details of my educational or employment background at the companies where I worked as a temp. I'd heard that it was common for temp work to be undertaken by people experiencing crises or changes of career, and that highly qualified temps avoided prejudice and misunderstanding by not discussing their backgrounds. Accordingly, I remained closed-lipped about my PhD and experience. Indeed, I would have felt humiliated to be doing menial work if everybody around me had known of my background. Equally, I knew that boasting about my past jobs and education could annoy or offend people in similar jobs with whom I worked closely, some of whom openly resented the promotion of university-educated people. With my background a secret, however, I was happy to be paid to work in a climate-controlled environment in which small talk and frequent tea breaks were the norm. In time, I met temps who were fleeing divorce, tragedy, debt, or loneliness, stories which in turn enabled me to situate my own experiences in the larger context of life's misfortunes.

Although it was disconcerting to be in a menial job after completing a PhD and having my research published in international journals, I derived tangible benefits from temp work. I was paid adequately to well, had constant employment, extended my computer skills, gained experience in the finance and retail industries, and escaped some of the harmful effects of the continuing university crisis. I also enjoyed working with people who were courteous and harboured no grudge against me, although we ultimately had little in common. In addition, I learned that the placing of inordinate responsibility on casual university teachers is paralleled in the business world by situations in which temps are required to serve as trainers and perform other supervisory tasks. Working in industries with which I was unfamiliar also gave me an outsider's perspective of political situations and hierarchies in which I was not a key player. This, in turn, enabled me to situate my experience of academic politics in a larger context. While I wasn't seduced by the materialism and management-speak that I encountered in the retail and finance industries, I gained insight into those who work in the business world and the cultural differences between the private and public sectors.

The social significance of my academic background became clearer to me when I was playing the role of a temp. My preoccupation with concealing my past had blinded me to the possibility that companies at which I worked might mirror my deception, gaining information about me from my agency and then playing along with my secrecy. Hence, I worked for an insurance company for more than six months before realizing that some of the managers knew I had a PhD and that they had been surreptitiously observing me. I became aware of this situation only after a male manager began to single me out for suggestive stares in the hallway when no one else was about. Initially confused by his tendency to behave as though he knew me although we almost never spoke, I eventually pieced incidents together and concluded that my predicament was less secret than I'd thought. Over time, this guessing game enabled me to regain a sense of where I stood in relation to the non-academic world, and thereby gradually rebuild my self-esteem. Whereas the Australian university crisis stirred in many academics a self-hatred that mirrored the way they felt they were perceived by the larger society, it was refreshing to work in an environment where those who knew about my background were neither unimpressed nor preoccupied by my PhD.

Yet, despite instances of mutual curiosity, I ultimately had little in common with people at the companies where I was a temp. Having come from an educational environment in which knowledge is freely exchanged and academics are not expected to create spreadsheets, in the business world I had few opportunities to exercise my intellectual capabilities or to perform any significant role. A PhD and teaching experience have little value in the insurance industry and seemed to position me as merely an interesting novelty. As a temp in the business world, I also encountered political scenarios that seemed as formidable and complex as any instance of university politics. For these reasons, I felt increasingly that I could only ever hold a marginal position in the culture and occupational hierarchy of the private sector.

The experience of working in subordinate roles as a temp made me consider changing my life's direction once more. Months spent stuffing envelopes and sending faxes gave me ample time to think, not only about the research I was doing on weekends but also about what I came to perceive as my failed academic career. As a commonplace temp, I could not avoid negative confrontations with the myth of meritocracy, the "view that those who are worthy are rewarded and those who fail to reap those rewards must also lack self-worth."[7] Meanwhile, doing a boring job increased my motivation to work on research outside work hours. Although (and perhaps because) I had limited spare time, my research became more important to me than ever. It became a means of fighting the fear that I might otherwise waste many years in a menial job.

Eventually, the increasingly intolerable monotony of my job prompted me to resume seeking an academic position. I had grown accustomed to spending my lunch breaks in the library of a nearby hospital that housed a university medical school. I used the library to access the Internet for academic research purposes while my oblivious co-workers lunched. Initially this arrangement seemed a clever way of sneaking some research time into my working days. Yet, as the months passed, my lunch breaks came to seem too short for research tasks. Sitting in the library one day, near a patient who brought his drip-feed stand with him while checking his email, I wondered: Will *I* ever be rehabilitated from this place? Patients and medical students came and went, but I felt that I'd never escape the routine of shuffling papers by day, making furtive trips to the library and spending weekends writing papers while other people shopped and mowed their lawns. I had to escape the monotonous yoke of temporary administrative work.

Yet I didn't want to return to any of the university settings of my nightmarish experiences. Nor was I keen to remain in Melbourne, where, despite the presence of family and friends, I was haunted by bad memories and kept running into dim-witted former social contacts. I wanted an academic job that required me to relocate. To achieve this goal, I became more of a workaholic than I'd been before. Between eight-hour days in my insurance job and weekends spent on research, I spent most evenings typing applications for continuing university teaching jobs, within and outside Australia. I'd come home from work and spend hours on the computer before collapsing into bed. I'd get up at five-thirty in the morning and search the Internet for job advertisements before going to work. I scarcely had time to cook, eat, clean or launder because even my Friday and Saturday nights were spent writing applications.

After a few unsuccessful attempts prompted me to compile longer and more detailed dossiers to meet the demands of the cutthroat academic job market, the drought broke and I was offered interviews for several jobs. I'd feared that my two-and-a-half year exile as a temp would prevent me from returning to academe, but within six months I succeeded in attaining a continuing teaching job. My new job was at a university in a small city where I could start a new life, and from which I could easily return home to visit family and friends. Unlike some of the people I met in my new job, I was happy to relocate and to leave behind the big city's traffic, impersonality, and inflated sense of its own importance. While my transition back to full-time academic work was stressful, it was infinitely more pleasurable than facing an unrewarding job.

Yet I was haunted by my previous bad experiences as an academic, which wielded a sobering influence on my new life. For this reason, I formed a number of resolutions on the eve of my return to full-time teaching. I resolved to be wary of alliances with those whose political or personal strategies include divisiveness, personal attacks, playing the victim, or paying inflated compliments. I also resolved to use in my new job the interpersonal communication skills that I had valued in working with administrative workers. Fairly or otherwise, university work had convinced me that many academics are poor team players because they are uncommunicative and behave inconsiderately, impolitely, and carelessly in situations requiring interpersonal skills. In my previous academic life I had tried to know the names of and engage with administrative staff, but I now placed greater value on the role of administrators in the academic world. Although being a temp taught me that I wasn't well suited to administrative work, temp work had a positive role in helping me rebuild my life.

Casual teaching work enabled me ultimately to advance myself, but it also precipitated my loss of trust in social institutions, friendship and the Western dream that hard work and determination are inevitably rewarded. Just as the Australian government's withdrawal of funding from universities followed an international pattern, so the universities' crisis of meritocracy has echoed effects on other industries of downsizing, mergers and economic globalisation. Although my decision to sever my dependency on sessional teaching work helped me to rebuild my life, this break was prompted by trauma and fuelled by disillusionment with Australian academe and politicians. Casual teachers need to take charge of their own lives and learn from the experiences of casual workers outside the academic world. Adjunct teaching work constitutes an extremely unstable basis for encountering life's misfortunes.

Notes

1. Stanley Aronowitz and William DiFazio, *The Jobless Future: Sci-Tech and the Dogma of Work*, (Minneapolis and London: University of Minnesota Press, 1996), 15.

2. "Ockham's Razor: Crisis in Our Universities," Radio National, Australian Broadcasting Commission, August 19, 2001. <http://www.abc.net.au/rn/science/ockham/stories/s347931.htm> (December 1, 2003). unpaginated.

3. Paul Fussell, *Class: A Guide through the American Status System* (New York: Simon and Schuster, 1983), 18-19.

4. R. Morley, "Under Control: Dick Down Under," *Manufacturing Systems Magazine* (September 1996): 108.

<http://www.barn.org/FILES/Manufacturingarticles/97/article9709.htm>
(May 14, 2004). unpaginated.
    5 Richard Hoggart, *The Uses of Literacy* (Harmondsworth and
Ringwood, Australia: Penguin, 1958), 84.
    6.Ibid., 84.
    7. Katherine S. Newman, Falling from Grace: The Experience of
Downward Mobility in the American Middle Class (New York: Free
Press; London: Collier Macmillan, 1988), 16.

Bibliography

Aronowitz, Stanley, and William DiFazio. *The Jobless Future: Sci-Tech
    and the Dogma of Work.* Minneapolis and London: University of
    Minnesota Press, 1996.
Fussell, Paul. *Class: A Guide through the American Status System.* New
    York: Simon & Schuster, 1983.
Hoggart, Richard. *The Uses of Literacy.* Harmondsworth and Ringwood,
    Australia: Penguin, 1958.
Morley, R. "Under Control: Dick Down Under." *Manufacturing Systems
    Magazine* (September. 1996): 108.
    <http://www.barn.org/FILES/Manufacturingarticles/97/article9709.ht
    m> (May 14, 2004).
Newman, Katherine S. *Falling from Grace: The Experience of Downward
    Mobility in the American Middle Class.* New York: Free Press;
    London: Collier Macmillan, 1988.
"Ockham's Razor: Crisis in Our Universities". Radio National, Australian
    Broadcasting Commission, August 19, 2001.
    <http://www.abc.net.au/rn/science/ockham/stories/s347931.htm>
    (December 1, 2003).

Excellence and the Adjunct Teacher:
Looking Backward 2005-1988

Rudolphus Teeuwen

The place is the Netherlands, the time the late 1980s. Returning from the US to teach at the literature department of his student days, the author finds academic life there much changed. Excellence has started its reign, but this excellence is *administrative* excellence, empty of content, the excellence that Bill Readings would come to define in his 1996 book *The University in Ruins*. The hiring of fixed-term teachers is one manifestation of this excellence. Several others are also described. Then the place becomes Taiwan, the time the mid-1990s and onwards. The author has exchanged adjunct teaching at home for full-time employment abroad. Reflections are made on the differences in treatment and status of adjunct teachers in the US, Western-Europe, and Asia. The changing face of adjunct teaching in Taiwan is described, with some predictions of the effects of administrative excellence on the future of English teaching at Asian universities.

Adjunct Teaching (the Netherlands); Adjunct Teaching (Taiwan); Adjunct Teaching (USA); Adjunct's Disease; Administrative Excellence; Differences in Academic Cultures; Foreignness

I came to recognize this only after the fact, but I was an adjunct teacher for four years. Part of the reason for the late onset of my awareness was that I am talking about a time, 1988-1992, when the systematic use of adjunct faculty was only just beginning, especially in the place of which I am speaking, the Netherlands. The very word "adjunct" was not used in education there, and it still isn't. A Dutch equivalent of the term was - I'll come to that - but that term's very clarity made that no warning bells went off, primed as all educational ears there are for euphemism rather than frankness. Another reason is that, in many respects, adjuncts are treated much better in Dutch (and, generally, in Western-European) higher education than they are in the US. Thus one can shrug off questions of rank and privilege, especially if one is naïve, as I was. And if one is, as I also was (it seems so in retrospect at least), still glistening with youth and ambition, one can think of one's temporary and terminal contract as merely an anteroom to a much better permanent position. No such position came along, though, until, in 1995, I emerged in Taiwan. But I anticipate.

In 1988 I returned to teach at the Comparative Literature Department of the University of Utrecht, the department I had left as a student seven years earlier for further studies at the University of Pennsylvania. I was still ABD upon my return from the US and saw the justice in not yet getting a permanent position. But the department had changed completely over those years, and so had the way higher education was organized in the Netherlands. The three professors who had mattered most to me as a student had all left the department.[1] New professors had come in or came in the same year I took my position, but to me the department still stood as a monument to vanished minds.

Dutch doctoral students, meanwhile, had turned into junior faculty members with modest salaries and pension plans in exchange for which they wrote their dissertations, had meetings with their professors, and did some occasional teaching. They didn't receive much regular instruction themselves, as far as I could see: in part they were doing what in the UK is called a "PhD by research," and in part they were adjunct teachers. I think the new status of PhD students at the time was the first manifestation of the intention to adopt the "Anglo-Saxon" model of education that has now swept all of Western Europe. In my eyes, the effort was testimony to the misunderstanding and confusion that govern acts of translation and cross-cultural apprehension. But perhaps it was a welcome misunderstanding. The importation of this "Anglo-Saxon" system allowed the government to present a desired reduction in spending on higher education as a systemic overhaul.[2]

Something that had also changed during my absence was the organizational structure of Dutch universities. This used to be a model of logic and simplicity: schools were divided in departments and professors of various rank belonged to a department in which they taught and did research. But in the late eighties teaching, research, and administration started to develop their own divisions, with different sources of financial and institutional support. The three areas intersected (or failed to do so) in unpredictable and original ways, and these points of intersection or dissociation tessellated into fiefs over which an increasing number of people could come to feel important. Go to the website of any Dutch university now and try to figure out where the English Department is. Often it won't be there: various parts of it will be scattered across coils of administrative razor wire.

In the waning years of the last century, many units old and new in the life of a Dutch university suddenly came to be headed by a *directeur*, a Dutch loan word from the French that doesn't mean "director" but designates functionaries at the highest level of corporate or public management. A CEO or CFO of a private or publicly listed company is a *directeur*, and so is the highest responsible manager of public institutions such as hospitals, museums, schools, or prisons. The word was never used, however, in connection with universities and, fresh back again into the Dutch language, I heard a ring of operetta in this term's new, academic application - and to hear it refer simply to coordinators or conveners of one thing or another. It was the future speaking, though. Often these *directeuren* (after a year of one-day-a-week re-schooling and spoiled weekends?), started signing their letters about sports days and salary scales, merit pay and money streams, restructuring and streamlining with that tell-tale addition to their names, M.B.A. Real *directeuren*, meanwhile, especially those who worked in the corporate world, started to abandon the Dutch word entirely and to take on the corresponding English terms to bring out distinctions that the new, "entrepreneurial" university had hoped to erase.

1988 was eight years before Bill Readings would publish his *The University in Ruins*, and another seven years before I would read it. The book is an energetic blend of neo-Marxism, deconstruction, and postmodernism and not at all the elegy that the title promises.[3] Its analysis of the pass to which universities have come feels devastatingly accurate; its relatively upbeat outlook for the future needs all of postmodernism's abstraction as well as all of a promising young scholar's professional faith. The book is primarily concerned with North-American universities but, whether as early adopters of American practices or, more likely, in response to the general *Zeitgeist*, the University of Utrecht and other Dutch universities of the time uncannily complied with Readings' analysis. Thus, the educational establishment in the Netherlands quietly but quickly abandoned the ideal of the university as a place of *Bildung* where teaching and research are inseparable and where the unity of the nation-state is culturally and scientifically forged. The very notion of the nation-state came to look quaint in the face of ideals of European integration and facts of globalization, and *Bildung* lost its legitimation and direction. Even if we follow Readings in his refusal to mourn the decline of the nation-state and the sort of education it gave rise to, it is hard not to regret what took *Bildung*'s place at the heart of the university. The university's new ideal, Readings argues, is "excellence." Excellence is good, of course, but not if it is a "dereferentialized" ideal that does not specify what it is that a university should excel at, and then sticks to it. With such a steadfast ideal missing, excellence becomes an ideal of performativity, of responsiveness to market demands. The quality of a university or any of its units becomes an administrative, financial, and quantitative criterion, one, that is, without content.

One of the forms that administrative excellence began to assume in Dutch universities of the 1990s was that of "modularity." Courses had to fit many possible study paths of students unable to make up their minds about what they studied while they studied it. And in order to qualify for financial assistance students had to study this at a prescribed minimum rate of academic success as expressed in credits earned per semester. Course modules offered at Dutch universities also had to fit seamlessly with modules students might take at other European universities, and vice-versa, lest students would take courses "in vain," i.e., without being able to get credit. This would mess up their access to financial assistance: ideals of excellence quickly become an interlocking and self-validating system. In fact, this self-referentiality is exactly what replaces reference to content. As students were turned into people who attended university and performed at least a stated minimum amount of studying, with the object of their efforts left grammatically and existentially dangling, the financial underpinnings of their efforts no longer moved beyond fiscal prudence to concerns of merit, need, promise, generosity, or national pride. Needless to say, the new enthusiasm for adjunct teachers served that same accounting ideal. The replacement of *Bildung* by "excellence" enabled the divorce of teaching and research as much as it did that of students and study or financial assistance and any non-automated response to characteristics of individual students.

The University of Utrecht had embraced excellence. It looked grandiose to me in its brocaded business suit but with Bill Readings' book still in the future I didn't realize what was happening. Besides, my department did have its attractions. For one thing, there were a few scholars in the margins of the department's empiricist emphasis with whom I developed a very good rapport. They were foreigners, German and Irish, who themselves had studied at North-American universities. The German colleagues clearly were unhappy with the department's dominant approach and, more obliquely, with being German among the Dutch.[4] Their sort of unhappiness resonated with my faded nationality and intellectual pride, and gave me that heady sense of belonging with erudite outsiders, with cynical rebels. I would have done better to keep my head down a bit: I probably came to look an unlikely prospect for preferment in the eyes of those who had real influence in Dutch academia.

For another thing, the department allowed me to teach a very wide spectrum of courses. Service courses were among them, sure, but even those were relatively meaty introductions to literary theory for various groups of language majors. I had to teach those at inhospitable hours sometimes, but I could also teach thematic courses for undergraduate students and even a graduate seminar. I directed an MA thesis for a straggling "old-style" student, one of a group forever again created by the educational system's rage for newness. I probably had the very newness of the system at that time to thank for the latitude it offered me. I threw myself happily into teaching, expanding my range and experimenting with formats and approaches, never once checked, visited, or doubted by my colleagues.

As I worked with gusto on my teaching I also developed, alongside my naïveté, a form of cynicism combined with dreams of grandiose success and delicious revenge. Many adjuncts will recognize this. In my case this took the form of looking at my institution the way Lytton Strachey looked at the religious life in "Cardinal Manning." There was a Manning in my department and a Hurrell Froude, "a clever young man to whom had fallen a rather larger share of self-assurance and intolerance than even clever young men usually possess."[5] Their zeal stood out against the equivalents of Strachey's portly Church of England divines who "sank quietly into easy livings."[6] For myself I couldn't decide between being Cardinal Newman or Strachey himself. Facile stuff, this, I know. It is that combination of anger, envy, and pride that Michael André Bernstein (in *Bitter Carnival*) defined as *ressentiment*.

In every dream home a heartache. With semesters also abolished and replaced by five eight-week modules a year, the new system could be very responsive to fluctuating teaching needs. The percentage of my appointment was readjusted upward and downward countless times throughout my four years. It must be said in gratitude that the department's chairman never failed to get more than our department's share in additional teaching allowances for his adjuncts: restrictions become challenges to good administrators. Still, at every percentile downturn I looked in deeply felt melodrama at the yet paltrier sum deposited in my bank account, thought of *Ladri di biciclette* or Shakespeare's Sonnet 29, and cursed my country, not always quite *à propos*. Wasn't I a married man? Wasn't my wife, too, fresh back in Holland and still finding her feet? Couldn't I run circles around my colleagues? Why must Holland punish and humiliate her native sons for having left? The Dutch have a saying for this: "*Opgestaan is plaats vergaan.*" Leave your seat, lose your seat.

My job title of *toegevoegd docent* ("added teacher") was still very new the year I came in, and unambiguously denies its bearer institutional essentiality. It translates the Latin "adjunct" into unvarnished Dutch, an example perhaps of the cool, minimalist clarity with which Dutch newness sometimes superimposes itself, until it is absorbed by

them, on cluttered old structures. I was still so much a Candide, so full of
trust in the benevolence and dedication to cultural excellence of the Dutch
system of higher education that I didn't even feel the insult, the exclusion,
and the cynicism of dereferentialized excellence expressed by that job
title. The only sting of the position that I was aware of was that it was
terminal. After a maximum of four years you would be turned out of your
job, and the quality of your teaching couldn't save you. No one in the
department, no one teaching at the university was happy with this
revolving door of hiring and then firing entry-level teachers. As more and
more academics became less and less dimly aware of what the university's
turn toward excellence really meant, many came to feel betrayed and
threatened by this development. Still, as these things go, no one whose job
wasn't also on the line was very upset about the practice of hiring to fire
either.[7]

In the governance of an academic department at a Dutch
university (and this is common throughout Western Europe) everyone
participates. Students, administrative personnel, adjunct teachers, PhD
candidates, professors - we all attend or are represented at general
meetings, committee meetings, and gatherings to plan departmental
events. So, in teaching and governance the various forms of exclusion of
which adjuncts in the USA often complain so bitterly do not exist in the
Netherlands. This reflects a rather sympathetic levelling instinct within
Dutch culture that makes that hierarchical differences aren't insisted upon
if this can be avoided. Because of this cultural habit, adjunct teachers are
treated with collegiality while they are around, and are given all available
institutional support. But meanwhile a clock that you have managed to
ignore is counting down somewhere, and the submerged hierarchical
differences will suddenly resurface. On that cue the excellence with which
you may have performed your job will be cancelled by the bureaucratic
excellence of things as they are. No one you have worked with is
personally responsible for your dismissal, and expressions of regret at your
leaving are sincere. Only when for an adjunct teacher the moment arrives
of final handshakes and the sight of backs turned, she realizes that all
along she had been marked a sacrificial lamb to the cruel God Government
so that the department may live.

*

I took my dismissal harder than I should have. I had unwittingly
come to identify with the department but it, of course, had not done so
with me. To be an adjunct is to be denied this mutuality even though, in
Holland at least, all the marks of it are offered. Academics the world over
do check out colleagues to see who is competition and who is not, and by

an act of institutional protectionism adjuncts are not. In an American context this means that no undue respect, consideration, or institutional support needs to be wasted on adjuncts. In a Dutch context it means that such signs of humanity can be safely bestowed upon them. I should have appreciated these real benefits while they lasted, shrugged it off when they stopped, and let myself roll smoothly into the safety net of the Dutch welfare state until I could find my feet again. I sulked in my tent instead. I also vigorously applied for jobs, finished my dissertation, and ate the humble pie that comes with unemployment benefits.

To be unhappy in a welfare state is to be utterly alone. We Dutch, generally, are good at happiness, and often lead the well-rounded lives that score high on the happiness scales developed in the social sciences.[8] We cultivate friendships, develop engaging hobbies and, while hard working, still have a relatively relaxed attitude to work and career. Our stakes in happiness are thus numerous and diverse, and both potentially cumulative and safely compensatory. A system of state health care, education, unemployment and invalidity insurance, child support, and old age pensions, meanwhile, takes the edge off many worldly cares, even though the expense and administration of this system with its systemic quirks and bureaucratic kinks are sources of irritation all in themselves. Still, a welfare state is nothing to sniff at. But, as an academic, I had accustomed myself to more unforgiving US ideals, to the high stakes, high intensity, and single-mindedness that make devastating failure much more likely than benign, quiet success. I felt myself losing in both cultures, contaminating the phlegm of the Dutch outlook with the high-strung nervousness of the American, and destroying American confidence with Dutch resignation to the way of the world. I have never recovered full membership in one or the other culture and ten years of living and working in Taiwan hasn't turned me into a Taiwanese. But at least in Taiwan there is a tolerance for poorly translated beings such as me.

Taiwan's academic habits and institutions themselves are clearly modelled on American examples and many Taiwanese teachers and scholars who were educated in the 1980s and 1990s did their graduate work at American universities - often generously sponsored by the Taiwanese government who wanted to engineer its own "great leap forward" in a matter of one or two educational generations.[9] Many of my colleagues now are such teachers and scholars, and some of them would recognize some unfinished translation work in themselves. Still, such is the strength of Chinese culture that, once back in Taiwan, most of the returned are enveloped again by the dynamics of their native culture. And, like in the Netherlands, the genius of this place too discourages that frightening characteristic of the most impressive of American academics: a single-minded absorption in one's work. Family strongly ties the Taiwanese to a world beyond their immediate personal or professional focus. In a different way from how this works for Dutchmen - the Taiwanese, for instance, tend not to have hobbies or take long vacations - the Taiwanese still spread their investments in life's potential satisfactions in a manner that makes me look here as driven as the serious American that I resembled in Holland and that, any serious American would notice, I no longer am. Another factor that aligns Taiwan with Holland rather than the US is size. Small countries both, Taiwan and Holland make it equally impossible for members of an academic field not to know everyone else in it. This fosters in both countries a partial reliance on personal acquaintance for professional advancement, a situation considered morally compromising for all but the highest levels of academe in the US, and therefore discouraged with the help of unwritten prohibitions (e.g., institutions do not hire their own fresh graduates; one cannot attain a high professorial rank without first serving in a lower one) more easily maintained in large academic communities.

If you are reading this, you have also heard or read stories about how rewarding it can be for a literature PhD to teach high school or community college, to edit and translate manuscripts, to work for software companies, newspapers, government, the church or the hospitality industry, or to go into business for oneself. I ended up doing the more timid of these things myself, but half-heartedly, pressed and prodded by the Dutch unemployment benefits office. That office, understandably, is no respecter of the nice distinctions that teachers derive from the kind of institution at which they teach or of the fact that academics prefer not to see themselves primarily as teachers at all. So it was job interviews for me at high schools in small towns and villages, and school principals who hired me for a couple of hours a week against their better judgment because their schools received a premium from the government for taking someone off the unemployment rolls. Administrative excellence again. It turned out not all bad: humility is a virtue that needs to be forced a bit (but why was *I* the one that needed to be taught it?); high-school teachers make the kindest colleagues (they work together with little or no professional jealousy!); I taught Dutch, the one subject I had an old, never-used teaching license in, and thus was forced to pay attention to my native culture again (but how insignificant that culture seemed to me in its high school outfit!); and high schools and community colleges bring you closer to something that, in comparison to the life I had lived for very long, felt a fuller, more variegated, and unfiltered world.

I know people who faced their personal job crises with the spirit and grace that allowed them to make a go of new careers outside of university teaching, but I never could surrender myself to the new turn my life was taking. In high school teaching I missed the shadow world, the bookishness, the immersion in thought that universities allow even, clandestinely, their adjunct literature teachers. I missed the slow thinking, that academic hybrid of idleness and discipline, that only jobs in humanities departments offer (no matter how busy and fast such jobs also are) and that is necessary for good work (no matter how paltry the results of such thinking often are). I knew I had much to be humble about as an academic but decided that I needed to keep on having much to be humble about. Books simply are my main method of attacking life! I did get my wish. Coming to Taiwan was to me a move to stay in literature, in academics, in the cave.

Four years of adjuncthood, three years in the wilderness: these seven years of unrequited professional love have disabled me from feeling any deep sense of professional inclusion or belonging. I know that quite a few ex-adjuncts share this feeling, even if they eventually succeeded where they didn't at first. It is a sort of adjuncts' disease. We love being professors of literature more passionately probably than colleagues who started out on the tenure track and know not of life outside of it. We chose the profession against the counsel of wisdom, stayed loyal to it even when it shut us out, and didn't just roll into it by the act of indecision that is luck. But we are wary of the profession as an organizational entity with its structure of conferences, distinctions, grants, gate-keeping mechanisms, and prominent scholars. What rings hollow to us in this is the implicit belief that a profession is something carefully fostered by the grave and judicious. In part it is, of course, and we need gravity and judiciousness. But the profession is also a game of hazard - something you do not realize until you lose. Wasn't the astronomer in Johnson's *Rasselas* who considers himself employed in regulating the seasons an exceedingly grave and judicious man? Jacques Barzun says of a profession that it "in one of its aspects is a collection of people captive to a set of ideas."[10] We simply aren't captive to the full set of ideas. Still, we ponder questions of how our profession works and operates with great insistence, driven by that matter of personal interest that can even be a chip on our shoulders: why didn't they want us from the start?

Speaking just for myself again, I feel great gratitude to Taiwan and particularly to the academic department that picked me up when I was drowning and that continues to treat me with kindness and respect. But I think I am right to put that down to individual luck rather than professional design. It is not that I feel that our profession is particularly fraudulent. We just, for better and for worse, do not have a clear and shared idea of what our profession is and what constitutes good work in it. This makes for professional disenchantment for almost all of us, with the exception perhaps of those who immerse themselves in the people-oriented aspects of the profession, the busyness of committees, organizations, and overflowing agendas, or the interaction with our students. Otherwise, the humanities offer most of their practitioners very little resonance. Authors of excellent books, men and women who took their profession very seriously, are forced to ponder, more often than not, an attenuated version of Bishop Berkeley's philosophical question: does a tree falling in a forest make enough of a sound if only a few people heard it fall? Professional disenchantment becomes even a sympathetic trait - and this only in the humanities - when those among us who actually thrived in it, who drew crowds to their falling trees, profess it. The expression of professorial disenchantment has become a sub-genre of the burgeoning field of life-writing: think of Alvin Kernan's *In Plato's Cave*, George Steiner's *Errata*, and the greatest, most beautiful of all in this type of memoirs, Frank Kermode's *Not Entitled*. These books chart the high road to disenchantment, the disenchantment that mixes with the melancholy of old age. My adjunct's disenchantment took the low road, and mixed with the indignation of youth. This is a type of disenchantment that you can survive and put behind you (but not without difficulty), and that you can follow up on (if you can reinvent your relationship with the profession) and that could even still yield the right (if you can fool yourself a bit) to some of that tonier disenchantment.

Here in Taiwan I took up the permanent position that I am enjoying to this day and here I stopped being an adjunct. What little more I have to say about adjuncts I say about other people, not myself. And the adjuncts I see around me now, in Taiwan, are different again in status, outlook, and ambition than American adjuncts are, and Dutch ones were, and than I was.

When, in 1995, I became part of a kernel of permanent full-time faculty members at a Foreign Language department in Taiwan, there was a transitory group of American, Canadian, and South African part-time teachers swarming around it, around us, doing most of the undergraduate language instruction.[11] They were mostly male, often single, and no longer in the blush of youth. There were some interesting courses but also many mind-numbing ones for them to teach: service courses in English to students barely literate in the language and without the intention to do something about this. But they didn't mind: being an adjunct to most of them was about having a life and making a living, and the university offered them that chance. Being around them felt like living a bit part in an eighteenth-century sea novel. They were "characters" who set off our academic blandness: adventurers and Asia lovers, life philosophers and square pegs, home-schooling missionaries and United States drop-outs, unbuttoning puritans and entrepreneurs on the make, professional failures at home and "coloured" South Africans caught unemployed between apartheid and the ANC ascendancy. They were all without criminal records and with MAs but not necessarily in English and not usually very recent. They weren't colleagues in the sense that we shared a profession: none of them was the frustrated scholar that I had been, or even the lover of literature or of English words that you might expect to gravitate toward a department such as ours. They weren't intellectuals, at least not the kind who "think they owe it to themselves to be delicate, tentative, and easily bruised."[12] Some of them though (in those days just before blogs) were robustly writing books on Taiwan, humorously trying to make sense of a bewildering place while their eyes were still fresh. I recognized the impulse. In such contemplated books there is always a chapter on traffic in Taiwan (and the local conviction that nothing that isn't in your field of vision has the right to exist) and one on stray dogs (and how their heart-rending fate seems to rend hardly a Taiwanese heart).[13]

Except for a South African I came to know who had lost his job as a history teacher at home, these adjuncts never seemed to experience anything traumatic about their status. They were not brooding on neglected superiority as I had done. None of them aspired to being a full-time professor of literature, although some might hope for a full-time position in one of the "Applied English" programmes that abound in technical colleges in Taiwan. They saw a language department of a university as a place where skills are taught, skills they respected because they themselves did not quite possess them (how to do "research," how to write, how to read literature and don't ask why). We were always hiring new ones as they would always suddenly move on; they were utterly expendable because they always expended themselves. We couldn't pay them well: there are government pay scales we have to obey and those haven't been revised in years. We didn't treat them very well but we had few complaints: they knew they were favoured foreigners compared to how the Taiwanese treat their construction workers and domestic helpers from Thailand, Indonesia, Vietnam, and The Philippines. We felt superior to them in a way reflected in this paragraph of mine.

Around the year 2000, though, a different breed of adjunct started applying for our part-time positions. The new adjuncts are younger, as likely to be female as male, and as likely to be Taiwanese as foreigner. They see a language department as a place where exactly four skills are taught: reading, writing, listening, and speaking. They would say so because most of them are recent graduates from British, Australian, or American MA-programmes in fields such as TESOL, Education, Applied

Linguistics, or (would you believe it?) Curriculum Design. Such programmes have mushroomed in recent years and cater specifically to the hunger for English in places such as the Middle East, East Asia, and Eastern Europe. Some adjunct teachers plan to return to graduate school for a PhD in these fields after a few years of teaching practice in schools such as ours and saving up money. Those without such plans basically choose adjunct teaching itself as their profession. And, with their expertise and certificates, the new adjuncts do indeed turn adjunct teaching into a profession rather than the mark of professional failure or academic cruelty. Because these new adjuncts feel good about what they do, they make universities here feel better about themselves. Increasingly, Western and Australian universities are losing their monopoly in educating adjunct English teachers for the Asian market, as Asian universities themselves are designing their own MA programmes in TESOL and Applied Linguistics. These home-grown TESOL departments are staffed with professors, mostly local but also foreign, who went back for a PhD.

In some respects, the professionalization of language teaching is the perfect solution to the woes of adjunct teaching in contexts where adjunct teaching actually means teaching English to non-native English speakers. Local university departments can now begin to supply a large part of their own needs for adjunct staff, talented adjunct teachers now have a recognized profession in which they can obtain PhDs and full-time employment, and the growing recognition of their profession will give adjuncts the power to push for improved terms of employment, and for the right to teach content courses in their field, one with its own forms of research, its theories, and its discussions. And most importantly from a wider point of view: professionally trained teachers of English might well prove better teachers of English. I am all for the four skills, and if the new breed of teachers can actually get students in a place such as Taiwan to read, write, speak, and understand English, then there is hope for literature teachers as well.

But the professionalization of adjunct English teachers in Asia is also a victory for excellence in Bill Readings' special sense of the word: an excellence emptied of content. The new adjuncts let universities here off the hook while making them look good. Universities here can outsource onerous labour cheaply to professionals that look great on paper and in brochures (they are specially trained!), and that do not lurk menacingly in hallways as the slightly scary adventurer-teachers of before sometimes did. These new adjuncts' brisk professionalism feeds perfectly into universities' ambitions to have classes going as close as possible to "24/7." Their sense of going up in the world if they are asked to teach classes for special target groups (managers, participants in fast-track MBA programmes, teachers) seems that "win-win" situation of dream business models. Certainly, universities will pay these adjuncts better than the professional failures or adventurers of before. Excellence more than anything else has its price and Asian universities are just as willing to shell out for reputation, position in rankings, and attractiveness to students as their Western counterparts. It is also true that some professionals in TESOL or Applied English will be hired full-time, will do research, and start journals. They will also be the ones asked to manage a growing army of enthusiastic, kind, and capable professional English teachers who, for all their dreams and aspirations, will never join the university's faculty for real.

In this respect nothing much will change for adjuncts. After universities here will have quickly absorbed and rewarded the first generation of TESOL MAs, ABDs and PhDs, these graduates too will start to develop the frustrations of thwarted ambition long since known to the literature folk across the hallway. The entrepreneurial university that created TESOL as a niche market will eat most of its children, and Asian universities will start to resemble closely the grumbling hives of their Western counterparts.

Notes

1. Wim van den Berg had left for the University of Amsterdam; Mieke Bal for SUNY Rochester and after that the University of Amsterdam; and J.J. Oversteegen, the professor who I had admired most, had taken early retirement. I still remember the shock I experienced in May 2001 when, surfing the Internet, I suddenly found out that Oversteegen had died almost two years before.

2. The changes in European higher education of which these were the early Dutch stirrings came to a head in the 1999 Bologna Declaration. In this declaration, 29 European countries commit themselves to a common degree system consisting of two phases, a three-year BA degree and a one or two-year MA degree. By now, some 40 European countries have signed the Declaration, and 2010 is the year by which a "European Higher Education Area" should exist. This BA-MA type of degree system already existed in the UK and in France (as, of course, it does in the US, be it with a four-year BA there), but it meant enormous changes in countries such as Germany and the Netherlands where university studies typically were articulated more complexly and took much longer than the 4 or 5 years of the "BAMA" structure now being phased in. With European higher education systems losing their national particularities, they can now compete for students throughout Europe especially if they teach more and

more of their courses in English. But this switch to English, Bob Wilkinson rightly argues, is harder to do well and culturally responsibly than people in government, education, and administration seem to realize. See Bob Wilkinson, "Where Is English Taking Universities?" Learning English Supplement, *Guardian Weekly*, 8 March 2005, 1+.

3. There is unintentional elegy in the act of reading this book anyway. In 1996, the year of publication of his book, Readings (1960-1994) had already died much too young in an air crash. Diane Elam, his colleague at the Université de Montréal, took care of the final editing of the book and wrote a foreword. In the book's "Library of Congress Cataloging-in-Publication Data" only Readings' date of birth is given.

4. The Second World War cast a shadow over German-Dutch relations at least until the close of the twentieth century. The Dutch army was vanquished by the Germans in a matter of days in May 1940 after which, under German occupation, the Dutch - a tiny minority of collaborators excepted - busied themselves with resistance, sabotage, and the saving of Jews. That, at least, was the story. The Dutch were slow to divest themselves of this metonymic heroism and the implicit virtuousness of their military feebleness. These national myths of bravery and innocence informed until very recently the way many Dutchmen felt they could approach Germans. German culture, on the other hand, had started its huge and ongoing project of *Vergangenheitsbewältigung* (the coming to terms with its past) in the 1960s, some twenty years after the end of the war, and some thirty years before the Dutch first seriously attempted to look realistically at their behaviour in the years 1940-1945.

5. Lytton Strachey, "Cardinal Manning," *Eminent Victorians: The Definitive Edition*, introduced by Paul Levy (1918; London: Continuum, 2002), 9-107, p. 16.

6. Ibid., 14.

7. I don't see the term "toegevoegd docent" any more. The Dutch language seems to have fled to the kinder, gentler Latin of junior docent. The humanities departments of the University of Utrecht have also abandoned the 5-module academic year again, now for a quarter system.

8. The Netherlands ranks a joint second (with Sweden and Denmark, and after Iceland) on the net happiness index of the 54-country World Values Survey Happiness Index. The index is based on 1995 data. It is hard to believe the survey results, though. On the question, "Taking all things together, would you say you are: very happy, quite happy, not very happy, or not at all happy?" an alarming 96% percent of about 1000 surveyed Dutchmen report to be quite or very happy. This percentage is 84 for the USA, 87 for Britain, and 72 for Germany (listed as "W.

Germany"). As far as I can tell, Dutch happiness is a recent phenomenon. In the Holland I remembered upon my return in 1988 (i.e., the Holland of the 1970s), happiness was a sign of insufficient sensitivity and you wouldn't be caught dead happy ("More Than Money").

9. Taiwanese students still travel for their educations, in fact such travel is a growing part of Taiwanese students' lives. But rather than students pursuing excellence, it more and more becomes excellence (Bill Readings' kind) pursuing them. Foreign universities, stripped of government funding at home, prey on Taiwanese students and their parents at "education fairs," exploiting complex motives in the Taiwanese and offering them overseas experiences that are often tailor-made for them and thus largely drained of authenticity. The motives of the Taiwanese include a desire for status, distinction, and employability at home as well as a desire to forge or keep alive a family's connection with the US or Canada (where some students were born when their parents worked toward their PhDs) in case of trouble in Taiwan's fractured relationship with the Chinese Mainland.

10. Jacques Barzun, "Toward a Fateful Serenity," in *A Jacques Barzun Reader: Selections from his Works*, ed. and introd. Michael Murray (New York: Perennial-HarperCollins, 2002), 3-11, p. 8.

11. In Taiwan, the term "adjunct" isn't used. The division is that between "full-time" and "part-time" faculty. Part-time teachers, of course, typically spend more hours in the classroom than full-time teachers do. They do not teach "content courses," but only courses that draw upon their ability as native speakers of English; they are not involved in the governance of the department, and are lucky if they have a shared office. They will often teach night classes too for the many subsidized special programmes that typically spin off Taiwanese universities: English for government employees; English for high-school teachers; English for students of the English Language Centre; English for the Two-Year Technical Programme. They often combine their jobs at the university with jobs at other institutions or companies and with teaching private students.

12. Jacques Barzun, "James Agate and His Nine Egos," in *A Jacques Barzun Reader: Selections from his Works*, ed. and introd. Michael Murray (New York: Perennial HarperCollins, 2002), 92-103, p. 96.

13. Australian Chris Murphy actually succeeded in turning such observations into the sort of book all expatriates here seem to contemplate at some point of their stay: *Four Years without Socks: An Expatriate Teacher in Taiwan Tells Tales out of School* (Rosanna, Vic. [Australia], Innaminka Ink: 1999.) The stylistic ghost of Clive James hovers over the

book, but that is not a bad one as ghosts go. And Murphy is very perceptive about life in Taiwan, as well as honest about how his deeper ignorance about Taiwan enables him to see the surface of it. He is silent on one thing, though: the apparent lack of empathy of many Taiwanese with animals, and the careless cruelty into which this often turns. It is perhaps Murphy's Australian anti-sentimentalism, or his determination to keep things light, that makes him turn away from this aspect of life here. Taiwan's unlucky dogs do feature prominently, though, in the best fictional account so far that an expatriate writer has given of life in Taiwan. Eric Mader-Lin's novel *A Taipei Mutt* (Taipei, Cheng Shang Publishing House: 2002) shows life in Taipei through the experiences of a street dog (actually a man changed into a dog by a female magician). It is a comic, satirical, and unsentimental novel but contains, as implicit indictment, the best description of the horrific skin conditions to which societal impassivity condemns Taiwanese street dogs (see pp 154-55).

Bibliography

Barzun, Jacques. "Toward a Fateful Serenity." In *A Jacques Barzun Reader: Selections from his Works*, edited and introduced by Michael Murray, 3-11 New York: Perennial-HarperCollins, 2002.

___. James Agate and His Nine Egos." In *A Jacques Barzun Reader: Selections from his Works*, edited and introduced by Michael Murray, 92-103. New York: Perennial-HarperCollins, 2002.

Bernstein, Michael André. *Bitter Carnival:* Ressentiment *and the Abject Hero*. Princeton: Princeton University Press, 1992.

Mader-Lin, Eric. *A Taipei Mutt*. Taipei: Cheng Shang Publishing House, 2002.

"More than Money," 7 Dec. 1998, (20 Oct. 2004). MORI 2004. <http://www.mori.com/pubinfo/rmw/morethanmoney.shtml>.

Murphy, Chris. *Four Years without Socks: An Expatriate Teacher in Taiwan Tells Tales out of School*. Rosanna, Vic (Australia): Innaminka Ink, 1999.

Readings, Bill. *The University in Ruins*. Cambridge, Mass.: Harvard University Press, 1996.

Strachey, Lytton. "Cardinal Manning," In *Eminent Victorians: The Definitive Edition*, introduced by Paul Levy, 9-107. 1918. London: Continuum, 2002.

In and Out of a Japanese Doctoral Programme

Terry Caesar

The specific frustrations teaching in a new doctoral programme at a Japanese University are detailed in narrative form by a foreign professor on a fixed-term contract. These frustrations become the opacities of Japanese organization, from which he is necessarily excluded, often to comic effect. The experience turns on the crucial distinction between the way things are officially (and collectively) supposed to be and the way things unofficially (and personally) are. A doctoral programme at a Japanese university is not presumed to be publicly representable in terms of this distinction.

Doctoral Programme; Rules; Organization; Director; Japanese; *Tataeme*; *Honne*; *Senpai-Kohai* System; Director; MA Students; Ministry of Education.

> *Japan, in particular, disgraces itself with its third-rate universities.*
> Nicholas Kristof & Sheryl WuDunn

A knock at the door. I'm downloading folk music from Napster. It's the director of the graduate programme! He wants to instruct me about the dates for the examination of the MA theses of my two advisees. Will Wednesday a week after next be all right with me? It will. "About half an hour," he adds, and then leaves. I turn back to my computer screen and turn up the volume of something by the Cincinnati Dirt Band.

It's taken two years to regard the knock so casually. Even now I haven't managed as successfully as I might think, since I almost blurted out, "can the candidate fail if she doesn't do well?" At my former university, the relation between the written and the oral phase of a performance for a Master's degree was clearly established; the one had to be accomplished before the other was permitted, and even then a poor oral performance would cost the candidate the degree. At my present university, who knows?

Of course I could ask. In a sense, I've been asking since I got here, bit by bit. No questions so grand as, what's the purpose of the programme or why do students enter it? Instead, minor matters, such as what's the name of my class and how can I order texts for it? About the first thing: apparently my graduate classes have vague, commodious titles - "Seminar in American Literature" or "Textual Studies" - that fit very nicely into the carefully unspecific, non-committal, open-to-consensus cultural fabric. About the second: by now I'm fairly confident that I gave the right office worker the correctly filled-out form, despite the fact I still can't read a Kanji of it.

Much of my relation to my position would change if I could read Japanese. (Or was not the only full-time foreign employee in the entire university.) I can still recall my utter amazement at discovering that the whole MA programme existed in textual form! Even down to credit hours. For all I know in the little booklet - which a secretary late one morning last semester was about to deposit into a drawer, before I begged her to pause - there's even a statement of aims. But to whom to look to ask, and then translate? The essence of my position here is that I always have to ask. Nobody's telling.

In any case, I don't, or can't, especially care about the MA programme. I've been hired for another purpose: the new PhD programme. Why should Mukogawa Women's University want a doctoral programme? Best not to ask. First things first - if the university does indeed desire one, what does it need to satisfy Ministry of Education requirements? Well, among other things, me. That is, a senior professor in American literature with plenty of publications (mine were rated tops - whatever this means - the director eventually told me) on the graduate faculty. Then apparently all would be in place. I've signed a four-year contract, in accordance with the Ministry's mandate of an initial four-year cycle, the first year to get the programme in place.

But why does the university want a doctoral programme? Two years later and counting - slowly - I'm no more sure than I was at the outset, when the director introduced me to the department and compared me to the new manager of the local baseball team, the Hanshin Tigers, the Japan League's perennial losers. Poor Tigers. They finished last again that year, last the next, and are last so far this year. At least the difference between the manager and the players is clear and their performance takes place in public. Mukogawa's doctoral programme continues to be veiled in so much stealth and secrecy it still eludes me, while the director manages everything from graduate faculty meetings (conducted only in Japanese) to oral as well as written examinations for entrance into either the MA or the PhD programme (each conducted only in Japanese). Initially hailed as the manager of the team, I'm in fact more comparable to a groundskeeper. What sort of game is this? Does it have any rules? Is there ever a winner?

-1-

I remember my surprise, halfway through my first semester, to discover quite by chance that one, no, both of my graduate courses in fact last the whole year! What I had hastily planned as one semester courses, on the American model, were in fact year-long courses, on the Japanese model.

Which is more true: that I could have been expected to know this, or that my new Japanese colleagues could have been expected to tell me? Based on what I know about Japan now, the answer seems easy: neither one. To a foreigner, Japan is guaranteed to be a mysterious place initially, no matter how many books he reads before the plane touches down; I had read everything from Patrick Smith's *Japan: A Reinterpretation* to the wonderfully-named Boye Lafayette De Mente's *Behind the Japanese Bow.* Japan is the world's most famously insular culture, which *is* insular, and proudly so, because everybody has been able to take so much for granted for so long that no organizational space exists to accommodate a foreigner.

Instead, all is proscribed, formal, relational. In these terms, I arrived as an anomaly. A senior professor, I could not easily be translated into the master-disciple, or *senpai-kohai* system, whereby, in part, the new person is "mentored" (to use an American idiom), with respect to everything from the lay of the land in department politics to the correct local procedures for how to check out books from the library, keep a complete, up-to-date record of class attendance, and order paper clips. Nobody told me anything. Everybody expected me to know everything. I wondered if the experience was akin to some sort of Buddhist monastery where the monks - smiling all the time - were engaged in an elaborate, almost unconscious pattern of action designed to initiate the new novice by humiliating him.

And where was the abbot? My new colleagues seemed scandalized that the chair of the English department didn't speak English. Was this why he didn't greet me? Or was it because of his conflict with the graduate director, a prominent Shakespeare scholar, apparently my official boss? In time, I learned that most of the department despised both men - the one (retired from another university) felt to be flagrantly deceitful and conniving, the other (also retired from another university) perceived as remorselessly sour and dismissive. But of course outwardly all would no more speak openly or at length of such things than they would speak of their spouses or even our administration. I remember walking with a colleague after lunch one day. The name of Mukogawa's vice-president came up. Wasn't he the son-in-law of the president? Yes, my colleague confirmed, "but we don't speak of these things in public."

What do you do at work when nobody tells you anything? One thing is, learn to ignore memos. I'd always hated memos, and had written a whole chapter on them in one of my books. Now, since every single one was written in Japanese, I couldn't read them even if I loved memos. By my second semester, certain things were clear: how to tell the ones that were significant (they had numbers), how not ever to ask students to translate any (they knew nothing about context), and which colleagues I could trust to help (if I got them at the right time). The rest of the memos I just discarded, along with my inhibitions about doing so. Another thing you do is even simpler: relax. If you're invariably going to get some procedures wrong, you may as well learn to enjoy the minor scandals of, say, *not keeping the class attendance book properly*. I never quite succeeded in enjoying these scandals, though I tried hardest with this particular one, probably for good Freudian reasons.

But there are two main things you do when nobody tells you anything. One is, read, and the other is, write. It developed that, like all full-time Japanese professors, I had my own budget for books! (As well as for supplies and travel. The first is a most generous category, justifying the order of refrigerators or televisions for the office.) Thousands of yen - and this isn't counting either your section budget, much less the departmental budget. Gradually I realized that I could order up my own library. So I did, and learned to read with sweet abandon. All I had to do is to go downstairs to the library when the latest batch of books arrived, have them checked out permanently to me (or rather until I left, at which time the books would revert back to the library), and say *arigato* to a woman in a full-length white lab coat who spoke not a syllable of English. Sometimes I even said "thank you" in English, just to provide a genuine foreign frisson.

Writing was, and is, an even rarer consolation. By the end of my first year I paid my scholarly debts principally in the form of a long, densely footnoted article on the representation of Japan in recent American fiction, and was completely free to write about anything. I wrote the memoir about my father I'd wanted to attempt for years. After our first cherry blossom spring, I just sat down and wrote about it. A trip to Thailand? Immediately upon return from summer vacation, a long travel piece. Singapore and Malaysia? Another long travel piece. And in between assorted short articles on such local themes as attending sumo or being a *gaijin* as well as lots of book reviews on professional subjects. I'd never had so much time to write in my life during semesters, except while on sabbatical. Here I wasn't on sabbatical.

And yet I wasn't teaching in any way comparable to the past thirty years. Conversation classes took no preparation time at all. Literature classes took a little, and graduate classes a little more. But all classes only met once a week for the Japanese standard ninety minutes. A grade could be waived like a wand over any performance, and no student would complain; perhaps, I reasoned, such is the free license granted to college years by Japanese society, students didn't even care much about grades. (The central administration cared only about attendance.) By the end of my first semester, it was obvious that the grad students didn't expect to be asked to read very much per week. Forty pages made them groan. I was pleased to try to make them happy. Forty pages just demanded an hour or so from me. I spent many more hours reading books about Japan.

In many ways, Japan became for me far more compelling to read and write about than to live, especially in academic terms. In academic terms, Japan disintegrates on contact for a foreigner, because the terms are highly personalistic from the start and remain so. Karel van Wolferen states: "Japanese loyalty is directed solely at a group or person, not a belief or abstract idea."[1] More specifically, Ivan Hall explains: "Japanese universities do not have a sorting system based on a period of apprenticeship followed by peer review leading to tenure."[2] Difficult as it is to generalize for every university at all levels, I believe the following statement is accurate: social networks - radiating from universities attended or common professional friendships - are utterly decisive, not only for hiring but for professional movement or success of any sort. Van Wolferen again: "*Jinmyaku* ["personal veins," as in mineral deposits] are much more widespread, and of incomparably greater importance, than old-boy networks in the West.[3]" I may have been more anomalous because my hiring was not part of any network than because I enjoyed no *senpai*, if we grant that a distinction can be made, which it probably can't, at least not to Japanese.

Oh, the sweet opacities of Japanese organization! There's lots of time to muse upon them if you don't have to attend departmental meetings. (I didn't.) Eventually I worked my way to van Wolferen's seminal study, *The Enigma of Japanese Power*, while teaching an MA course on popular culture to six students and another on American short fiction to one. The one with one student began with three. The third dropped after the first week, leaving a note under my door that she was "concerned" since I had said I would "look unfavourably" upon a student who had more than two absences. The second dropped the next week. No note. The one who remained said that this student is really only interested in Middle English phonetics. What? Why should a Japanese graduate student even care about Middle English phonetics? But by then I knew the simple answer: one of her professors taught a course in this subject. Had the department judged it so important that one of its regular courses be devoted to it? Of course not.

Instead, the department just chanced to have among it someone who specialized in Middle English phonetics. How did his presence come about? (No women taught in the graduate programme, although one functioned as the director's minion.) You may as well try to penetrate to the core of the organizational enigma itself. Van Wolferen's point is that there is no such core. I wasn't here, though, to concern myself about such high mysteries, or any mysteries at all. I was merely here to embody something called "American literature," because the doctoral programme required such a person (and, I suppose, such a subject). So at the beginning of my second Mukogawa year, I was very excited. For whatever reason it existed, in whatever form it consisted of, and to whatever number of students it had accepted - complete mysteries all - the doctoral programme was about to begin.

-2-

Accounts varied about the number of students. The usual number given was, two. One was a recent graduate of the MA programme. She worked in a sort of departmental office. Her English was pretty good. The other was an area high school teacher. Apparently the director feared his English was not so good. He wasn't clear about a possible third student, who was either from far north in Hokkaido, currently in Hokkaido, or had something else to do with Hokkaido. In my mind, she became "the Hokkaido student." She never materialized. A year later somebody told me that in fact she was never in Hokkaido at all but had worked as a secretary in the Japanese department, one floor above English.

Excited, I say. My first doctoral class had been scheduled. Alas, it had no content. But not to worry. The director had been at his casual best in his suggestion. "Give them something to do with criticism," he advised. I proceeded to survey the professional journals in English in the library (not a bad selection) and to draw up a tentative short list of articles. We would read one per week, mostly but not exclusively in American literature. I would get some sense of their critical vocabulary, if any. (The overwhelming majority of courses in English at Mukogawa, as at most Japanese universities, have to do with language, not literature.) They would learn - well, I wasn't sure exactly what, because much depended on them. But it would be something suitably . . . doctoral, I was determined.

The first meeting was scheduled for Saturday at 2. An hour before, the minion called on the phone. Class cancelled. What! Why? Because the students work. One teaches high school, the other does something else. But wait, I thought this was precisely why the class had been scheduled for a Saturday, at this particular time. Then I stopped. Best to say nothing or make no protest, like a good Japanese, and instead only nod, while superiors spin their airy organizational nothings. Perhaps, I thought, there really *is* no PhD programme after all. The director & minion are just trying to save face. "We'll let you know," she concludes. Perhaps there really is a programme. Just not today.

A week passed. There was never another call. Should I have made a point of checking with one or the other? The director, though, was usually elusive, while the minion was always hysterical. Best, I reasoned, to show up the next Saturday as if somehow there would be students in the room. But there were none. Had I really expected that there would be? Of course there remains a doctoral programme. Proof: me. I'm here. In a sense, the programme doesn't even need students. The best explanation of why it existed in the first place was simply that the President of the university had always wanted a doctoral programme in English. More abstractly, how many times already had I read about the foundational distinction between *soto* and *uchi*? The innermost recesses of Japanese life depend upon this distinction. The former has to do with what you show to the world or the outside, while the latter is what you show to your intimate circle. This sort of thing is fascinating to read about. But it's hell to live.

During the next week, I asked the director about the missing-in-action doctoral course. Another surprise: it seems now there was never any course because the three students who were enrolled in the programme, had each opted for "English literature." (Two specifically for Jane Austen, subject of a long running course - one novel per year - taught by an old British friend of the director's.) Two others had indicated an interest in American literature (Steinbeck and O. Henry, respectively) but they flunked. "Maybe next year there'll be somebody in American literature," the man muses. I'm speechless. You mean there's no actual programme consisting of courses for all students? Each just works under a professor who's a specialist in "English literature?" But how can one "specialize" in the whole of English literature? And why this strict division between English and American literature?

I didn't pose any of these questions. It would just have begun another fruitless journey into terms - disciplinary, if not academic - that seemed to me completely ridiculous. Most likely, the truth was, again, personal. The minion lied (haplessly "ethnocentric" word!) for the director, who, in his turn, may have once lied - or something - to her. Maybe both were served up some sort of suitably doctoral story to the administration, while in fact continuing the MA programme by other means. In any case, how much did I want to get involved with this? Even if I wanted to, what power did I possess? (Any foreigner is automatically *soto*, ultimately.) Mine only to represent the Doctoral Programme, in the pure - and very Japanese - form of its Idea. But there was a final twist.

I returned to the scheduled room for a third Saturday, as if haunting the scene of a crime that never took place. Suddenly, to my shock, one of the students I knew to be in the programme - she of the Mukogawa MA - walked by. Where was she going? To class. What! Yes, her class in the doctoral programme. It seemed that it was taught by the director. Its subject? Wayne Booth's classic, *The Rhetoric of Fiction*. She and another student, the male high school teacher, were meeting in the director's office. After she left, I waited a few minutes, then walked upstairs, and past the director's office where, sure enough, there he was, with the two students, speaking of course in Japanese, while undoubtedly going over selected passages in the book and translating them into Japanese.

I felt as if I had witnessed the scene of the crime. But to whom to report it? Why didn't the director tell me about this class when we chatted the week before? Why was he teaching it now? Whatever happened to the decisive boundary between English and American literature? Of course it's easy for a foreigner to see deceit here. It may be just as easy for a Japanese to see care. The director, it could be said, was simply sparing both the programme and me embarrassment - the one because the worthiness of the high school teacher remains uncertain, the other because his English isn't very good. Many things could indisputably be said, among them that in fact by now my actual participation in the programme could be dispensed with, as being in some senses an embarrassment of its own.

So back to the consolations of writing. What else to do? The next week I began to write an essay-review that I had agreed to do some weeks previous. One of the books was, of all things, Mark Currie's *Post Modern Narrative Theory*. Currie begins with Booth! It seems narrative theory of the past forty years proceeds from a critique of the sort of naïve formalism and "general idealities" enshrined in *The Rhetoric of Fiction*.[4] (29). But I doubt very much if, back in the doctoral classroom, the director and his students were engaged in such a critique. Back in that classroom, it was still 1961, the year *The Rhetoric of Fiction* was published. In terms of this classroom, there was no need to know the theoretical developments of the subsequent forty years, much less to be able to write a review of them.

-3-

During my second year I acted as the advisor to two MA students. One (an exceptionally well-read retired businessman) wrote his thesis on a short story of Bernard Malamud. The other (whose English was quite limited) wrote about the image of the geisha in six post-war American films. The director liked the Malamud thesis. It was solidly formalist. He didn't like the geisha thesis. "Sociology," he snorted. But, like her much older colleague, the student passed - I never found out if this was the correct word - her examination. "Just as well she wrote in English," the director assured me afterwards. "It would be nonsense in Japanese." Why bother to reply that in fact what he had just said struck me as nonsense, much less to suggest that the study of English had changed a bit during the last forty years? I looked forward to next year. Another doctoral course had been scheduled for me.

In part inspired by the director's example, I chose another classic, Henry Nash Smith's *Virgin Land: The American West as Symbol and Myth*. My thought was that we could read it during the first semester, and then develop a critique during the second semester, using a couple novels about the West, as well as some selected essays by New Western historians and Smith's own reconsideration of his book. It was very much to my purpose that it wasn't "literary" in any narrow sense. The study of American literature has never been, and American Studies (or Cultural Studies, for that matter) seemed to me especially suitable for students who really have no background in literature, whether in some circa 1960 formalist sense or any other. What the hell, I might have reasoned, if all else failed, we could watch movies. I didn't know the half of it.

A week or so before the new semester, I met with the director, who assured me that I would have "at least two" students in the doctoral course. The reasons why this particular intelligence had to wait until the week before to manifest itself - as it appeared - eluded me. But on with the programme, at last. One student, though, was rather weak, he said. In fact, she had failed the examination last year. But she had taken it again, was still mad to enter the programme, and couldn't easily be refused this time, mostly - the director intimated - because the institution needed her money. I shrugged. At least I could expect to teach one course in the programme for which I had been hired. I didn't even groan at the mention of Steinbeck, who was, it seemed, the great passion of this particular student, a middle-aged woman. At least Steinbeck was better than O. Henry.

Come the great day. I walked into the room. One of the students turned out to be from my initial MA courses, a nice, dry, shy, reasonably intelligent young woman. The other was visibly shaken at my appearance, and turned to my former student for a translation as soon as I said good morning and asked how she was. Then she turned on a tiny tape recorder in front of her on the table. It was state of the art. I don't remember what else I said, now to both students, as the new one continued to tremble, her eyes bulging, her face stricken. The poor woman was absolutely terrified. Under the circumstances, it did not seem best to give an overview of the historical development of American Studies or to set the study of *Virgin Land* within the ideological critique of the New West historians. What to do? I wanted to flee the room myself.

I asked them what they had read of American literature. After some consultation with the former student, the new one finally blurted out to me, "Steinbeck." The former one thought some more and eventually pleaded, "E.M. Forster?" (In fact the subject of another of her courses, as I later found out.) Pointless even to sketch a characterization of American studies, or to focus upon the problems of a specifically literary study within it. Instead, I picked up my copy of *Virgin Land* and gesture at the cover. There are the words, "symbol" and "myth." I explained what each of these words means, while trying to figure out whether to speak to the former student, who could understand me, and to the new one, who clearly couldn't. The woman was in a hysteria of attentiveness. But she couldn't speak. I asked the former student to translate selected words into Japanese. Each time after the translation the new one nodded furiously.

Finally I asked the one to ask the other what percent of what I'm saying she can understand. "10%," she - through her colleague - said. Then she covered her face in her hands. How to convey that I want to do the same thing? What *can* we do? Blessedly, I'd thought to bring Jonathan Rabin's article on Pacific Northwest painting in the March *Atlantic Monthly*. It has pictures. We can literally see something of one nation's response to one idea of itself by looking at pictures. In this case, one picture is not only going to be worth a thousand words. It's going to be worth a whole language. The new student calmed down a bit as I pointed at the odd Indian here or the distant ship there. Is one picture "classical?" Best merely to define it as "rational." The new student consulted an impressive electronic bilingual dictionary. "Romantic?" We decided upon "emotional," now engaged in consensus-building, like good Japanese.

Neither of the students knew the word, "Puritan." As one punched it into the machine, and then both read what it said, the former student (re)translated for me. Sounded pretty accurate, although by the time we all get the information on the table I'd forgotten why I brought up the word in the first place - other than because it's just hard not to say something comprehensive about "American literature" without mentioning the word, "Puritan." The former student gave me a piece of paper. I wrote the words, "nature" and "civilization." As we continued to peruse the pictures, I tried to illustrate their progressive development by pointing at one word, then the other. Each time, careful nods by the one student, passionate convulsions of the head by the other. I also pointed at certain sentences of Rabin as I read them, slowly. Comprehension of some sort was wordlessly indicated, in respective ways.

Onward through Rabin to the end, by which I was pointing once again to the cover of *Virgin Land*, this time now bringing up Hokkaido, and wafting through the air some speculation about how imaginatively barren the vast land to the north seems to be for Japanese, in such contrast to the West for Americans. But this sort of thing only seemed to confuse the former student, not to mention the new one, and then I got confused again about what to ask the one to translate for the other. After an hour and fifteen minutes we were all exhausted. Time to stop. I declared that we must all try our best. The new student got up and bowed. Then she produced an envelope, with photographs of herself and her daughter, dressed in Halloween costume! It seems she was in Hawaii with her husband last Halloween. "Very nice," I declared, perusing and smiling hard. The woman smiles and bows again.

Fortunately, the director was in his office. "I was afraid of this," he uttered, after my account of the class. "We had to accept her." But of course he has to concur that I can't teach her, much less that the former student isn't being justly taught if she has to act all the time as a translator for the new one. What to do? The director wondered if the new one wasn't headed for a nervous breakdown, whatever we did. He thought putting her into the other MA level course in American literature taught by a Japanese colleague might indeed satisfy her for a year, while she attempts to improve her English. (Also she might be able to get lost in the seminar of the director's former British colleague, who seems to have exhausted Jane Austen and so moved on to Thomas Hardy - a novel a year, as usual.) But eventually she'll have to get past me, because it's American literature that she wants to study. Why? She likes Steinbeck. Again, why this crucial division between English and American literature? As well ask to call the Ministry of Education, who probably insists upon it. Meantime, a paradox: I'm at once the only reason there can be a doctoral programme in the first place (those Ministry requirements) and the only reason - now, anyway - why it can't easily continue.

Oh, well. Back in the doctoral classroom of the present with my remaining doctoral student (looking more chipper than I would have been if I'd been her), we bend to the task. At first the task is, well, national. "I thought all the people in the first two chapters were British," she said of *Virgin Land*. Maybe the Ministry of Education in its infinite wisdom knows more than I think. On into James Fenimore Cooper. Perhaps our best class of the semester turns out to be when the student, at my request, tapes a network television showing of *The Last of the Mohicans*, and presents a few scenes for me in terms of two more of Smith's subsequent chapters. We had a good discussion. The whole book, though, is harder going than I'd realized - full of dense historical argument and political nuance. My favourite class to date is the one when we see together a wonderful old Western, *Broken Arrow*, with Jimmy Stewart and Jeff Chandler. The student insisted that she'd never seen a Western. Virgin land indeed.

-4-

According to a *Newsweek* report, the number of "PhD aspirants" last year in Japan was 62,488 - more than double the number ten years ago. The number of such aspirants pursuing a PhD specifically in English is virtually impossible to determine, much less the number of the programmes. It seems accurate to state that at present some seventy-five Japanese universities offer doctoral programmes in literature, a category from which "English" cannot be isolated and to which might be added, depending upon the university, other categories such as "Linguistic Education" or "Linguistic International Culture." Official information about Mukogawa's own programme (in Japanese of course) is contained in one page of a handbook, kept in the department office, listing basically one course, "Literary Research," in three areas: Linguistics, English literature, and American literature. Some twenty credits must be taken over a three-year period, after which in order to complete the degree there is an "oral assessment" as well as a thesis.

Good luck to the two students who entered the programme at its inception. I won't learn why they entered. Japan's Council of Universities, it seems, wants to boost graduate school numbers. The nation needs more specialists, although dissertations on Jane Austen might not be quite what the Council has in mind. But of course I'll never see either of these student's respective dissertations, which will be written in Japanese. They'll be awarded doctorates in a language which they don't necessarily have to speak or write, on the basis of courses in which (with the one exception of the director's former British colleague) they haven't even had to hear English spoken. With my departure next year, the native scholarship unfortunately necessary to launch the new doctoral programme will be gone, no longer necessary for the continuance of the programme, which, I'm told, merits a sum of money - I don't know how much - from the Ministry of Education, just to help get started.

Will I meet with another doctoral student next year, during the final year of my contract? Not likely. Will the poor woman of this semester past present herself to me once again? Perhaps. "I'll tell her that you will be waiting for her next year," the director chuckled, in his best avuncular manner. But I won't be waiting. If she really wants to try again, I'll insist on the prerequisite of a conversation first. We might be able to discuss the weather. We won't be able to discuss American studies. Unless I refuse to care about whether or not she and I communicate about something more than the chances of rain tomorrow. Granted, there's already a logic in place by which I could, or even should, refuse to care. And it can't be denied that there's a certain wonderment to be had in actually teaching for an entire year in English a student who doesn't speak English. In college, it happens all the time in first year courses (especially with junior college students). Nothing special there. But on the doctoral level! This would be a rare distinction, even for a Japanese university.

All that would be necessary, in fact, would be to say nothing about it. "It is socially acceptable in Japan," Van Wolferen explains, "for 'reality' to consist not so much of the results of objective observation as of an emotionally constructed picture in which things are portrayed the way they are supposed to be."[5] He has not directly invoked another polarity underlying the whole Japanese way of life, that between *tataeme*, or the official position, the way something is supposed to be, and *honne*, the unofficial circumstance, the way something actually is. But the truth of Van Wolferen's words depends upon this distinction. A translation into English only misleads, though, because "supposed to be" conveys little of the sense of encouraging people to do or believe their best, whereas "actually is" neglects the pejorative connotation, of something revealed that shouldn't be - at least in certain contexts. In addition, *tataeme* partakes of the world of groups, whereas *honne* is more or less strictly personal.

Kerr uses this idiom to make a no-nonsense claim: "Japanese universities are one giant *tatemae*_erected to the idea of advanced education."[6] (He especially lambastes graduate schools, whose funding is poor, research accomplishments few, and even physical plants dilapidated.) Yet finally, it seems to me, such a conclusion is too easy. I don't dispute it. My own experience gives me no basis for disputing it. But my own experience in Japan now includes Japanese terms, through which my experience should acquire a larger social setting, to which I should be responsible. Moreover, in Japanese terms my experience is never more wholly mine - in the most private, unfortunate and unrewarding sense - than when it disdains the social world in which everything, including one institution's doctoral programme, has its meaning. Granted, some *tatemae* is better than others. Some is more necessary than others. But the fact of *tatemae* can no more be dismissed than the social and ethical work of value itself, without which no society can function.

If an actual Japanese university wants to establish a doctoral programme for itself that has very little basis in fact, so what? To Japanese, the basis of the programme is not the fact, but so to speak its aspiration to the fact, which includes an understanding - and solicits an agreement - that "mere" factuality accomplishes very little, at least at the outset. We must trust that the programme will come to manifest itself, in time. Meanwhile, best to speak of it in ideal terms. And there is a final thing: even if these terms can't be realized - from some point of view outside them - they can still function as if they were. Kerr himself provides an excellent example in an earlier chapter on the Bubble economy. After discussing the way the Ministry of Finance and banks have conspired to inflate assets on paper or how the stock market has been abandoned as a forum for companies to sell equity to the public, he pauses. Why, therefore, has so little changed? Why hasn't Japan's financial system gone under?

"The paradox lies in the fact that money is to a great degree determined by society and its belief systems," explains Kerr. "If everyone agrees that Japan's failed banks are still functioning, then they function. If everyone agrees that unrealistic land and stock values are acceptable, then this is indeed so."[7] The same with the educational system. If everyone agrees that Japan's universities are still functioning, then they function. Some might term them third-rate. But such a judgment plays no significant part in the belief system out of which these universities emerge, and into which they release graduates. Furthermore, if everyone agrees that Mukogawa's doctoral programme is acceptable, then it indeed is - and there's the end of the matter. Foreigners be damned. The purpose of such a programme is to produce PhD's for Japan, not for anybody else.

Elsewhere, Kerr returns to the question of money. What is its nature? Does it have invariant laws, apart from politics or culture? It seems there are laws, even if their effects, insofar as Japan is concerned, "will not necessarily show themselves as classical theorists would predict."[8] Thus, the inflated equations of a bank in Tokyo may show up in a reduced equation for a pension fund in Osaka - not to mention a plan to cement over a stretch of seashore in Hokkaido. Just so, if Japan is willing to maintain a "stratospheric" national debt in order to forestall economic collapse, we can say that the nation is willing to maintain an enormous educational debt in order to forestall intellectual collapse. Effects might be felt in a classroom somewhere in Iwate or a research agenda established in Tokyo. But if the system works for Japan, it works, period.

The only trouble is, well, me. Not me personally - barren of *tatamae*, filthy with *honne* as I am. Instead, "me" as the site of the way a discipline cannot avoid some intersection with the outside, where the intricate belief system in which it's embedded inside Japan immediately ceases to be intelligible. This may be true - although not equally true - of every intellectual discipline. It's sadly true of English especially. Notwithstanding the similarities between finances and educational procedures, there is one enormous difference insofar as the discipline of English is concerned: the money is minted abroad, and retains its value on the world market because it's minted abroad. Therefore, even when a nation reprocesses and manufactures English as its own currency with as much care and elaboration as Japan does, it still must suffer the suspicion of having produced something counterfeit. *Tatamae* be damned.

Is this why the brightest or most ambitious students of English in Japan continue to pursue graduate study abroad? (So at least I've observed.)

How can the Ministry of Education, or the Council of Universities, or even their own universities prevent them? It can do something worse, though: it can mock them. For all I know, many of the doctoral programmes in English at Japanese universities are good ones. But few are going to perceive them as equal to any in England or the United States. However, if doctoral programmes in English such a Mukogawa's proliferate during the next decade in Japan, as there is ever reason to believe, bad programmes will drive out good programmes - perhaps even ones where the language is minted - as inexorably as bad money drives out good. If this fails to happen, then, contra Kerr, there really are no laws about money and, contra my experience, it will become possible to write a dissertation in Japanese on Middle English phonetics in the novels of John Steinbeck.

For better or worse, whatever my own final year brings, it won't be the opportunity to direct this particular dissertation. I do expect, however, to direct the MA thesis of the best student - pretty good by any standards - in the programme, while continuing to enjoy the isolate blessings (so inconceivable to my Japanese colleagues) of not having to attend department meetings. I'm not running out of subjects to write about, but perhaps I'm running out of books to read about Japan. How much can you seek to know about a nation, especially as a function of what you can't live, or live out, there? Already there are days when I daydream about convening an impossible meeting of selected administrators, and my director. Not his unbearable minion, although, what the hell, we can include his old British colleague, whom I've still never met.

Set down that Middle English lexicon, I imagine myself saying to all assembled. Time to go forward! Let's see if we can even circumvent the Ministry of Education. We must boldly leap from, say, 1961 to 2001! The brave new world before us - I would continue - lies on the Internet. Everyone agrees! If we want to get our new doctoral programme its deserving market share, we have to go online. We need to consider what we can offer in doctoral education that no one else in Japan has had the vision to conceive. No more nonsense about *tataemae*. We must "try our best" (how the Japanese love this cliché!) to be pragmatic. In plain old American English, let's go for it. (If only the words had the same snappy force in Japanese.) We must all work together to find a way to download a doctorate.

Notes

1. Karel van Wolferen, *The Enigma of Japanese Power* (New York, Vintage: 1990), 169.
2. Ivan Hall, *Cartels of the Mind: Japan's Closed Intellectual Shop* (New York, W.W. Norton: 1998), 93-94.
3. Van Wolferen, p. 110.
4. Mark Curry, *Postmodern Narrative Theory* (New York, St. Martin's Press: 1998), 29.
5. Van Wolferen. p. 8.
6. Alex Kerr, *Dogs and Demons: Tales from the Dark Side of Japan* (New York, Hill and Wang: 2001), 302.
7 Ibid, p. 95.
8 Ibid, p. 279.

Bibliography

Currie, Mark. *Postmodern Narrative Theory*. New York, St. Martin's Press: 1998.

De Mente, Boyle Lafayette. *Behind the Japanese Bow*. New York, Passport Books: 1995.

Hall, Ivan. *Cartels of the Mind: Japan's Closed Intellectual Shop*. New York, W.W. Norton: 1998.

Kerr, Alex. *Dogs and Demons: Tales from the Dark Side of Japan*. New York, Hill and Wang: 2001.

Kristoff, Nicholas and Sheryl WuDunn. *Thunder from the East: Portrait of a Rising Asia*. New York, Knopf: 2000.

Smith, Patrick. *Japan: A Reinterpretation*. New York, Random House: 1997.

Van Wolferen, Karel. *The Enigma of Japanese Power*. New York, Vintage: 1990.

Deprofessionalizing

James Kirwan

The author reflects on the course of his working life over the past fifteen years, how it has taken a very different direction to the one he had originally envisaged, and the way in which his image of the academic life has changed since the time when he became a postgraduate.

Academia; Publishing; Career

This will be a short contribution, and a personal one. The task that the editors have set - to recount and reflect on my experience as one whose "scholarly achievement has not translated into institutional success" - renders it necessarily short and personal, as I have few reflections to offer. Over the years I have, quite deliberately, avoided theorizing on the reasons for the direction my career has taken, and, indeed, one of my incentives in becoming involved in this project is to see what more detached observers than myself might make of that direction. Moreover I do not know how common my story may be: I have no basis for theorizing. But, to the story.

I received my PhD from Edinburgh University in 1989, at the age of 28. At that time my first book, a version of my thesis, was already in press at Routledge. I have been told since that this constituted some kind of achievement but at the time I was not aware that it could be seen that way, and, bless my innocence, as the failed job applications rose into the scores I began to think that a mere single book must be far below the average output of the average postgraduate. I confess that I did not get out much.

I had devoted my whole time at university to research and writing - to the extent of completing a second book on an entirely different subject from my thesis even before the first book came out. At an early stage in my university life I had noticed that sitting around talking about research and doing research were mutually exclusive activities. For a variety of reasons I had chosen the latter course. My erudition was unusually broad; my ignorance of academia was boundless.

Between 1987 or 1988 and 1990 I applied for more than a hundred jobs, without ever getting an interview; except once, for a job in Hong Kong that had changed from a literature to a linguistics post by the time the interview was held. My only contact with most of the institutions I applied to were the cards acknowledging receipt of my application material. Only one university - in Denmark - contacted me after the rejection to explain that, while my application had been strong, it appeared that my present research was not principally orientated towards literature. This was fair comment; by 1990 I had already been trying to get my second book (*Beauty*) published for over a year. I toted the idea of this book for a couple more years, accumulating letters from editors saying that while they themselves would be interested in reading such a book there was no market for one. When I had come to the end of my list of likely publishers, I put the typescript away in a drawer.

Any sensible person would have given up the idea of an academic career by this point. In fact I had tried to give up much earlier. I had drifted on into postgraduate research in literary theory through a love of ideas and arguments but had found myself in a discipline obsessed with names and slogans. My years of independence since have done nothing to instil in me that collegiate spirit of tolerance that can laud old ideas as breakthroughs, trivia as important contributions, and second-hand sketches as erudition, that can pretend it does not see when a very little gold, or tin, has been hammered to a great extent. But even before my thesis was submitted I was already largely disillusioned by the deadening triviality (demanded by professionalism) of the whole academic enterprise. In fact the CV I am using to check my dates is the first draft of one I sent to the supermarket chain Tesco. They, like the other companies I wrote to around 1989-1990, found me overqualified.

Then, one day, standing at a job notice-board in a corridor in Edinburgh University, I met someone who knew someone who knew someone who was looking for a teacher to recommend to a college in Japan. A few months later I started work in the college. I had sometimes been counselled by other postgraduates and on one occasion by an academic (my landlord) to devote less time to research and more time to networking. To which I had priggishly (and prophetically) replied that if that was what it took to succeed then I would rather fail. I had, however, two consolations regarding the way I had finally obtained a post: firstly, I told myself it was not really favouritism if the people involved did not know you, and, secondly, the alternative appeared to be social security.

I threw myself wholeheartedly into my first job. So wholeheartedly that at the end of four years I realized I had done nothing in that time - "holidays" included - except prepare and teach. I had contributed five papers to the college journal because I had been asked to do so, but all were excerpts from either the work on beauty, or others - on hermeneutics and on Kant - that I had written before leaving Britain.

I returned home in 1994 and stayed there a year applying for jobs in Britain and Europe. It proved to be simply a repetition of my previous job-hunting experience: few replies and no interviews. When an ex-colleague wrote to me of a tenured post in Japan I applied and was accepted. (By this time, I had no qualms about getting a job through contacts.) It is at this point, anxious to be closer to my now widowed mother, that I must have started to think about "professionalizing" myself, for I see I published several papers, contributed a couple of chapters to books, gave papers at seven international conferences, and wrote half a dozen reviews between 1995 and 2002 (a period that also covers the birth of my two children). The "turn to beauty" of the mid nineties benefited me to the extent that when I decided to try again with my *Beauty* in 1997 it was picked up by the first company I wrote to - Manchester University Press - and published in 1999: ten years after I had written it. The work on Kant that I had begun before leaving Britain the first time was published by Continuum in 2004, and a book on sublimity I started in 2001 was published by Routledge in 2005.

This productivity was largely the result of the nature of the new job. Though I had been told that I would be teaching practical English - conversation, composition, and practical reading - for the first year only, and after that literature and culture, nine years later I was still teaching exclusively practical subjects. ("It's a buyers' market," said the president on the day I signed the contract.) Some of my foreign colleagues were resentful of this, and of the fact that even after nine years we were still teaching more courses than newly hired Japanese faculty members, but I found myself quite content with the situation - once I had worked out a way to teach practical English: a subject of which I knew nothing. I felt badly for foreign colleagues who wanted to teach their own subjects, and for my students, who deserved better than an amateur English teacher, but the ease of class preparation left me ample time for writing. Nevertheless, throughout the period I continued to apply for jobs in, or at least close to, Britain, without result. In 2004, I changed to another university in Japan (this time without the aid of contacts) for the sake of a better salary; the cost of transporting a family of four from Japan to Britain annually in order to visit my mother being too much for the salary I had. My mother died two days after the new job began.

*

So here I am. I feel I have been very lucky in a sense. I have tenure, and a good salary. The university has the kind of library facilities and research grants I could have only dreamed of for the last nine years. Nominally I am no longer teaching exclusively practical subjects, though such is the language level of the students, and their endemic lack of motivation, that it is, practically, still a matter of teaching English. But I am content with that. While I have greatly enjoyed giving conference papers, I find the idea of regularly standing up before young adults on the pretext that one is more knowledgeable or, in some way, quicker-witted than they are about anything that really matters, rather dubious.

And "the profession"? I find it difficult to see myself as engaged in anything that resembles a profession. I teach for the university that pays me, and, if I write again, I will write only about what interests me. My acknowledgements pages have been, and will probably remain, empty of the names of colleagues and grant-awarding bodies. My attempts to professionalize myself are at an end now that there is no longer a pressing practical reason, and this piece is the last thing I intend to write to a deadline. The unfinished books on exoticism, taste, erotica and pornography, and hermeneutics, will remain unfinished at least until my children are older: as a mere hobby, writing books is, for the moment, too time-consuming.

I would certainly have written the first two books at a more leisurely pace if I had been able to foresee that their completion was not going to make any difference to whether or not I got a job. I regret now that I spent so much time upon them. I do not mean that I wish I had spent the time professionalizing myself - networking, writing what I knew could be published rather than what I thought worth writing about, adding those precious millimetres to the CV. If I had been fully convinced from the beginning that this was what was required I would never have attempted, as I did, to get into such a profession. Who would? For what? No, it is the summer days spent in libraries that I regret. And if, academic as you probably are, you are tempted to admire the feat of completing two publishable books before the age of 30, just think how you spent your summer days in your late twenties. Something was lost.

*

And the course my working life has taken? Certainly it is not what I had in mind when I became a postgraduate. But I have never felt that the world owed me a living for doing what I wanted to do. After the first two years of looking for a job I felt that my PhD was about as useful as a certificate in lamp lighting, but I could not claim that anyone had twisted my arm to undertake it. At the outset, of course, I had thought that scholarly achievement was sufficient, and I consistently mistook the realism of those around me for cynicism. Perhaps I should, by rights, have got the kind of job I was then seeking - in recent years I have met several English-speaking colleagues who want to know why I do not work in Britain or America. Perhaps they are right, and there is something amiss. Since I never had an interview, at least I have the consolation of knowing that, if there was any injustice involved, it was purely impersonal. When, towards the end of the century, I got around to comparing my own record (and work) with those of others who held the kind of jobs I once wanted, the mystery seemed only to deepen. Perhaps I was spectacularly unlucky; fell through every crack that was going. Perhaps, after all, the race is not to the strong; it would hardly be a novel discovery. Frankly, it does not matter now.

And to my fellow gypsy scholars? Well, I am not sure I can claim to be a gypsy. I am where I belong. I am at home (with a typhoon roaring outside my window). However, to those who feel themselves to be in some kind of predicament I offer two observations. If you really are a scholar, then being a gypsy one probably has more advantages than disadvantages. (I am not overlooking the purely practical problems, like getting hold of secondary literature.) If, on the other hand, you are not really a scholar but simply someone enamoured of "the profession," then I can only recommend that you find something worthier to love.

Education in Taiwan and its International Perspective: Cultural Mimicry's Synecdochic Fallacies

Christopher J. O'Brien

This paper examines cultural mimicry as it appears in Taiwan's educational system and its roots in unsuccessful imitations of Western school systems in China. Chinese administrators committed a type of error which can be termed a *synecdochic fallacy*. In this kind of mistake, gaps in understanding are filled in by unconscious stereotypes about the group being copied, or else by commonsense notions drawn from one's own culture. When any element of the preconceived image appears to match up with the original, the entire image is often wrongly supposed to have been verified: a secondary error which the author calls a *misconfirmed assumption*. Both of these types of errors are typical of the Taiwanese educational system of today.

Taiwan's native English-speaking teachers, though often holding full-time positions, are literally adjunct: auxiliary and subordinate to the local teaching staff, largely because of faulty assumptions of the two types described above. Educators in such positions are urged to help teach students to overcome mental inertia, avoiding such errors and trying to perceive the Other more clearly, in hopes of eventually correcting many of the fallacy-based problems with imitative educational systems, leading their countries towards fuller mutual understanding between Easterners and Westerners.

Cultural Mimicry; Stereotype; Taiwanese Education; EFL; International Relations; Racism

Close to a decade ago, I felt like a pretty popular fellow. No fewer than seven schools were vying for my affection, and I sat down at my desk in Changhua, Taiwan to sort the offers out. This group of suitors represented about 70% of the schools to which I had sent my résumé, with a debonair mug shot affixed to it, as is customary here, and cover letter, following a brief search on the Internet with the keywords "Taiwan foreign teacher hiring." Most of my respondents sent me a packet with brochures, job application forms, and a brief, personal note asking how soon I could start teaching. A couple even sent me class schedules for the subjects I would teach. I suppose I had a charismatic CV.

I consider intellectual and scholarly earnestness to be highly important, so my first goal was to determine which of these schools seemed to have the highest educational ideals and standards, in order to determine which job offer to accept. I put the salary information aside at first, and examined the pamphlets. What struck me, here as on the various homepages I had seen, was the almost obsessive demand to be seen as "a technical college with an international perspective," or as "the local university with the global outlook," or any of several equivalent, self-serving clichés.

As a reader who has always been fascinated by word roots, and a PhD student who had been learning about the critical movement of deconstruction, I decided to set the words "international perspective" at war with their meanings . . . just to see who won. I inferred, from other information in the promotional materials I'd been sent, that the phrase had a "buzzy," generalized connotation, intended to suggest that the schools in question were modern, trendy, sophisticated, culturally eclectic, and, in short, prepared to get up and boogie to the world beat. It was also probably meant to contrast with the same traditional, conservative, Sino-centric attitude that prompted Mother China to name herself "the Middle Kingdom." However, the choice of the word "perspective" seems in my mind to indicate both a lofty vantage point, and a significant distance between the viewer (the college) and what the college sees. Therefore, the literal meaning of "international perspective" was either that the college is located in Taiwan, but is aware only of events happening abroad; or else the faculty members all look at the college with the critical, muddled gaze of a foreigner.

These significations are unintended, surely, but there is some truth in them. As a statement of a college's expertise with foreign languages and culture, I can assure you that an "international perspective" is little more than hype, in the main. Later experience working for several such schools reinforced the idea that they were not so much modern or sophisticated as imitative of schools that their administrators consider to be so, such as those in the United States. So, in a sense, these schools do have some kind of international perspective, because they are looking at Western schools from a distance, and trying to mimic them - while failing to perceive or evaluate both the results of this mimicry at their own institutions, and the reasons why the Occidentals behave as they do. The problem is that this distance interposes a haze of fancy and misinformation in between the two cultural hemispheres, impeding cultural exchange and understanding, which balks both the Taiwanese colleges and myself. I have crossed the dividing gulf and eschewed the limitations of an international perspective in favour of a first-hand view, and now hope to see through and deconstruct that miasma of stereotypes and unfounded assumptions. I have dubbed the tendency to act on incomplete or erroneous data, mistaking it for complete and accurate information, the *synecdochic fallacy*.[1]

Synecdoche, normally, is a technique used by authors and poets as part of their craft: it is the kind of metaphor in which a part is named, but the whole body is signified; or the larger group is named, but only one part of the group is really meant. The kind of synecdoche that I am examining here has a slightly different character from that employed in English literature. It is usually employed unconsciously, producing confusion, and leading to miscommunication and error. When it is noticed at all, people disdainfully say, "she has leapt to conclusions," as if they never do such things; in fact, synecdochic fallacies are well nigh universal. A typical example occurs when a former Taiwanese exchange student boasts, "I'm familiar with the school system in America," but in truth has only briefly observed a small section of a single school, and then presumed the whole system to be just the same.[2] In the present case, the part that has been perceived of education or culture - either genuine or fictionalized - is not merely taken, but actually *mis*taken as being representative of the entire educational system, or for the culture in which the system is situated.

Cultural and educational mimicry between the East and the West, marred as it is by misunderstandings, is symptomatic of a larger pattern of cultural and social interaction. I believe that this pattern - in which an incomplete transmission of information is mistaken for the entire message - is just the bugbear that makes real, deep communication between any two beings so hard to achieve. Regrettably, such errors are inevitable when two formerly unacquainted groups first meet each other. This is the nature of the present relationship between the educational system in Taiwan and its counterparts in the Western world, particularly the United States.

I will return to my crowded desktop of 1997 now, to see what other fallacies may be found. At first, I concluded from my favourable rate of acceptance letters that Taiwan was a superb place for expatriate teachers to come for work: seven job offers came of my first batch of résumés, five of them for full-time lecturer positions! Five full-time *college-level* education careers, with suitable salaries, in the offing, when I had despaired of finding even one in the USA, and I had only hoped for a middle school position teaching general music and chorus. At this point, readers might wonder how I can even claim to be an adjunct teacher, one of the world's educational proletariat, since my ship had came in so grandly. Well, do not make assumptions based on these external factors yet; wait until you see the details in better focus. When my ship came in, I discovered that it was little more than a dinghy.

Since I moved from my family's home in Virginia to Taiwan, almost nine years ago, I have lived here as a foreign English teacher. Expatriate educators like me get full-time teaching jobs here quite often; in fact, few university departments of foreign languages, English-centred kindergartens, or supplementary schools are without any foreign teachers. Like our part-time counterparts in America and elsewhere, we full-time foreign teachers have certain disadvantages, when compared with the main body of local teachers. The phrase "adjunct teacher" is typically used to refer to part-time educators, I know, but though plenty of expatriate teachers are hired full time, I still feel that we are adjunct in a more literal way: we are at once auxiliary, and also subordinate to, the local teaching staff. Faculty lists at Taiwanese departments of applied foreign languages are typically composed of the names of local teachers,[3] with a couple of genuinely foreign language users tacked onto the bottom. Like literary or human appendices, we can be removed without danger to the body, and furthermore, we can be replaced more readily.

Compare an expatriate teacher's qualifications to win a teaching job at a Taiwanese college to those of the locals. Though there are minimal qualifications, schools are much less picky about us than they are about their local staff, and are often unconcerned about our actual educational or working background. Newly-hired local English teachers at the college level now need a PhD (though a few years ago an MA or MS was sufficient), and many departments either require, or strongly prefer, a TESOL or English degree. In contrast, I know of no foreign teachers whose training specialized in teaching or working with English in America, and few who have earned any kind of education degree . . . but I personally know a juris doctor, a biologist, an accountant, and a computer programmer who are currently training Taiwanese youths in the use of past participles and the way to pronounce the letter L. Also, one music teacher: myself. It makes one suspect that schools only sought to add me to their staff in order to display my face upon the departmental flag: the flagstaff around which new student recruits may rally.

Though some foreign teachers do get full-time positions with salary and benefits, compare how we and Taiwanese educators are used. We similarly provide nearly all students with the English training that is universally required of undergrads, and we know that it is our lasting impression that students will take with them; hence, we too must make an effort to be pleasant. But ours are also the faces that will make an impression on thousands of total strangers, since our faces have more marketability. In some extreme cases, for example at English supplemental schools - the omnipresent so-called "cram schools" - our faces can nearly become company logos, appearing on all corporate billboards and posters.

The part-timers at Western schools were chosen for their credentials or abilities; we were chosen mostly for our genes. As I came to understand this truth, I realized that, to the chairpersons of the Departments of Applied Foreign Languages, all my reference letters, official transcripts, descriptions of past teaching jobs, and cover letters were as nothing compared to the little two-square-inch photo of my face; and all those job offers were due mostly to its presence on the front of my application.

It becomes more and more evident that the main motivation to hire foreigners is a financial one, not primarily involved with didactic ideals. When I was working as a kindergarten teacher about six years ago, my all-English language school was recruiting foreign teachers. Like most such schools, it advertises itself as an "American English" school, though I was the only American connected with the school during my year and a half there. One morning, two candidates came in. One, a white man who spoke English fairly well, but as a second language, spoke with a strongly non-American accent. The other was what we call an "ABC," an American-Born Chinese man whose parents were both from Taiwan, but who grew up in the States. To look at him, one would suppose that he was Chinese, but his English was perfect, and he also turned out to be fluent in Mandarin and Taiwanese. The school president's decision was outrageous, but quite predictable: he chose the first gentleman, who had graduated with a degree in mechanical engineering at a non-English speaking university, and rejected the American, an education specialist whose major had been TESOL (Teaching English to Speakers of Other Languages). This is typical of the hiring decisions that happen each school year on this island: the choice was made according to the most relevant qualifications for the school's priorities, which are clearly not related to education. Perhaps the school owner had misheard the quote from the battle of Bunker Hill, and thought it said, "Don't hire until you see the Whites. . .and their ties."

Of course, for those certain foreigners who, though they hold master's degrees, came over to Taiwan mostly to land a soft job, and have little interest in teaching, this tendency is a lucky break. They sometimes get to appear on TV or on a promotional DVD, earn a decent salary, and teach for approximately half of the number of hours that are considered "full-time" office work in the West. And since their classes are largely skills classes instead of content classes, their educational and professional background hardly matters at all, because theoretically any educated native speaker can understand spoken English, speak it, read it, and write it reasonably well. Many such people have even been told, often on an Internet homepage, that they can "get rich quick," but they are quickly undeceived - and any experienced educator would be likely to laugh at their supposition that any teaching job could be considered easy.

For many of us, it is our first experience as an ethnic Other at large in an alien society. For those who take pride in being educators, and take the study of English seriously, this kind of superficial treatment feels just like racial discrimination - despite the fact that we are favoured, and not rejected, for racial reasons. For some of us, this fact is not made less denigrating by the salary or insurance benefits we receive. Oddly enough, Caucasians like me find themselves hired as "token Whites," accepted not for personal merits, but primarily to obey laws. These are not equal opportunity laws, however, as our counterparts representing ethnic minorities in the States sometimes encounter, but laws of supply and demand. Many of us feel sullied by such a job when we turn our minds to the situation, for we are not valued much for our hard work, our arduous training, or our skill at imparting knowledge to thirsty young minds. We are only selected for one of the few attributes about which we can feel no sense of accomplishment - the colour of our skin.

I would like to think that I was hired because, despite my Taiwanese colleagues' extensive and specific training in teaching English, my familiarity with my native language goes deeper than a second-language user's could hope to go. But if that were a recognized and valued truth, then these core "skills" courses would be the sole dominion of the expatriates.[4] Such is not the case. In fact, few of the courses we teach differ from those of our co-workers in terms of course titles or levels at all. Also, if that were true, the schools would hire more of us - after all, we are no more expensive to hire, nor, lately, any harder to recruit. We must conclude that it was not because of our teaching or linguistic prowess that we were hired so eagerly by the schools.

I suspect that another major unofficial motivation to hire us is that the departments of foreign languages need someone to proofread their official correspondence, notices, English-language publications, and web pages - preferably for free, on the basis of us doing them a friendly favour. Our function is that of ghost writers - the ones with the skill, who get no credit, but do most of the work.[5] The revisions their papers need are seldom the "quick double-checks" that the writers suggest. This is the sort of "favour" that can take days of editing and guessing the intended meaning of sentences. Major rewording is usually sorely needed, though the work can be entertaining enough when taken on with a sense of humorous distance, as the attempt to match Chinese grammar to English words is often pathetically comical. Though this proofreading "service" is not done for direct gain, it is intended to deceive foreign strangers who have not otherwise formed any impression of the writer: to make the local writer appear to be fluent in English. The eventual goal is still to receive some benefit from the writing, without having earned it, nor having even purchased the right to it. It is misleading advertising for a product which earns a profit, but from which we receive none.

One wonders what secrets these presidents and professors might be betraying by requesting this editorial service. After all, the president of a school declaring its "international perspective" is boasting that he has the necessary skills to lead his university into encounters with foreigners. A professor of English is *professing* that she has a command of the English language, and is a *master* of the language - right?

But when they ask me to rewrite their attempts at English composition, they hint that my role in the composition must be kept "hush-hush." The idea is: don't let me be revealed as a sham (just one letter removed from "shame"). They expect the readers of these finished drafts to collude in a synecdochic fallacy; namely, that the undersigned has flawless English ability, and that the article is proof of it. Just like a stolen passport, or the diplomas that are *purchased*, not earned, at the first college where I worked, the paper actually proves something else entirely, but only to someone who is in the know. What such ghost-writing boils down to is intellectual abuse, a sort of identity fraud, and plagiarism - although we are participants in our own degradation.

The temptation to betray this insolent form of trust is present at each new request for a proofreading "favour," and it grows each time. So far, I have withstood the temptation for two or three reasons; I cannot tell which of them is strongest. First, I know that my guilty conscience would bother me too much afterwards, if I intentionally left broken English in an "as is" condition, or worse, if I inserted some blatantly offensive message into my colleague's article - even if it were a statement of truth, such as "I graduated with a PhD in English teaching, *despite my abysmal level of ability in that language.*" Second, I am not in a position to laugh it off if I were discovered and fired from my job - or, my paranoia suggests, if I were forcibly put off the island.[6] And third, I would be *so* disappointed if nobody noticed.

Perhaps, these educators pass their drafts on to me just to gain "face," that Asian concept which has infected the West in recent centuries; the term itself, like the French *façade*, emphasizes the superficial nature of the idea: "I want to gain face with these people: let me borrow yours." Though nominally we are hired to teach, we actually serve as our schools' attractive packaging, window dressing, or advertising. Indeed, I have twice been videotaped - and then exploited by my school for publicity purposes. Television viewers see my image just long enough to get the only message they are meant to: "Our school has Western teachers." And, one is meant to infer, "learning from white teachers assures that, if your son or daughter attends this university, he or she will surely learn to speak just like a native speaker of English." When students arrive, however, they discover that the foreigners are actually very few indeed - my current school has exactly two teaching my language. This is an example of what some call "bait and switch" in advertising: a kind of metaphor uttered with malice aforethought.

Another implication that television viewers might form based on these commercials is that faculty members teach with the excellence of professors at American schools, such as the world-famous Ivy League universities in New England. Indeed, Western educational systems have stellar reputations in the East, if the history of Chinese education is any indication, for after East met West, the traditional ways of schooling changed rapidly and profoundly - surprisingly enough for a country that had considered itself the centre of the world for millennia.

Centuries before the empire's general populace had formed any particular opinions about the West, China's had established traditional schools that were quite unlike those in place today. Sometimes known as Confucian schools, they had been connected with the imperial government since the Tang dynasty (618-907 AD), and their primary function was to train male students for a stratified series of governmental placement exams.[7] The curriculum was based on the Classical canons and their teachings about human relationships, and geared to prepare pupils for becoming benevolent governmental bureaucrats; those who did not progress to the higher-level exams were considered qualified teachers instead.[8]

This was the system that was predominant in China when the "closed door" policy came to an end following China's 1842 defeat in the Anglo-Chinese War. Though some Chinese were aware of the outside world (the peasants were probably not among them), the imperial government intentionally and pointedly ignored it as much as it could afford.[9] After losing this war to the British, many countries started to take advantage of China's military helplessness to arrange exploitative trading agreements.[10] The Chinese realized that isolationism had to end, in order to compete with the rest of the world. Schools began to teach about Western industrialism, weaponry, and languages.[11] In 1895, another humiliating defeat by Japan, as both nations had been fighting over Korea, led to the conclusion that, according to Chinese professor of education Lu-Dzai Djung, "the educational system should be fundamentally changed. Japan was strong because of her adoption of Western education."[12]

Djung, writing in 1934, was probably reflecting his country's feelings of self-consciousness, obsolescence, and inadequacy when he stated that after the 1900 Boxer rebellion, the schools "in the capital cities of the provinces [were] turned into *modern* universities or colleges."[13] In 1932, echoing the same underlying devaluation of China, Becker et al. suggest - in the midst of asserting the nobility of China's heritage - that "China has only to adopt the scientific and technical equipment of [Western countries] . . . to attain a standard of culture as high as that of America or Europe."[14] Both writers' statements betray their mental equation of the West with modernity and high culture, and China with old-fashioned, more primitive culture.

More objectively, the writers of 1932 provide a useful, though rather blunt comparison: "Until the Renaissance, the European conception of teaching remained what, in China, it still was thirty years ago [in 1902]: dominated exclusively by preoccupations of a social and religious nature. . .[and] founded on knowledge of texts. . . ."[15] This observation underlines the prolonged period of educational stagnancy on one hand, and the new, startling tumult of imitative reforms on the other.

After that, to summarize, the history of Chinese education (following its story from the Manchu Dynasty, its downfall in 1911, to the peregrinations of the Republic of China, which governmental body has been residing on the island of Taiwan since 1949) has been a shifting pattern of several kinds of cultural mimicry. The most important influences were Western. Japan was the first of these models, as suggested above. Prominent in its approach were its imitations of Western education, with its concentration on science and its democratic innovation of teaching all youngsters, instead of only children of the rich or powerful; China admired the system, initially, because in their opinion, the Japanese had successfully adapted the Western model to Asian citizens. Then, the gist of what they had perceived of the American model was copied directly, starting with 1922 legislation that duplicated the pattern of elementary, junior and senior high school, college, and postgraduate schools, and the collegiate credits system.[16] There have been other shifts since then, but the American model is clearly still dominant; however, nationalist strains recur from time to time, and even outside of school, many of the old ways linger on.

A contemporary photograph included in *The Reorganisation of Education in China* suggests a dual track of mimicry that is still being followed today. It shows students and faculty members of the primary school in Nanking, China, standing with a few foreign visitors (a detail of the photo is shown below).

Figure 1: students and faculty members of the primary school in Nanking, China, standing with a few foreign visitors (In Becker et al, *The Reorganisation of Education in China* [1932])

The styles of clothing here indicate a marked contrast in gender roles or images: the Chinese men, one sporting a fedora, are dressed in three-piece suits (known as "Western attire" in Mandarin) and the boys are dressed in pseudo-military uniforms: perhaps these are prototypes of the uniforms that are still required in Taiwan's elementary schools. The one adult woman and the little girls from school are dressed in traditional garments, the models for which were certainly designed long before the parents of any of them were born. Some may interpret this as showing that the men wish to emulate the modern Westerner, departing from their cultural roots, while the women and children have maintained a truly Chinese standard.

However, I want to propose the idea that the latter group's choice of clothes is just as imitative as the men's is. People tend to forget that, as generations pass on, much of their lore vanishes; the traditions linger on, but the real motivations behind them dissipate. The women and children in the photograph are also imitating another culture - the ghost of China Past. Their attire is less foreign to them than the Western mode, but only in degree. It is no better fitted to the needs of the present day than the clothing is to the present location. In both cases, most participants are embracing the external markings of otherness, the apparel and actions, without a fundamental conception of what brought them about. Exactly the same disparity of gendered clothing is displayed each year on television news at the time of the Chinese new year: the newscasters are probably better informed than their ancestors about the West, but no more authentic, perhaps, than their grandparents were in 1932.

In fairness, I should mention that the Western men standing with the teachers in the photo are perhaps also following an old style with no better reason than that it has become traditional. This same sort of cultural fadeout can be vividly seen in family rituals and celebrations. My mother in law, who came from Mainland China to live in Taiwan as a youth, insists that we follow certain customs, which sometimes surprise my wife as much as they do myself. Though we dare not ignore Mama's serious demands now, we will probably not follow them ourselves in thirty-five years, and indeed will likely forget about them. When I asked her why, the best justification I got was "because it's traditional."[17] This is another example of a society going on autopilot, and it is not only the East that tends to do this. Especially during holidays, Westerners tend to follow suit, engaging in age-old rituals in order to keep tradition alive, or perhaps undead.

In these synecdochic fallacies, an action is observed by outsiders - often, children - without being taught about its motivation. Imitation is encouraged, but (particularly in mystical rites) regardless of whether the action has any real efficacy, uninformed mimicry will certainly have little meaning for this later generation. For them, the ritual is mistaken as the important part, instead of the ritual's purpose.[18] When some lament that youngsters nowadays are departing from traditional ways, they are showing themselves as a species of Ayn Rand's "second-handers," but placing their sense of value in the approval of people who no longer exist.[19]

The most widespread and insidious of synecdochic fallacies is the idea of a universal "common sense" that is assumed to be shared by all humanity. This is a treasured myth: common sense is strictly cultural in most respects, with core concepts common only to a specific group, and it is learned, not inborn.[20] Imitating the actions of Occidental schools in Asia fails because the teachers' and students' basic assumptions about life are dissimilar to those of the Western models. Though they are, in the obvious external details, nearly identical, Taiwan's educational system is, inwardly, quite different from America's. Differences in heritage may explain the fundamental distinctions. Generally speaking, America's essence is the concept of freedom and independent thought, but China has long favoured an emphasis on conformity. One of the multiple reasons for this difference is overpopulation, which itself is largely due to a cultural stress on siring large numbers of children in order to have a proprietary work force for agriculture, and the insistence on having at least one boy to carry on the family name. Having too many students, and too few teachers, has led to a string of drastic departures from the Western model. When conformity is used as a means of reducing complexities in order to retain control, people's differences do not magically vanish, yet they do often dis-*appear* - meaning that the leaders who wish to save their time and effort cease to see the complexities of the situation.

In a crowning irony, this strong push to conform seems to have originated in foreign consultants' well-meant suggestions to follow the example of schooling in the United States. We know from Ruth Hayhoe that in early stages of the reorganization of education, following the fall of the Manchus and the success of Dr. Sun Yat-sen's revolution in 1911, Chinese education was an emulation of American schools, especially in the decade between 1922 and the time of Becker's report.[21] However, due to lack of funds (among other reasons), it is clear that admission to the schools was limited and arbitrary; the result was that the well-off families' youngsters were often the only ones who could afford this education.[22] Another vexation was the popularity of the "Normal" or Teachers' Colleges, which had produced more qualified teachers than the current system could easily employ, despite the reported excess of schools that had been built, due to the relatively low number of participating students.

At that time, a vast majority of Chinese were illiterate, including those in the government.[23] Part of the reason for this is that most commoners had to work to earn a living from an early age; most students were children of rich nobles. Becker and his colleagues condemn the wastefully low teacher-to-student ratio, as well as the numerous schools in which the government had installed expensive libraries and scientific labs, regardless of their superfluity.[24] They recommend that the school system be made more democratic, so that all Chinese youngsters, or nearly all, may attend school;[25] - this is counsel that Djung ardently offers as well.[26] Their report states that teachers at the primary level have about 20 students in each classroom, which amounts to fewer than nine million children enrolled in all. They suggest that the number of students per classroom be raised to 50 for each teacher, which would make room for more than 22 million children altogether - much closer to the universal education goal that the Americans were already achieving.[27]

It may well be that this report, or other contemporary reports with similar conclusions, became the Republic of China's stimulus for making education compulsory and for and taking that system and its policies with them when they crossed the strait seventeen years later. Briefly, this situation led to classes with what American schools would consider too high a student to teacher ratio, which led away from student-centred education, and brought a push towards conformity and order. Student participation in class decreased, and harsher discipline was instated than the United States' laws will permit. Over-full classes further led to an obsession with standardized tests (no doubt supporting the decisions with false ideas of similarity of purpose between the new exams and the Confucian imperial exam system), in order to save wear and tear on teachers, which brought students and teachers to a consensus about the priority of rote memorization as the best way to pass these examinations. Today, elementary school classes usually have about 45-50 students, and when I arrived in 1998, they had more like 60; typical college classes still have 60 students. The outcome is that the teachers seldom understand - or even consider, it seems - the students' personal learning needs, and the students seldom understand the subjects they are tested on very deeply. Success on exams is mistaken for learning accomplishment by teachers, parents, and students alike. In common parlance, Taiwan's students might be accomplished at "book learning," but not so much at application, despite the empty claim that mine was a department of *applied* foreign languages.

In fact, even the accomplishments in data memorization are short lived. By now, it seems, they have adopted a "bulimic model" of education: they tend to purge their minds of the tested materials after the quizzes, to make room for the next batch of trivia, thus keeping their minds nice and slim. Little or no nutritious or useful information is retained by the brain. This drastic flaw in the system is so obvious that even Taiwan's Government Information Office has been obliged to comment on the situation on its website - in the English portion of it, at least.[28]   The Ministry of Education's own site emphasizes pluralism, creativity, independent thinking, and the arts, but students here have seen little evidence of these touted priorities at their own schools, as they frequently attest to me in conversation.

These three phenomena - the imitation of Western school systems, the mimicry of clothing, and the overcrowding of classrooms that led to the systematic purging of previously-regurgitated material - I see as more examples of synecdochic fallacy. In each, the mimicry in which the Chinese and Taiwanese people are engaged indicates an imitation of surface forms, of actions and procedures, without any internalized, "gut" understanding of the motivations behind the actions. They adopted American educational law but could only follow its word, since its spirit remained inaccessible. The first students who underwent this transformed style of education had no context from which they could comprehend their strange, new form of instruction. Becker et al. attest that, in the 1920s, Chinese students studying in Europe and America "brought home, unmodified, ideas of institutions and methods with which they had become familiar during their studies . . . which, in Europe and America, were intimately associated with the temperament peculiar to the several countries, nations, and peoples." [29] Yet they applied the foreign ideas anyway. Becker insists that the conditions of life that had created the American educational system, and made it so distinct from those in England and Europe, are not at all those of China of 1932.[30] These factors, among others, ensured that the graft of new life could not take hold with any remarkable success among the minds of the Chinese. Specifically, agrees Hayhoe fifty-two years later, the idea of self-motivated learning - so crucial to students in the USA - was central to school reform movements in the 1920s and '30s, but "Chinese schools had neither the material resources nor the intellectual atmosphere for the individualized learning. . . ."[31] Though Taiwan (the new home of the same government's power) speaks of reform, it is difficult to see how to implement it when East and West still lack a mutual base of understanding. The two cultures are still, to a large extent, out of communication.

At the time when my desktop had letters of acceptance jostling each other for attention, all these realizations were yet to come. After considering the various job offers, and their related paraphernalia, I contacted one of the schools and arranged for an interview. My first visit to its Department of Applied Foreign Languages exposed me to the disparity between the educational systems in the East and the West, which on the surface had hitherto appeared to be quite similar. On arrival, the first thing that tipped me off that the department was less internationally minded than its ads had suggested was the office of the department itself. Aside from the brand name on the copier (it was an "X" word) and several imported textbooks, the public area of this room sported almost no writing in English or, indeed, in any foreign language. It seemed, in many ways, to be a mockery of a "real" (that is, American) English department, where already-skilled undergraduates honed and perfected their skills. But I knew that no comedy was intended; this kind of parody was, in some participants anyway, undertaken with the best of intentions.

Teachers from the Eastern and Western educational systems might be quite mistaken in their impression that they have made real contact. Clearly, there were signs of mimicry displayed in the department of applied foreign languages that I was working for: the trappings of American colleges. Some teachers, who had actually spent time earning degrees in the States, displayed souvenirs of their schools at their desks. Others decorated their cubicles with Disney characters, posters in English, and their college textbooks - I say *decorated*, because I never saw anyone consulting these tomes. However, what convinced me that the college did not really have an international outlook was this: I was asked to work exclusively on Sundays. Though such a demand is not the best way to win a Christian's support, I considered my financial situation and decided to accept the offer.

Soon, the time for my début arrived. I had been assured, before ever arriving in Taiwan, that every one of the island's youngsters was required to study English from the first year of junior high school, through senior high school's senior year. Therefore, each of these adult students had studied English for a minimum of five years before they started to earn their associate's degrees. This was encouraging. I myself had studied Spanish for five years as part of my public education, becoming nearly fluent, so I assumed that these students were *at least* conversant in English. Well, you know what they say about what happens when you *assume*.

Please consider the following paragraphs, which describe the beginning of my first teaching day at that Institute of Technology. They form a pair of perceptions, somewhat Blakean in character, representing first what I expected, and then the pain that comes when a dreamer awakens, and is disillusioned.

Innocence
China. *The wise, middle-aged teacher steals sagely into the room. The students, who have been reviewing notes and practicing their skills, instantly fall silent as they perceive their master; they rise in unison. With a blend of respect, awe, and dread, they bow deeply and, as one, they chant: "Good Morning, Mr. O'Brien." As they take their seats, the lesson begins promptly. The learnèd professor lectures and the students take copious notes. At exam time, the brightest pupil is a source of pride and admiration for all her classmates, and the professor feels that teaching is a great honour.*

Experience
Taiwan, Republic of China. *The inexperienced, rather young American lecturer ventures into the room. He sees a female teacher standing at the podium, who turns irritably and informs him that his classroom is across the hallway; she gestures expressively. So he enters the opposite classroom. The students, wolfing down breakfast sandwiches and soybean milk and tossing their waste onto the floor, are middle-aged. They perceive their teacher and instantly, with a blend of curiosity, excitement, and ridicule, exclaim, "Whooooo!" in unison. Since they promptly*

*leave their seats to greet and examine the lecturer, there is almost
no way to begin the lesson. As the learnèd professor begins to
lecture, the students pass copious notes. At exam time, the
brightest student is the source of answers for all her classmates.
The professor, feeling most unprofessional, feels that teaching is a
great burden on him.*

Thinking back, I now realize that I made three telling errors, all
due to assumptions or stereotypes that blinded me to my real situation.
First, I identified myself with that paradigmatic Confucian schoolmaster of
the fabled past, and failed to differentiate myself from him; in my mind, I
was just a teacher, the same as he was in his time. As a former amateur
actor in school and community plays, I formed some Stanislavskian habits,
which included putting myself into the shoes of a fictional character. As it
turns out, this character, the wise, bearded mandarin, was just as fictional
as the king in *Cinderella* or Olin Britt in *The Music Man*. Second, I
mistakenly took the orderly, respectful, and studious Asian youths of
cinematic fame as reliable representatives of what I could expect all
students on this hemisphere to be like: respectful of their elders, silent, and
probably wearing a period costume, complete with hair worn in a long
queue or pigtail. Third, nostalgic and traditional as Chinese culture is in
general, modern Taiwan is still *not* identical with ancient China.

Like the eclectic trappings of the department of applied foreign
languages, my notions of education in Taiwan had been composed
piecemeal. Stories I had read, movies I had seen, anecdotes that had been
told to me by Taiwanese classmates, schoolyard jokes from elementary
school, and the like all formed a part of the presuppositions which I took
into that classroom. If my stereotyped expectations were ever lacking in
detail, I no doubt filled in the gaps by using my imagination, and
incorporating some "common sense" elements based on my own
schooldays. In the hodgepodge of mixed media, hearsay, and fantasy, my
assumptions about Taiwan's education system were entirely typical of
stereotypes in general.

In short, I unwittingly made a foray into Orientalism, but I
discovered my folly. My Taiwanese wife alerted me to the events of the
real world quite soon, successfully catching my mind's eye. Although I
had learned much, perhaps more than most Westerners ever do, about
Taiwan and Chinese culture by that time, I discovered that my
preconceptions had nearly usurped my sensory perception. In fact, if my
initial glimpse of the class had sufficiently resembled the imaginary scene
I had expected, it is likely that I would have considered my preconceptions
to have been confirmed.

This happens frequently, in fact. After the anxiety about what to expect has been overcome, many people tend to let down their guard prematurely and go into autopilot mode. Feeling reassured, they carry out their plans, become self-absorbed, and consequently stop observing their real surroundings critically. As in Poe's "The Purloined Letter," sometimes an important item is left in the open, but its external appearance is blindingly obvious in its seeming normalcy. Since it looks like what we expected to be there, it remains entirely unnoticed. I could elaborate, but perhaps it is enough to mention that I call these examples of synecdochic fallacy *misconfirmed assumptions*, and that they can lead to plenty of mischief, which is only occasionally intentional.

When we allow our behaviour to be dictated by habits and by perceptions that have been blindfolded by stereotypes and assumptions, we can tend to skim around on the surfaces of life. Having data is not enough; we must see beneath the surface and understand things of value as deeply as we can - and check more carefully to see which unnoticed things might be of such value. One of the most potentially damaging synecdochic fallacies involves bad learning habits. I see evidence of such bad habits every day. If, for example, an incompetent English teacher trained my student when she was six years old to mispronounce as common a word as "she," I can find it the work of months to help her overcome this fundamental error, because it has been rehearsed wrongly for twelve years, and internalized; the mistake is literally inaudible to her by this point. If, as youngsters, we are taught in a shallow way, this often becomes our educational paradigm: we stop expecting that school can be any more than that. Later teachers might be better, but by the time our learning habits are formed, we might not even recognize their superiority, and go about our business of learning in the usual cursory manner. This mindset can poison a student's entire learning life, often lasting beyond the school years. But if our teachers show us the truth behind the image, get us intellectually excited, and stimulate our curiosity, we might just become the self-motivated students that all teachers love to have in class - and bring up our youngsters in the same way, being their first and most influential teachers.

As a wise person once told me, one has the right, and the power, to choose whether or not to be offended by others' thoughtlessness. Certainly, if a "gypsy scholar's" main goal is only to be gainfully employed, well, he is. If it is, instead, to be respected, he should consider whose respect would be more meaningful: his employers', or his students'. If his students' respect is more important to him, he might make major progress by trying to rid students of a mindset in which synecdochic fallacies are the norm. And, if love of teaching and a desire to help students achieve their own maximum potential are paramount, then we "Gypsy scholars" teaching our native language abroad must be in the best position of all. Several colleges' worth of freshmen are our pupils, and we have the potential to help each of them free themselves from the chains of habit that force them into synecdochic fallacies every day. We are the roots of the academic tree, and from us students might just draw their nutrition for life - a life of intellectual freedom.

Notes

1. Synechdochal fallacies are surely mental habits of the human race in general, and especially characterize anyone's perceptions of the Other in any form; to assume that I am proposing such errors to be the sole domain of Asians would be to commit another such error and miss the paper's point. Witness the Americans' current interest in tae kwon do and feng shui, and their relatively superficial understanding of these things; even many Asians tend to imitate the observable actions of traditional arts without comprehension of their motivations.

2. The synecdochic fallacy, like the literary one, can also be found in the reverse order. For one example, if a teacher in Boston meets only one Taiwanese exchange student with poor speaking ability, he might suppose, from what he has heard elsewhere, that such faulty oral skill must be exceptional. Since the teacher knows that all students on Formosa study English from grade school up until senior high, he is likely to assume that what he has experienced is atypical; in this case, the assumption is wrong. Other configurations of the synecdochic fallacy are possible, but this paper focuses on how people extrapolate faulty assumptions from minimal information.

3. Taiwan is only a third of the size of my home state, Virginia, so I tend to think of anyone from the island as a local resident; I mean, here, teachers who are citizens of Taiwan.

4. One exception might be classes in grammar, which most people seldom learn much about in regards to their own languages; Taiwanese teachers have studied English grammar much more comprehensively than I have, for example, and I have to struggle to educate myself in it.

5. Long-insular China has a phrase for non-Chinese: "foreign ghosts." Thus, these scholars have unwittingly added a new twist to the term "ghost-writer."

6. This has actually happened, so my nervousness is not entirely unfounded. One of my American co-workers was forced to leave his job recently, with plausible enough excuses - though his infractions of school policies were hardly more outrageous than those of other, local, teachers. The unofficial reason had to do with his low level of achievement with several activities that the department had been counting on him for, such as maintaining the English part of the school's website. He was sought out for these projects as a volunteer; these favours were mentioned nowhere in his contract as requirements.

7. Ruth Hayhoe, ed., *Contemporary Chinese Education* (Armonk, NY: M. E. Sharpe, 1984), 29.

8. "In other words, teaching itself was, while not exactly dishonorable, an indication that the instructor had failed to move on to the real goal, that of governance." (Hayhoe, 32).

9. Lu-Dzai Djung, *A History of Democratic Education in Modern China* (Shanghai: The Commercial Press, Ltd., 1934), 2.

10.Richard Hooker, <http://www.wsu.edu:8080/~dee/CHING/OPIUM.HTM.> (October 11, 2004); Djung, p 6.

11. Djung, 2-4.

12. Ibid., 4.

13. Ibid., 6, emphasis added.

14. Becker et al, 27.

15. Ibid., 30.

16. Hayhoe, 38; Becker et al, 25.

17. The other justifications were mostly of the old-wives'-tale, superstitious sort. For example, one must not whistle during the "ghost month," for fear of attracting the attention of spirits.

18. This sort might be called "fly-on-the-wall" imitation, to borrow another literary term: the properties that can be seen, heard, or otherwise sensed are imitated, but the new generation has no access to the thoughts or feelings of its elders or ancestors. It is the old division between the body and the spirit, in a different setting.

19. Rand's characters discuss her idea of "second-handers" in *The Fountainhead*.

20. Probably, even within one family, no two members of a cultural group share all of the same basic assumptions that make up their personal common sense, due to distinctive influences throughout their lives. In effect, one might say that the things one holds as "common sense" form the core of his or her private culture.

21. Hayhoe, 38.
22. Ibid., 65-66.
23. Djung, 7.
24. Purchasing impressive technological items for the classroom is common in Taiwan's universities today; contacts at a variety of such schools report that few professors are able to operate most of them, so that they usually go unused. At my own school, no manuals are available to explain their features, and furthermore, their buttons and remote controls are marked in Chinese; even the computers in our classrooms in the department of *foreign* languages all use the *local*-language edition of the operating system.
25. Becker et al, 62-63.
26. Djung, 11
27. Becker et al, 62.
28 ."Critics of the system, as well as many students, feel that exam-takers are forced to memorize vast amounts of pedantic trivia, which are regurgitated during the exams and then forgotten. . . . [this] permeates the entire school system." (Government Information Office [Taiwan]. <http://www.gio.gov.tw/taiwan-website/5-gp/yearbook/chpt18.htm.> [September 21, 2004]).
29. Becker et al, 23.
30. Ibid., 26.
31. Hayhoe, 39.

Bibliography

Becker, C. H., M. Falski, P. Langevin, and R. H. Tawney. *The Reorganisation of Education in China*. Paris: League of Nations' Institute of Intellectual Co-operation, 1932.

Djung, Lu-Dzai. *A History of Democratic Education in Modern China*. Shanghai:The Commercial Press, Ltd., 1934.

Government Information Office (Taiwan). <http://www.gio.gov.tw/taiwan-website/5-gp/yearbook/chpt18.htm.> (September 21, 2004).

Hayhoe, Ruth, (Ed.). *Contemporary Chinese Education*. Armonk, NY: M. E. Sharpe, 1984.

Hooker, Richard. http://www.wsu.edu:8080/~dee/CHING/OPIUM.HTM. (October 11, 2004).

From Adjunct to Tenured: Both Sides Now

Judith Caesar

The essay examines several issues, all based on the writer's personal experiences, but all leading to the conclusion that the system of hiring adjuncts to teach composition courses is grossly unfair. First, the essay considers the problems facing composition teachers who teach outside the United States. Second, the essay considers how college administrators seem to view the hiring of adjuncts predominantly from an economic rather than educational perspective. Adjuncts are seldom given any training or orientation that would help them understand the needs of their students and they are seldom observed or evaluated. This, combined with the low salaries and little respect that adjuncts are paid, raises serious ethical questions about the practice of hiring adjuncts. Many adjuncts seek to become full-time, tenure-track teachers within their departments, not realizing what an extremely difficult process this can be given the internal politics of many departments. The best solution for the adjunct may be to try to qualify for full-time teaching at another university, since it seems unlikely that this exploitive situation will end in the near future.

Adjuncts; Temporary Full-Time Staff; Middle East; Hiring; Fairness; Tenure

I can only speak from my own experience, and that experience has made me very cynical. What I say is true of the universities at which I have taught. There may be thousands of universities all over the world to which my inferences do not apply, for all I know. But from what I have seen directly, I have concluded that adjuncts are hired only to save money, with no concern for the quality of the students' education, and that when adjuncts are able to make the transition to full-time faculty members, they do so much more on the basis of their interpersonal skills than on their pedagogical ones. This is true both in the US, where I often was an adjunct, and in the Middle East, where I was interviewing and hiring adjuncts. That so many adjuncts continue to teach well despite these factors is a credit to their integrity and professionalism. Would that more college administrations shared these traits.

Let me begin with some background about where I teach, to put my experiences in context. I am currently an associate professor on continuing contract at an American style university in the United Arab

Emirates, most of whose top administrators are American. Although this university is accredited in the United States and has a curriculum and faculty comparable to good state universities in the US, we have a very different student body. In the US, the majority of students speak English as their first and only language and have been through the US public school system, after all. Here, while some of our students are monolingual English speakers, most are bilingual - English and Arabic, Farsi, or one of the many languages of the Subcontinent. This makes them more culturally sophisticated than their American counterparts, but it also means that the grammatical and rhetorical structures of the language with which they are more familiar often seem more natural to them than the structures of English. While some of the students are native Emiratis, most are the children of ex-pat Arab, Iranian, Indian, and Pakistani professionals working in the Gulf, who want their children to have an American style education without sending them to fend for themselves in a foreign culture. Some students have gone to elite British or American system private schools where English was the language of instruction, the majority of the teachers were native speakers, and teachers used the most up-to-date western methods. These students speak and write English with native speaker fluency. Others went to less elite private schools where English was the language of instruction, but where the teachers were from the Middle East or the subcontinent and the emphasis was on traditional rote learning. Others went to public high school, where Arabic was the language of instruction and English was just one class among many. The minimum TOEFL score required for entry here is 500, which is somewhat lower than that required of foreign students at most American universities. However, because English is widely spoken in the UAE (it's the common language that binds the ex-pats, who outnumber locals 4 to 1) and because our students watch American movies and TV, most of them speak and understand spoken English with native fluency. Most are also quite bright.

The problem is that most also have varying degrees of trouble with written English. In any composition class that I have taught here, we have three or four students who write excellent English but need a bit of help with style and don't yet know how to write a term paper, like students in an honours freshman comp course in the US. Some are fluent but have problems with organization, critical thinking, and development, like the average American student or slightly worse. Yet many others still have problems with grammar and sentence structure, in varying degrees of severity, but they are ESL errors, different from the ones our American composition textbooks teach them how to correct. And yet these students might be able to organize and develop their ideas well, sometimes better than the more fluent students. Teaching such a mixed group of students requires inventive, sensitive, intelligent, and flexible instructors, teachers who can figure out that grammar errors don't signal poor intellectual skills, just a weaker background in English, teachers who are not just going to play ESL spoken language games with students who already speak English fluently, and teachers who can understand the several different types of first language interference that are causing the students to make the sort of grammar errors they do. How does one find such teachers? For me, the question was not merely rhetorical. For one year, I did my stint as chair of the English department and in that capacity I oversaw the hiring of adjuncts. Of course, I have also served on search committees, where we also tried to find such paragons.

However, when I was teaching in the United States, I did not have a tenured or even tenure-track position. I usually taught as a temporary full-time (TFT) assistant professor, which is somewhat better than being an adjunct because I was paid at least the minimum salary for an assistant professor and had a full-time faculty member's benefits. But I have also taught as an adjunct for $2,000 a course. I taught for three years as an adjunct while I was working on my doctorate, and later, after I had my degree and publications, when I wanted to teach in the same city as my husband. I have been a temporary full-time assistant professor at five different American universities and an adjunct at four others. (I also taught overseas, as a foreign expert in China, an assistant professor in Saudi Arabia, a Fulbright professor in Egypt, and a logistically supported scholar in Japan, but these were all systems in which foreign professors were assumed to be temporary). So I have looked at the situation of adjuncts from both sides before attaining my jaundiced views.

Looking back on the experience of being a non-tenured professor, a few things now strike me as strange. At only three of the nine different universities did anyone ever come in to the classroom to observe my teaching. Of course, most of these universities asked students to fill out evaluation forms, but it was never clear to me exactly how these evaluations figured in the administration or department's decisions to offer another contract. At some schools, they were simply given to me personally and I had no idea who else saw them, if anyone. I assumed that they were just a teaching aid, a way for teachers to understand what they might be doing wrong. (In fact, as teaching aids, they were not particularly valuable, unless I wanted to take seriously my students' advice to make sure the part in my hair was straight and throw away that ugly green blouse).

When I first started teaching, I wasn't very good at teaching freshman writing, always at least half of my job, since like many literature graduates, I had no idea how to teach composition and had to figure it out for myself by trial and error. What made teaching writing particularly difficult for me was that I had gone to a college which had no freshman writing programme (students all had high SATs), so I was teaching courses that I had never taken. I had no idea why my students had the sorts of writing problems they did, and I had never even seen before the kinds of mistakes they were making. Fortunately, since my students had learned some skills in high school and would pick up others from their reading and writing for other classes, I don't think I did too much damage even in those early years. Moreover, I was still usually offered contracts, so I figured that my good intentions and conscientiousness must have been noted. However, it seems to me a little odd now that I was never asked to submit a course syllabus to any department. And in no place that I taught did anyone ever talk to me about department policies or standards, much less about the most effective methods of teaching composition. When I first began teaching, I could certainly have used some friendly advice, I realize now, but at the time, I mistook this lack of guidance for official confidence in my abilities.

Looking at the problem as a department chair charged with hiring adjuncts has been enlightening. When I took over as chair, I was alarmed to discover that the university's policy was to schedule as many sections of freshman composition as there were students (and projected students) required to take them, regardless of the number of full-time teachers available to teach them. The dean assured me that no North American university scheduled only as many sections of classes as it had teachers. (Hello! We aren't in North America!) The remaining sections, he told me, could be made up with overloads and adjuncts. There simply wasn't enough money to hire enough full-time teachers to cover them, he said. In fairness, I'd like to add that our university, unlike most in the US, actually paid adjuncts the same amount per course as full-time instructors would earn for teaching an overload. The university saved money by not having to pay benefits that would otherwise include an education allowance for children and free housing. However, the more attractive salary didn't make it any easier to find adjuncts.

Thus, in August, I was charged with the task of finding adjuncts to cover about 30 sections of freshman composition, and I needed to find adjuncts in a hurry. The number of experienced adjuncts we can hire here is much smaller than in the US, for several reasons. Here in the UAE, universities are not allowed to issue work visas for adjuncts, since they are not full-time contract employees. Our adjuncts have to be here on a spouse's or a father's residence visa. (All of our adjuncts have been expats, since educated Emiratis are generally wealthy and well-connected enough to pick and choose, and they do not choose to be adjuncts).

Usually, the adjuncts have either been ESL teachers working full time elsewhere or they have been faculty wives who had MAs, but not MAs in English or Composition, or they have been faculty wives who had taught high school English. The problem is that teaching college level composition is not the same as language instruction, and having an M.A. in something doesn't mean that one can teach freshman comp to a mixed group of students like ours. Unfortunately, our dean didn't see the distinction, and most of the resumes came through him.

Worse, we had no system to give them any help or training, and still don't. The other composition instructors and I were too overworked ourselves to be much help, since teaching such mixed classes requires so much individual instruction, at least if the teacher is conscientious. Since adjuncts are not required to go to department meetings, they often didn't know the kinds of problems that other teachers faced and discussed. And not having taught at the college level before at what was supposed to be the equivalent of an American university, they have no way of knowing the standards that were expected of students and the kinds of work these students would be required to do in their upper level courses. (I remember trying to explain to one adjunct hired for the summer that yes, students really did need to know how to do library research and cite correctly using APA form, since their courses would require term papers and their professors would blame the English department if their students didn't know these things. He had thought all he had to do was "get them talking and participating.")

Of course, smart teachers figure out a great deal on their own, but it takes time - a semester or two, at least. But my point is that they shouldn't have to. And while they are in the process of learning, adjuncts (and new teachers of all sorts) can do more damage here than inexperienced teachers in the US, since we do have bright students who want to know exactly why something is wrong and will become exasperated if the teacher can't explain, for instance, why it is incorrect to write, "Although social life in Italy differs from life in my country, and considering me as a kid at the time, I felt comfortable and wasn't shocked or confused." Obviously, you can understand the student's meaning. It may take a moment's thought to realize that the writer has tried to add an idea in a modifying phrase when it should have been part of the subordinate clause. But someone who had never learned formal grammar (a social studies or science major, for instance) could well look at a sentence like that and just know that something was really wrong without being able to begin to explain what it was. I am also aware that since written Arabic doesn't use much subordination and one can add ideas to a sentence with "and" (*wa*) very freely, our Arab students tend to get tangled in their sentences once they go beyond the simple and compound sentences demanded by basic language competence. But this is not self-evident, and the textbooks don't explain how to deal with these kinds of mistakes. However, each teacher has to look at sentences like that, which s/he will never have seen from a native speaker, and figure out exactly why they don't work, because the good students will want to know. And of course, a sentence like this may appear, as this one did, in the midst of a relatively cogently written argument, which leaves one with the problem of how to grade the overall paper.

I don't know if other chairs are in similar positions of needing to find adjuncts and not having any time to either select them carefully or train them. I expect that in the US, universities have fewer uncovered sections scheduled and certainly they have a larger pool of experienced candidates to draw on. But the number of freshman composition sections listed as taught by "staff" rather than a professor's name on university schedules suggests that in fact, many universities rely on adjuncts or graduate students to teach basic freshman writing courses. And I would guess that it is for same reasons: it is cheaper to pay an adjunct $2,000 a course than to hire a full-time instructor at $35,000 a year. At a time of soaring college costs, I can sympathize to some degree with the motivation, but not with the results for both student and adjunct.

Because of the urgent need for someone to teach those classes, immediately, adjuncts do not go through the same screening process as full-time or tenure-track faculty, or at least they do not anywhere I have ever taught. No search committee reviews their resumes or interviews them, they are not asked to come to campus and teach sample classes or give presentations, and they are not asked to submit samples of their work to be reviewed by their colleagues. They are hired on the basis of their resumes and a brief interview with the chair. At least, I asked candidates about how they would go about teaching some of the basic elements of college writing, but I still wasn't in much of a position to be picky. I would guess that because of time constraints, few chairs even check to see if the information on the resume is true. I know I didn't have time to check, and no one suggested that I should. (It was only after the semester began that we learned that one British-educated teacher had graduate certificates rather than the graduate degrees she had claimed on her CV.) Under these circumstances, it is amazing that so many adjuncts are qualified, competent, dedicated teachers, as in fact the vast majority is. However, their colleagues don't know this and may treat them as "glorified secretaries" (not that there is any excuse for being patronizing to secretaries either).

Full-time temporary professors in the US are in a slightly different situation than adjuncts anywhere, but the professional result for them is much the same. TFTs are required to submit transcripts, letters of recommendation, and copies of publications. However, their colleagues never get to see their credentials at any college where I have taught. This puts the temporary professors in precisely the same positions as adjuncts in relation to their colleagues, that is, none of them know what her qualifications are, and some colleagues assume that the qualifications of both adjuncts and TFTs are weaker than that of full-time, tenure-track faculty. Of course, this is not necessarily true. When I was teaching as an adjunct after I had my PhD, I actually had more publications and experience than the chair of one the departments in which I taught, a fact which did not endear me to her. And after visiting the classes of our adjuncts here as department chair, I could see that many of them were excellent teachers, at least as good as their full-time colleagues. But no one else knew that, and I knew only because I decided on my own to visit the adjuncts even though there was no university policy requiring me to do so. And of course, neither I nor anyone else had any idea whether they were spending hours explaining errors and writing encouraging comments on student papers or just noting a few of the errors and slapping a "B" on them. Being an adjunct often means that no one knows how good you are, and, worse, no one seems to care.

The result is that both adjuncts and TFTs are in a kind of professional limbo. Their colleagues don't know whether or not they are competent and qualified, and while some kind and professional colleagues will make a point to get to know adjuncts and temporaries, others will view them as inferiors, and this attitude may to be conveyed to the secretarial staff and even the students. I had adjuncts come to me near tears because the secretary crossly refused to print out the class rosters they needed for upcoming classes. Admittedly, the secretary was obscenely overworked and this was enough to make anyone cross, but I noted that she never vented her vexation at full-time professors. I also found that students tended to complain more about adjuncts, and about much more trivial "problems." One student threatened to call the chancellor because an adjunct, following university policy, had dropped him from her course for non-attendance. Another wanted me to fire a teacher who had reprimanded her. The student had left the class to buy herself a candy bar and then interrupted the class again when she returned and started eating it, but she was outraged that the teacher should have "rudely" told her to leave. While I did my best to quash this sort of student nonsense, I don't think all chairs do the same. Moreover, I don't think this situation is unique to my university, since I had experienced the same kind of disrespect when I was an adjunct or TFT. At the time I had thought it was just my problem.

This brings up a very important question, something that is a bit of a paradox except that the logical puzzle provides no flash of deeper insight. Are adjuncts and TFTs to be considered qualified professionals or not? If not, why are they teaching at the university level in the first place? Why do the students have to pay the same tuition to be taught by an "unqualified" adjunct as they would to take the same course from a tenured professor? Why aren't adjuncts given supervision and training to help them become better qualified? If they are qualified, why aren't they paid proportionally, that is, an eighth per course of what a full-time faculty member teaching four courses a semester would earn as a yearly salary? If they are qualified, why aren't their colleagues encouraged to review their files, as they would with candidates for full-time positions, and then, having satisfied themselves, treat the adjunct with the same respect they would accord incoming tenure-track faculty? I'm afraid that the answer is that it is irrelevant to both administration and some colleagues whether or not adjuncts are qualified. Adjuncts will be assumed to be qualified enough to require no more help or guidance than any other professor, but they will often be paid and treated as if they were not. I also wonder sometimes why students who organize boycotts of companies using sweatshop labour do not realize that the academic versions of sweatshop workers are teaching their classes. Do they have no idea how little adjuncts are paid? Or do adjuncts just lack the glamour of exploited workers in far-away countries?

I realize that some people who are adjuncts don't really mind it. Women with small children may enjoy the chance to stay in touch with the intellectual world without having the responsibilities of full-time employment, and I don't blame them. Motherhood seems like more than enough responsibility for anyone. In a slightly different situation, a colleague told me that he had enjoyed his years as an adjunct. He hadn't been a graduate assistant while working on his degree, so adjuncting gave him the chance to acquire some teaching experience. He even whimsically compared it to being an apprentice in medieval times; after all, they didn't get paid much either, quite the opposite. Another adjunct, retired from full-time teaching, remarked how much he enjoyed just being able to go in, teach his classes, and go home, not having to worry about cranky colleagues or department politics. All of this adjunct bliss, however, is dependent on the adjunct having a spouse who is employed full time and willing to be the principle breadwinner. If these happy adjuncts were suddenly divorced, they might feel differently when they tried to support themselves on $16,000 a year. And after all, the medieval apprentices received food, shelter, and training, all denied the adjunct.

Thus, many people who are adjuncts would like to be full-time employees, and even accept adjunct positions with the hope of getting a "foot in the door." Those who use this tired metaphor haven't considered the usual fate of pushy salesmen's feet. Yes, sometimes adjuncts can go on to become full-time faculty members. But to do so requires the political skill of Bill Clinton and the circumspection of Jeeves. I say this in part because I was never able to make the transition from being an adjunct or TFT to a tenure-track position at the same university, but I was easily able to pass a continuing contract review and be promoted to associate professor once I had a continuing contract. This has led me to analyze the reasons why this supposedly difficult step is in fact so much easier.

For promotion and tenure, you are essentially competing against yourself. It's your job to lose, and the rules for keeping it are fairly straightforward. Publish. Volunteer to serve on committees. Avoid offending your colleagues. And, of course, teach competently. Even the last two are not all that difficult. To avoid offending your sane colleagues, all you usually have to do is greet them when you see them in the hallways, express professional disagreement politely even when others are not being polite, and keep your political and religious views to yourself under most circumstances. All that is required of you is that you not act like a jackass. Of course, some colleagues may dislike you anyway, simply because they don't like your age-group, gender, ethnicity, characteristic facial expression, taste in clothes, speech mannerism, or any number of other elements of your personhood which are difficult to alter. But if you are lucky, the normal members of the department will have spotted this colleague for what s/he is and disregard what this person has to say about you. Even with teaching, it is usually good enough if your teaching evaluations are at or slightly above the department average and there are no complaints about you.

Despite possible snares and/or bad luck, however, getting tenure is nothing compared to moving from adjunct to tenure track, because, in my experience, you will not be judged by the same criteria as outside candidates. This is because people know you. And this is part of the trouble. For adjuncts, it isn't enough not to have offended anyone. You have to have everyone like you. And to get a department full of cranky squabbling English professors to like you is an astounding feat, since if one person likes you it is entirely possible that someone else won't like you simply because the first person does. And of course, when a tenure-track position opens, it is usually only one position in a department that employs four or five adjuncts/TFTs, two or three of whom will also apply.

This means that your colleagues not only have to like you, they have to like you better than x, y, and z. The ensuing discussions can lead to vituperative search committees meetings and lasting factions in a department. In at least one department where I have worked, the department decided to forget about inside candidates and hire someone from outside instead, thus angering everyone instead of just one clique. I have seen a few adjuncts become full-time, tenure-track teachers. But these were people whose diplomatic skills could also have gotten them positions as international mediators, or who had the very rare good luck to have their hard work noted and appreciated. I didn't fall into that category, nor do a great many people who are good teachers and good scholars.

"But what about committee work, teaching, and publication?" one asks. If you are an adjunct, you normally don't serve of committees, so that is out. And in my experience, the teaching of adjuncts is considered by somewhat different standards than that of tenure-track teachers. Average student evaluations are not enough, or at least will not be enough to satisfy some members of the committee. On the other hand, if you are a woman and have high evaluations, you may be suspected of mothering your students rather than teaching them. Other times, adjuncts may never have been asked to participate in the student evaluation process at all. Probably no one will have observed your teaching. Consequently, the search committee will rely on how good a teacher they think you might be, and for this they will focus on chance remarks you've made about teaching, on gossip, and on whether or not your colleagues like you. As for publication, that can work either way. If you are at third-tier college where your senior colleagues have published little themselves, it can actually be a handicap. On the other hand, if it is a demanding college and you have been supporting yourself as an adjunct for a number of years by teaching at several schools, or have combined part-time work with full-time motherhood, you will probably not be as well published as outside candidates, nor will you be if you are the sort of adjunct who puts in extra office hours and writes long thoughtful comments on students' papers. Unfortunately, most of the adjuncts I have known fall into at least one of these categories, if not two.

The situation is not fair. In a fairer world, adjuncts would at least be paid at the same rate as their more fortunate full-time colleagues and would be treated with the respect their work merits. But as both history and literature teach us, the world is seldom fair. Personally, I do not see any signs of the academic world becoming a fairer place any time soon.

As for the answer to this dilemma, I can only give the one that worked for me, and it would probably have worked sooner if I had followed this advice at an earlier age. The sad truth is that throwing all your energies into teaching is not in your professional interest. Teach as well as you need to for your own self-respect, but be aware of the likelihood that no one else will know or care how well you teach. Instead of focusing all your intellectual energies on teaching, write. Write every spare minute you have. Send out everything you write and if your article is rejected with comments, rewrite it and send it out somewhere else. Subscribe to a call for papers list and see who is publishing what. Instead of going out for a drink with your colleagues (where you might say something silly anyway) go to the library and read the scholarly journals. If you have a good record of publication, you have a decent chance of getting a tenure-track job somewhere other than the places where you worked as an adjunct. I did. Oh, and luck helps too.

Notes on Contributors

Judith Caesar is an associate professor of English at the American University of Sharjah, United Arab Emirates. She has written two books about teaching and living in the Middle East: *Crossing Borders: An American Woman in the Middle East* and *Writing Off the Beaten Track: Reflections on the Meaning of Travel and Culture*, both published by Syracuse University Press.

Terry Caesar, back from Japan, continues in the profession as an adjunct professor at various colleges in and around San Antonio, Texas. He is also a columnist for a new on-line publication, *Inside Higher Education* (http://insidehighered.com). He is author or co-editor of seven books, the most recent being *Traveling through the Boondocks: In and Out of Academic Hierarchy* (State University of New York Press, 2000). Other books of his are *Forgiving the Boundaries: Home as Abroad in American Travel Writing* (University of Georgia Press, 1995) and *Conspiring with Forms: Life in Academic Texts* (University of Georgia Press, 1992). With Eva Bueno he edited the anthology *Imagination beyond Nation: Latin American Popular Culture* (University of Pittsburgh Press, 1999).

After eleven years as an adjunct, **Sarah Gates** now has a tenure-track position, Assistant Professor of English, at St. Lawrence University, where she teaches Survey of British Literature, Methods of Critical Analysis, The Victorian Novel, British Romanticism, and various courses designed for SLU's First Year Programme. She is happy to report that she will never have to teach Freshman Composition again, because SLU has no such course in its curriculum.

Steffen Hantke has published essays and reviews on contemporary literature, film, and culture in *Paradoxa, College Literature, The Journal of Popular Culture, Post Script, Kinema, Scope, Science Fiction Studies,* and other journals, as well as in anthologies in Germany and the US. He is author of *Conspiracy and Paranoia in Contemporary Literature* (Peter Lang, 1994) as well as editor of *Horror*, a special topics issue of *Paradoxa* (2002), *Horror: Creating and Marketing Fear* (University Press of Mississippi, 2004), and *Caligari's Heirs: The German Cinema of Fear after 1945* (Scarecrow Press, 2007). He currently serves on the editorial board of *Paradoxa* and has served as advisor to the book review board of *College Literature*. He is also chair for the "Horror" area at the Southwest/Texas Popular Culture and American Culture Association. He currently teaches at Sogang University in Seoul, South Korea, as Associate Professor for British and American Culture.

Janet Ruth Heller teaches English and Women's Studies at Western Michigan University. She has published a fiction picture book for children, *How the Moon Regained Her Shape* (Sylvan Dell, 2006) and many poems and scholarly works, including *Coleridge, Lamb, Hazlitt, and the Reader of Drama* (University of Missouri Press, 1990). She is currently Vice President of the Michigan College English Association and a Past President of the Society for the Study of Midwestern Literature.

James Kirwan is the author of *Literature, Rhetoric, Metaphysics: Literary Theory and Literary Aesthetics* (Routledge, 1990), *Beauty* (Manchester University Press, 1999), *The Aesthetic in Kant: A Critique* (Continuum, 2004), and *Sublimity: The Non-Rational and the Irrational in the History of Aesthetics* (Routledge, 2005). He works at Kansai University, Osaka, Japan.

Carla Love is a Senior Lecturer in German at the University of Wisconsin-Madison, where she has been teaching since 1980.

Cynthia Nichols is a long-time university lecturer in English. She holds an MFA in poetry from the University of Iowa, and her creative as well as scholarly work has appeared in a variety of journals and magazines.

Christopher J. O'Brien is currently a PhD candidate in the National Sun Yat-sen University in Kaohsiung, Taiwan, in English and American literature. He is interested in the interaction between the imagination and perception, and how stereotypes can influence and inform the senses. His dissertation is on the image of the stereotypical Gypsy figure in the Western imagination, as it has both shaped and has been shaped by creative art, mostly literature, from the fifteenth through the twenty-first centuries. He has a master's degree in vocal music education from Shenandoah University and a bachelor's degree in music history and theory from the University of Richmond (Virginia).

Kenneth H. Ryesky, Esq. received his B.B.A. and J.D. degrees from Temple University, his M.B.A. from La Salle University and his M.L.S. from Queens College CUNY. He is admitted to the Bar in New York, New Jersey and Pennsylvania, and an Attorney at Law in East Northport, NY., USA.

Dr **Lesley Speed** is a Lecturer in Humanities at the University of Ballarat, Australia.

Rudolphus Teeuwen is interested in the intersection of literature and philosophy, especially in the English and French eighteenth centuries, in the genres of utopia, and in literary theory. He published essays and reviews on these topics and edited *Crossings: Travel, Art, Literature, Politics* (Bookman, Taipei, 2001). He is associate professor of English at National Sun Yat-sen University in Kaohsiung, Taiwan.

Kathleen K. Thornton has been an educator since 1970. She taught high school English for 18 years before completing her doctorate and coming to the State University of New York at Albany, where she has been a lecturer for the last 16 years. In 2006, she received the inaugural College of Arts and Sciences Dean's Award for Outstanding Achievement in Teaching.